Leading for Refugees and Newcomers

Leading for Refugees and Newcomers

Cases for K-12 Schools

Edited by

EMILY R. CRAWFORD
BRYAN MANN
MEREDITH BITTEL
RYAN RUMPF

HARVARD EDUCATION PRESS
CAMBRIDGE, MASSACHUSETTS

Paperback ISBN 9798895570692

The Library of Congress Cataloging-in-Publication Data is on file.

Published by Harvard Education Press,
an imprint of the Harvard Education Publishing Group

Harvard Education Press
8 Story Street
Cambridge, MA 02138

Cover Design: Jackie Shepherd Design
Cover Image: Rysak via Adobe Stock

The typefaces in this book are Adobe Garamond Pro and Myriad Pro.

Contents

Foreword

In an era of unprecedented global displacement, migration has become one of the most defining problems of our times, reshaping societies, schools, and communities in deep ways. According to the United Nations Department of Economic and Social Affairs, there are more than 281 million international migrants worldwide, reflecting the growing sophistication of human movement.[1] This movement is driven by economic opportunity, family reunification, and climate-driven displacement. Within this broader migratory environment, forced displacement has risen to alarming levels: The United Nations High Commissioner for Refugees reports that at the end of 2024 more than 120 million individuals worldwide were living in forcibly displaced circumstances due to war, persecution, and human rights violations.[2] Ongoing conflicts in Sudan, Ukraine, Syria, and Palestine, combined with political turmoil in Afghanistan, Venezuela, and Myanmar, are ongoing drivers of mass migration. Simultaneously, natural disasters, economic crises, and structural injustices push millions to seek asylum in other nations, making subsequent resettlement and integration processes more complex.[3] Such astronomical numbers make it even more crucial to implement systemic solutions that extend beyond short-term humanitarian intervention, necessitating sustainable policy and long-term support systems—particularly in education, which remains one of the most critical domains in which to foster inclusion and social cohesion.

With this historic mobility of individuals, education is at once a significant space of inclusion and a location of conflict where inequalities remain. Schools become the first institutional contacts for immigrant and refugee students, pivotal to socializing them, teaching them language, and educating them academically.[4] Schools, however, are not merely locations of knowledge transfer but also the primary locations for identity formation, belonging, and civic engagement. The educational trajectory of refugee and immigrant students is shaped by an interplay between institutional practices, leadership vision, and policy contexts. The educational achievement of refugee students hinges not only on personal resilience but on the presence of culturally sensitive leadership, equitable allocation of resources, and positive policy interventions that recognize the unique strengths these students bring and also take into consideration the structural supports needed to ensure their full integration and academic achievement.[5]

At the heart of processes to welcome newcomers lies language acquisition, which remains a key determinant of immigrant students' academic success and social integration, though provision for bilingual education and multilingual teaching are also outstanding concerns.[6] Schools that invest in linguistic access and emergent bilingual programs significantly increase student achievement and long-term health.[7] Beyond language, peer relationships, teacher support, and community engagement play a crucial role in the experience of newcomer students.[8] Nevertheless, despite growing recognition of the importance of these factors, schools continue to operate under deficit narratives, depicting refugee students as problems rather than as assets and as resourceful, which reinforces systemic obstacles that prevent them from fully integrating into school and social life.[9]

The United States alone has resettled more than three million refugees since 1975.[10] Current refugee flows from Ukraine, Syria, Burma, and Central America have placed pressure on educational leaders to develop equitable, just, and sustainable support systems.[11] As immigration policy becomes increasingly stringent and national politics more divisive, school leaders' responsibility to receive, guide, and support refugee children has never been more vital. *Leading for Refugees and Newcomers* arrives at a pivotal moment, offering timely insights and practical ideas for educational policy makers, scholars, practitioners, and community leaders. The editors—scholars with expertise in educational leadership, policy analysis, and refugee integration—have assembled a group of leading researchers and practitioners who bridge theory and K–12 practice. This book moves beyond theory to offer a rich collection of case studies grounded in empirical research and teaching perspectives that explore important questions at the intersections of leadership, policy, and community work. The scholarship is ecosystemic and holistic; it recognizes that effective responses to migration require collaboration between schools, families, policy makers, and community organizations. Comparative and interdisciplinary in its approach, the book asks some fundamental questions:

- How do educational leaders build inclusive and culturally responsive schools for immigrant and refugee students?

- What leadership practices best promote the academic and socio-emotional achievement of displaced students?
- How can schools expand their partnerships with families and community organizations to strengthen educational opportunities for newcomer students?
- What is the role of educational policy in advancing equity and access for refugee children?

The book is divided into three interrelated sections to collectively illuminate the policy, pedagogy, and community dimensions of refugee education. The first section, "Policy and Administration," addresses the intersections of education policy, immigration policy, systemic barriers, and school leadership styles in order to provide policy-informed perspectives on how schools can better serve displaced students. The second section, "Within-School and Classroom Considerations," addresses teacher practice, curriculum adaptations, language learning strategies, and socio-emotional interventions required to foster inclusive learning environments. Finally, the third section, "School Partners and Family Engagement," highlights the role of families, interagency collaboration, and cross-sector collaboration in enabling long-term academic success and integration for newcomer students. Book chapters synthesize research-based practices, authentic anecdotes, and critical policy analyses to help school leaders, policy makers, and educators make new strides from traditional academic discourse toward actionable, evidence-based solutions. It transforms schools from bureaucratic accommodation sites to places of transformational empowerment and belonging. Rather than focusing on the simplistic goal of assimilation, this book argues for school communities to recognize and tap into the strengths, cultural wealth, and resilience of immigrant and refugee students. As the editors highlight in their introduction, educational systems must move beyond piecemeal interventions and embrace holistic, student-led responses that honor newcomer students' and families' premigration and postmigration histories, so that every learner can be assisted in reaching their full potential.

A CALL TO ACTION: THE FUTURE OF WELCOMING SCHOOLS

This book is a timely and critical contribution that continues the momentum of shifting the narrative from deficit frameworks of immigrants and newcomers to an asset-based, transformative justice lens—positioning migrant students as agents of change rather than passive recipients of services. With its emphasis on leadership, policy advocacy, and community engagement, this volume is a precious resource for educational policy makers, scholars, school leaders, teachers, and community stakeholders committed to developing equitable, inclusive, and sustainable learning environments. A work of scholarship, to be sure, this book is also a call to action—a challenge to educators, policy makers, and community leaders to reenvision the school as a place of sanctuary, empowerment, and possibility. With the understanding and strategies presented in this volume, we take a crucial step toward making sure that all children—regardless of origin, migration status, or sociopolitical background—are able to access an education that is empowering, transformative, and life affirming.

Khalid H. Arar, PhD
Professor, Educational Leadership and Policy
Editor-in-Chief, *Leadership and Policy in Schools*
Honorary Professor of International Studies, Texas State University
Honorary Professor, West Attica University, Greece

Introduction

Global conflicts such as the wars in Sudan, Ukraine, Syria, and Palestine and the climate crisis are forcing millions of individuals and families to make the harrowing choice to leave their homes. Refugees and asylum seekers venture into new lands, even though the policies and people in them tell them they are unwanted, that they present a problem. This reality begs the questions: *Who will care* for the most vulnerable in our world? *Who will have the courage* to recognize the shared humanity between the host country and the newcomer in these fraught political times? *Who will provide the education* and path to a better life that the children deserve? No child asks or deserves to be raised in violence and conflict, with little education or opportunity to lead a safe, stable life. As of 2024, more than 120 million people worldwide have been forcibly displaced, either within their own country or abroad.[1] The number of displaced persons around the globe continues to grow. The US has resettled more than 3 million refugees since 1975.[2] Recently, the largest populations of refugees being settled in the US come from the Democratic Republic of Congo, Syria, Afghanistan, Venezuela, and Burma.[3] More than 6.3 million Ukrainians have sought refuge in neighboring countries.[4] By mid-spring 2024, 187,000 Ukrainians had settled in the US in the wake of the Russian invasion.[5] Refugees from Burma, Central America and the Caribbean, and elsewhere also have also made up newcomer populations.[6] In many cases across the United States, public PreK–12 educators and school communities have risen to welcome refugee and newcomer students and families.

This book asserts that educational leaders, broadly defined, are in a critical position to help transition refugee and newcomer families into schools by providing them with the support and environment they need to integrate into their new communities. However, meeting this goal is increasingly challenging in the current, actively hostile political environment for newcomer families. The future is unclear with many unknowns likely yet to emerge. What is clear is that educational leaders are a keystone of their school community and there are strategies and networks they can use to improve their leadership practice.

WHY EDUCATIONAL LEADERS MUST PREPARE FOR IMMIGRATION POLICY IMPACTS

Schools have always been sites where sociopolitical and cultural debates are waged, but now is a time of heightened scrutiny of schools that extends from what curriculum and pedagogies get used to what books are included in school libraries. At the time of this writing, a sea change in US immigration policy has entailed putting refugee admissions on hold, attempts to undo birthright citizenship, and tighter restrictions on the ability to claim asylum.[7] Further, in January 2025, a presidential executive order declared that schools are no longer "sensitive areas" for Immigration and Customs Enforcement to avoid.[8] Such actions predominantly impact people with immigrant heritage and people of color, but leaders can expect there to be repercussions for entire school communities.[9] Specific to refugee populations, a halt to federally funded support for agencies heretofore responsible for ensuring that refugees have access to basic necessities and critical services like counseling jeopardizes the well-being and integration of refugees already present in the country.[10] Access to education itself is compromised as immigrant communities shift their behaviors in response to an immigration policy climate that promotes high levels of fear.[11]

The Universal Declaration of Human Rights affirmed education is a human right in 1948.[12] Although some attempts have been made to overturn legal precedent in the US, law and policy still guarantee every child in the nation a free, public K–12 education. Refugee children, no matter their legal status, are entitled to an education *equal* to that of their non-refugee peers.[13] Critical gaps in their access to equal educational opportunities remain. Research shows that refugee and newcomer students' educational aspirations are high, but they may arrive with minimal or no formal education; they may be learning English and may need support to address psychological or physical traumas.[14] However, educators and schools vary in terms of their readiness to meet newcomers' needs. District or school infrastructure and the strength of community connections may be too underdeveloped to provide the necessary support and cultivate students' sense of belonging.[15] Although educators may have established long-term trusting relationships with students, they can differ in their awareness of immigration policies and in their readiness to adapt to shifting policies that shape student access to and engagement in school.[16]

HOW LEADERS CAN USE THIS BOOK TO MEET THE MOMENT AND PREPARE FOR UNCERTAIN TIMES

This book equips preservice and in-service K–12 school leaders and other educational stakeholders with ethical, research-based, and equity-minded strategies for welcoming and integrating refugee and newcomer students and families into public schools. In this particularly challenging moment, educators need strong preparation that includes legal knowledge, research-based best practices, and access to resources and networks that can help them weather the dynamic immigration policy environment. Leaders must also be proactive in countering harsh, harmful discourses about the "deservingness" of refugee and newcomer students and families to an education. Leaders are integral to fostering a school climate that communicates to all staff and personnel that refugee students and their families belong and that considers how community partners can support them and complement their school's endeavors.[17]

The goal of the book is to prepare current and preservice educational leaders and other stakeholders to lead their schools and communities so as to bring about more equitable treatment of refugee and newcomer students by ensuring they have access to both K–12 schooling and a meaningful, quality education. This collection of case studies has two primary purposes: (1) to familiarize K–12 school leaders with the contexts, policies, and practices that influence educational access for newcomer students and families; and (2) to engage K–12 practitioners in a problem of practice related to refugee and newcomer students' experiences in school and their communities in order to grow their knowledge of research-based best practices. Researchers note that schools are particularly critical for immigrant families as they are among the first US institutions that refugee and newcomer families encounter.[18] Educators are essential to help refugees integrate into their new communities.[19]

Leading for Refugees and Newcomers is an edited volume of case studies based on real-life experiences that administrators, teachers, and other educators have negotiated to ensure newcomer students and families' meaningful integration and engagement in school. The book's contributors are scholars and practitioners who have studied newcomer education, and several of the authors have firsthand experience leading schools in these settings. There are seventeen chapters that aim to inform K–12 school leaders and practitioners, challenging them to create stronger, higher-quality, and more equitable educational experiences for the newcomer students and families in their school community. The book is divided into three sections: (1) Policy and Administration, (2) Within-School and Classroom Considerations, and (3) School Partners and Family Engagement. Readers can engage with the book from cover to cover, focus on one section at a time, or select a specific chapter that resonates with them or addresses a rising issue in their own context. Case narratives cover topics that range from refugees navigating US school enrollment systems for the first time to expanding learning opportunities for newcomers in a science classroom. Following each case study is a small section of readily accessible research that provides background for the issue and literature that connects readers with best educational practices. Each chapter includes discussion questions and activities to stimulate reflection and critical thinking and problem solving.

IMPORTANT NOTE ON TERMINOLOGY

In this book, we alternately and interchangeably use the terms *refugee* and *newcomer*, defining them as referring to children and youth who have immigrated for reasons outside their control within the past ten years, as these are the years with the most significant economic and social vulnerabilities.[20] The term *newcomer* is used to minimize stigma and to change deficit-informed perspectives that can be attached to other terms such as *immigrant*, *migrant*, and *refugee*, which are labels that carry different legal definitions and are often conflated and politicized. However, terms like *refugee* are used in existing studies and laws, and when referring to these, we use a consistent term for the sake of clarity. Chapters in this book may use other terms like *refugee student* and *newcomer student*. Readers should note these terms are not necessarily synonymous.

SECTION 1

Policy and Administration

The chapters in Section 1 cohere around issues of how education policy intersects with state- or school-level administrative agencies and its implications for the ways school leaders provide or deliver education to newcomer students. Rumpf and Crawford's chapter looks at the nuances of state standardized testing requirements and how they can create ethical conundrums for school leaders working with newly arrived students. The authors provide creative strategies for leaders to meet requirements while also remaining sensitive to newcomers' contexts. The chapter by Hussein, Stansberry Brusnahan, and Hassan takes on the complexities of immigrant and refugee families accessing special education services and resources, facing stigma associated with disability and autism in particular and overcoming communication challenges. The authors call on educators to work in culturally competent ways toward expanding refugee families' knowledge of disability, terminology, and US special education processes and supports. Chapter 3, by Cieminski, Davidson, and Gosselin, is concerned with requirements and pressures related to policies that push to increase student academic performance while also balancing sensitivity to newcomers' backgrounds, which can include interrupted or no formal education and experiences of trauma. This chapter illustrates how educators can perceive tensions around fairly allocating resources. Authors Brezicha and Guan situate their chapter in a community that is a new immigrant destination. They highlight how the school has formed successful, collaborative partnerships with a state-level agency and community organizations to support newcomers in schools by supplying resources—while also shifting community member mindsets to see newcomers as assets.

CHAPTER 1

Testing for "Success"?

Considerations for Assessing Student Growth in Content and Language

RYAN RUMPF, EDD

Independent Scholar, Kansas City, Missouri

EMILY R. CRAWFORD, PHD

University of Missouri, Columbia

ABSTRACT

Refugee and newcomer students have to learn a variety of new customs and cultures that are a part of the US schooling experience. The Every Student Succeeds Act (ESSA) of 2015 requires all students in K–12 public schools to undergo standardized testing. Yet, policies that test refugee students who are new to US schools and who are acquiring English present a dilemma for school leaders. This chapter explores the case of one district's response to standardized testing, including a state-mandated reading policy that required the principal to test newly arrived students on their English reading literacy levels. It also presents how standardized testing policies for newcomer students can raise ethical questions for school leaders. We then offer creative strategies that leaders can use to resolve conflicting testing policy expectations while remaining cognizant of and fair to newcomer students who are exposed to US standardized testing for the first time.

CASE NARRATIVE

Angeza was born in Afghanistan in 2014. She is the daughter of an educated father who speaks five languages, studied at university, and worked in the local school. Both of Angeza's parents had high expectations of her as a student. She attended school every day in Kunduz. Angeza is kind and respectful, and academically, she was one of the top students in her class.

Angeza and her family fled Afghanistan in August 2022, a year after the Taliban rose to power. The family's voyage took them first to Pakistan, then to Qatar, Germany, Canada, Wisconsin, and finally, in January 2023, to western Missouri. Angeza was very excited to go to school, but also nervous. Learning English was impossible in Afghanistan, yet she would soon have to do everything in English. She wanted to make friends but worried she didn't know how she would talk with anyone.

The refugee agency in western Missouri took the family to the local district's central office to enroll in the school, and after much paperwork, including details about her linguistic and educational background, Angeza was to begin fifth grade the following Monday. Before she left, one of the adults asked her to take an assessment in English to place her in English classes. She wondered why, silently, because she had already said she didn't understand English. For almost an hour, Angeza took test after test. At first, she did not understand what to do as the directions were in English. The adult in the room showed her how to select answers and advance to the next question. She tried her best to listen and choose an answer that seemed correct, but after a few questions, she started to click on random answers and advance the test so she could be finished. She did the same on each of the following three English tests. Angeza left the enrollment office feeling much differently than when she arrived, and incredibly discouraged. "This was going to be very difficult," she thought as the family returned home. She felt the stress weighing on her. She wished she did not have to return to school but knew that was not an option.

Angeza's experience would be the first of many standardized tests she would take at the school without understanding a word on the page. On her first day of school, her teacher logged her into a computer and asked her to take a math test; then, the following day she had to take a reading test. Both were in English. She was good at math and was one of the best readers in her class in Afghanistan, but she knew she had failed these tests. "I hope my parents don't see this," she thought to herself, feeling very disheartened. Two weeks later, she had to take a much longer version of the same English test she took during enrollment. She took one section of the test each day for four consecutive days.

After the English testing, she started to settle into her new school. There were two other Afghan students in her grade, and she was able to see them at lunch and recess. They became good friends, but she wished she saw them more often. The school employed an Afghan translator who came to her class to help her. At times, she would have work to do on the computer. The lessons appeared similar to the reading and math tests she took, but she noticed that the activities looked more like what her younger brother in kindergarten should be doing. Despite the childish look of the program, she still didn't understand what she had to do. It was in English. The Afghan translator explained how the program worked, informing Angeza that she needed to choose a number for her goal, and the next time she took the test, she would get a prize if she met the goal. "How will I do that if I don't understand it?" she asked the translator. "You can do it!" he replied. "The program gives you a path to complete, and if you work hard, you will get there." She didn't believe it.

Angeza eventually started to understand the routines in the school and started to speak a few words in English. The students in her class were kind and helped her when they could. Her teacher was nice. She used a translation app on her phone to communicate and taught Angeza hand signals to communicate emergencies. She was most comfortable when the Afghan translator was in the room, though. He did not translate everything, but made sure she understood what the class was doing. He even helped translate some of the quizzes for her.

At the end of the year, Angeza's entire class had to take important tests. It reminded her of the end-of-year tests she had taken in Afghanistan. These tests were sources of pride (or shame) for families. Some students had to repeat a grade if they didn't pass. She had to do well on the test. Luckily, this year, she had to take only math and science.

When the test started, Angeza was relieved that she was in a small group with her Afghan friends, and the translator was there. She was confused why he was not translating the questions, though. The teacher read each question and answer choice to her in English, but she did not understand. She clicked on answers when she could and typed her name when she needed to write something. At the end, she knew she had failed again.

The school year ended shortly afterward, which was a relief after the discouraging testing experience. After summer break, she did not want to go back. School was too hard, and she did not feel that she was learning anything. She thought she learned more from her parents at home. At the end of the first week, the school held an event where parents could attend and talk with the teacher about their child's performance on the tests from the previous year. "Oh, no," she thought, as she was given a translated flier to give to her parents. When she got home, she reluctantly gave the flier to them and admitted she didn't do well. "Don't worry," her father said. "You are a smart girl and will learn English; it just takes time."

After a few weeks, Angeza again had to take the reading and math tests on the computer. She understood more this time around, but she knew she did not do well. A few weeks after the test, her parents received a letter in the mail. Written in her native Pashto, it informed the parents that her score on the test meant that she had a "substantial reading deficiency." The school had developed a Reading Success Plan that detailed how they would help her, and the plan was sent to the state for monitoring. "I already know how to read, but not in English," she thought to herself as her parents comforted her yet again.

A Principal's Perspective on Newcomer Testing Practices and Policy

As the leader of an elementary program designed for newcomer and refugee students, I (Rumpf) serve many students like Angeza. The students come from around the world and have diverse backgrounds and educational experiences. Many of the Congolese students come from the Nyarugusu refugee camp in Tanzania. I have also welcomed Burmese, Karenni, Afghan, and Cuban students to the refugee program. The program also serves students from Venezuela and Colombia who have spent months traveling and endured the Darién Gap. We serve students from as far away as Mongolia and Kazakhstan, who are also managing the emotions of culture shock. The one thing that all students have in common is that they are just beginning their journeys in English.

As the program principal, I am charged with navigating the various assessment policies to ensure students are assessed fairly and the testing experience itself does not harm the students' socio-emotional well-being. I must organize practices around (1) district-mandated iReady testing, which monitors progress and must be administered three times per year; (2) Illuminate testing, which is administered quarterly, (3) the Missouri Assessment Program (MAP) for grades 3–6, and (4) the ACCESS test for English learners (ELs), which satisfies the English-language proficiency (ELP) testing requirement under the Every Student Succeeds Act (ESSA) of 2015. These tests are in addition to the testing required for other district programming (e.g., special education, gifted and talented)

Knowing that students must take certain assessments, the team and I proactively identify tests as invalid when the test language does not align with a student's language ability. After making this determination, we develop plans to exempt students from invalid assessments when possible. The most meaningful of the assessments are ELP tests, as they are designed to measure how much English students have acquired. Missouri is a member of the WIDA Consortium, which provides professional development and ELP assessments, the most important of which are the ACCESS tests for ELs. All students must take the ACCESS (Assessing Comprehension and Communication in English State-to-State); however, students who arrive in the United States during the testing window are exempt. They are exempt, because the students just took the WIDA Screener assessment, another ELP assessment among WIDA's offerings, for formal EL identification.

Locally mandated assessments are intended to measure growth over a school year, identify trends, and hold staff accountable. Missouri school districts can choose which assessment they use. The tool used by my district, iReady, has a Spanish version of the math test. The program has staff to translate for other students; this may not be the case in many districts across the country. The iReady tool yields meaningful information by allowing the team to collect valid and reliable data on a student's abilities. These tests also provide an online, individualized learning pathway for students that is routinely followed in classrooms. Because the test is administered three times during the school year, the team can use it to measure progress over time.

To the extent possible, I arrange for translation of math and science on the MAP assessment as well. The State of Missouri does not provide a translated version of its assessments, so districts that choose to translate for students must use human translators, which is an added cost, especially for districts without translators on staff. Further, organizing translation is complex and requires much time and training to prepare translators, most of whom are not frequently in classrooms during the year. Yet students still have to take the test as mandated by ESSA. My team and I support as many students as possible with translators and proactively address the trauma experienced by students who do not receive translation.

Reading assessments are different. We exempt the students from the progress-monitoring assessment and do not ask them to complete the online activities. Students are also exempted from all other district-mandated reading assessments for their first year. Students within their first twelve calendar months in the United States are exempt from the MAP ELA assessment, an exemption that ESSA allows, though there are no exceptions for students born in the United States. While ESSA regulations apply only to the state assessments, the twelve-month exemption was a compromise between the program and district leaders. I would certainly prefer to wait longer, because acquiring enough English to meaningfully participate in these tests takes longer than a year.

A key takeaway for leaders planning their assessment system is to realize that language acquisition takes time and language proficiency impacts the validity and reliability of standardized content-area assessments.

Testing newcomers in their native language, regardless of the primary language of instruction, is the only way to know whether the student understands the test.

Senate Bill 681 and Advocating for a Practical Response to Policy Expectations

Missouri Senate Bill (SB) 681 requires school districts, beginning in the 2023–24 school year, to assess any student enrolled in kindergarten through third grade at the beginning and end of each school year, as well as any newly enrolled student in grades 1–5. Any student who "exhibits a substantial deficiency in reading" or has been identified as potentially dyslexic is required to have a Reading Success Plan (RSP) on file with the Missouri Department of Elementary and Secondary Education (DESE). The provisions define a substantial deficiency in reading as "a student who is one or more grade level or levels behind in reading or reading readiness"[1]

SB 681 replaced a law that had mandated retention of students who had a deficiency in reading at the fourth-grade level; however, that law had an exemption for ELs. A crucial component of the new law mandated that identification of students needing an RSP be completed with one of four "state-approved" reading assessments, none of which included a native-language version. It is unclear why in the new law there is no exemption for ELs, and the prospect of forcing students to take a high-stakes assessment when they have no chance of comprehending it caused much anxiety among the team. If the policy was to move forward as written, every one of the students would be put on an RSP. Every year, for many years, parents would receive a letter saying their child has a "significant reading deficiency." The team feared this would negatively impact students' sense of self-worth and self-efficacy long term.

Immediately after seeing guidance on Reading Success Plans from DESE, I began exploring the local options and contacting area districts to understand what they would do. I also contacted state leaders. The district insisted on adhering to the state guidelines, and DESE insisted on adhering to the legislation.

I then advocated for a native-language literacy assessment, first at the district level then at the state level, to confirm or dispute the scores earned on the iReady reading assessment, since native-language literacy was not an approved option. DESE soon added language allowing the use of a body of evidence rather than a single test score. Fortunately, the program has an extensive multilingual library with books in fourteen languages, several of which are leveled readers. I also reached out to the district's director of diversity, who connected me with the Mexican Consulate. The Consulate provided several copies of textbooks and materials that included diagnostic reading assessments. After assessing each student's native-language literacy, we found that some students did need an RSP, but the majority of students did not.

TEACHING NOTES

Over the past two decades, standardized assessments have demanded an increasing share of time and resources in US public education in the United States, even though research shows that they can perpetuate social stratification.[2] ELs are the most tested of all student populations.[3] Every level of the education system has established policies that drive teaching and learning in classrooms. At the federal level, the ESSA mandates standardized assessments in reading and math for students in grades 3–8 and once in high school. In addition, students must take a science assessment once at the elementary, middle, and high school levels. Students who are formally identified as ELs also take a large-scale ELP assessment, which must be aligned to each state's academic standards, every year until they are proficient in English.[4] At the local level, progress-monitoring assessments, such as STAR, iReady, and Northwest Evaluation Association (NWEA) MAP, are given throughout the year. Some districts also administer interim ELP assessments.

Research is unclear as to what level of English proficiency is sufficient for a student to meaningfully participate in standardized assessments; however, the field of second-language acquisition research generally agrees that it takes between five to seven years to acquire the academic language used in schools.[5] Growth trajectories for ELs note tremendous progress in the first year or two of schooling in the United States, with growth slowing as students become more advanced and progress through the grade levels.[6] It is unsurprising that students who are in the early stages of English acquisition are unable to meaningfully participate in standardized assessments administered in English. Newcomer and refugee students, who are just beginning their journeys in English, do not understand the complex language of the tests. Test results are not valid for newcomers when they cannot understand the questions.[7] Test reliability is also a concern in the case of the student misunderstanding of test questions.[8] Further, in many cases, the technology needed to complete certain test items is often new or unfamiliar to these populations.[9] Therefore, test results are unlikely to inform educators of what students actually know and can do. They also raise stress levels in students and impact the students' identity, sense of self-efficacy, and motivation.[10]

Angeza was a successful student prior to coming to the United States. She knew she could read well, and so did her parents. This disconnect between what the school told them and what her family knew about her contributed to the othering the family felt from both the district and the community in which they lived. It also affected Angeza's drive and sense of self-efficacy. As leaders, we must set our students up for success, and the assessment system is an integral component of fulfilling that commitment. Students should never take a test that is not valid or reliable. Most assessment leaders, at all levels of education, frequently overlook this specific population in their mandates. It is up to all of us to make sure their needs are considered.

Discussion Questions and Teaching Activities

(1) Describe the process of enrolling refugee and newcomer students in your school district.
    (a) What does the district policy require?
        (i) What kind of information is collected that relates to the student's experiences with formal schooling and languages they speak?

- (ii) Who collects this information, and how is the information distributed?
- (iii) What do you see as strengths and gaps in the student enrollment process? What additional steps and/or resources can be used to smooth student transitions?

(2) What are the testing requirements in your state for English learners?
- (a) How does your district organize and conduct state testing for ELs?
  - (i) What exemptions exist and how are those decided?
  - (ii) What accommodations does your district provide and who decides whether they're appropriate for a student?
  - (iii) What do you see as strengths and gaps in the state testing process?

(3) What local, district-level assessments are required for ELs?
- (a) How does your district organize and conduct local assessments?
  - (i) Are there exemptions for ELs?
  - (ii) What accommodations are provided?
  - (iii) How can you make assessments meaningful and useful for decision-making purposes?

CHAPTER 2

Working with Socioculturally Diverse Immigrant and Refugee Families to Meet the Needs of Students with Disabilities

DEEQAIFRAH HUSSEIN
Minneapolis Public Schools

L. LYNN STANSBERRY BRUSNAHAN
Department of Special Education, University of St. Thomas

HASSAN HASSAN
New Century Charter School

ABSTRACT

This case study highlights the complex realities faced by Somali families navigating identification and special education for children with autism. It explores the impact of communication challenges; lack of disability and special education knowledge; stigma associated with disability; and access to resources on immigrant and refugee families. To best meet students' educational needs, schools must understand socioculturally diverse communities. This case study describes educational practices to meet the needs of socioculturally diverse children with disabilities. Recommendations for school leaders include the following four strategies for addressing the barriers and challenges immigrant and refugee parents encounter when a child is identified with a disability and receives special education interventions: (1) utilize socioculturally responsive communication; (2) increase knowledge and awareness of disability and special education; (3) address sociocultural stigma associated with disability in diverse communities; and (4) provide access to socioculturally relevant educational resources. Implementing socioculturally responsive practices is important as a lack of knowledge and difficulty navigating complex systems can prevent families from accessing the timely identification and intervention that leads to more positive outcomes for children with disabilities.

CASE NARRATIVE

The Abdi family, immigrants from Somalia, have six children. During preschool, the parents' gave permission for an evaluation of their three-year-old, Samatar, as they had noticed differences in his development. They found the assessments intimidating with unfamiliar language and embarrassing questions, such as "Is he toilet trained?" The school determined that Samatar had developmental delays and began providing early-intervention services. When Samatar turned four, the early-intervention team asked permission to do additional assessments.

The multidisciplinary evaluation team consisted of a special educator, school psychologist, social worker, school counselor, speech pathologist, occupational therapist, administrative designee, and language interpreter. The evaluations revealed that Samatar met the educational criteria for special education under autism. The family was shocked, not having realized that the evaluation was related to special education determination. The father didn't want the school to label his son due to the stigma associated with disability in his cultural community. The family shared that they thought special education services were for students with profound disability. The parents didn't have access to resources in their first language to help them understand special education. The mother knew the child needed support and persuaded the father to reluctantly consent to the special education interventions. The father stopped allowing anyone to come to their home and started taking only the older children to the mosque because he was worried about what others might think.

Now the school is seeking parental permission to evaluate the Abdis' two-year-old, Burhaan, who is experiencing delays. Since the challenges are not as visible as his brother's, the father believes Burhaan's needs might be addressed spiritually through prayer. The father does not want another child labeled and refuses to give consent. The mother would like Burhaan to have access to the needed educational services and wants the evaluation. Burhaan engages in solitary activities rather than playing collaboratively with peers. He faces challenges in social communication and sensory regulation, which are interfering with his learning. During circle time, he sits on the periphery, covering his ears and rocking. If a peer is in close proximity, he will physically hit them due to a lack of communication skills. Without the support provided in an individualized education program, administrators must follow district discipline policies to ensure student and staff safety. After several meetings with the school administrator and multiple school suspensions for behavioral challenges, the Abdis finally consent to an evaluation for the two-year-old.

TEACHING NOTES

School leaders require an understanding of socioculturally diverse communities to best meet students' educational needs. Many of these communities have been in the United States for only a generation or two, making them relatively new to American culture.[1] For example, Somalis began arriving in America in the 1980s as refugees fleeing a civil war.[2] Immigrants and refugees, like the Abdi family, face sociocultural shock and have to navigate unfamiliar educational systems.[3] The Individuals with Disabilities Education Act (2004) provides criteria that qualifies individuals for special education eligibility under categories focused on "disability." Children and their families' needs emerge from multiple intersecting sociocultural identities beyond just disability (e.g., nationality, ethnicity, race, gender identity, socioeconomic class, religion).[4] The intersection of disability and other sociocultural identities has an impact, as illustrated in Somali children experiencing disproportionate and delayed identification of autism compared to the general population.[5]

School leaders can employ the following four strategies to address the barriers and challenges immigrant and refugee parents encounter when a child is identified with a disability and receives special education interventions.[6]

Utilize Socioculturally Responsive Communication

When school leaders are working with families who do not speak English as their first language, the focus should be on socioculturally responsive communication, as poor communication can impact parental participation in aspects of their child's education.[7] Socioculturally diverse families report they are least responsive to communication conveyed through formal meetings or written materials, methods commonly used by educators.[8] Somali families report they do not have the language or know-how to voice their needs in educational meetings.[9] To avoid communication barriers, school personnel can define special education terminology. This is essential for languages in which words do not exist for disabilities. Mental health conditions are a foreign concept to some non-Western cultures.[10] For example, Somalis report being unfamiliar with terms such as *depression*, *anxiety*, and *stress*, which can lead to perceiving these problems as nonexistent in their communities.[11] Language barriers and a lack of socioculturally sensitive engagement on the part of school leaders and educators can hinder communication about developmental concerns and disability characteristics.[12] No words or definitive meanings for what disability entails can make it difficult for parents to seek identification, process, and accept a child's disability.[13] Schools must ensure that interpreters for parent-school communication are experienced, because some interpreters lack the language to accurately translate educational terminology and do not understand educational processes.[14]

Increase Knowledge and Awareness of Disability and Special Education

School leaders must provide a means for families to increase their knowledge of disability and special education processes. Some cultures define disability constructs while others do not.[15] Many Somali parents state they lacked a general understanding of autism or had never heard of autism before a doctor diagnosed their child.[16] Researchers report difficulties engaging Somali families in conversation about autism due to disability awareness and understanding and sociocultural sensitivity.[17] A lack of knowledge about typical development and disability characteristics can contribute to delays in recognizing signs and seeking evaluations.[18] Lack of knowledge and difficulty navigating complex systems can prevent families from accessing timely identification and interventions.[19] A child who presents no physical manifestation of disability can contribute to parents' reluctance to accept a diagnosis.[20]

It is important for school leaders to remember that immigrants and refugees were schooled in different systems, so they are unfamiliar with the US educational system and experience challenges understanding the educational responsibilities thrust on them if their child has a disability.[21] Parents note they are invited to meetings whose purpose and agenda they know nothing about. Instead of feeling like partners in their child's education, parents express frustration at being told what to do and what forms to sign with little explanation or context provided by the large number of school personnel in meetings, which makes them feel outnumbered and othered. School leaders and educators must take the time to explain to parents that they are important members of the educational team.[22] Families also say they need diversely representative and sensitive professionals to conduct evaluations and assist with the complexity of navigating services from a sociocultural perspective.[23]

Address Sociocultural Stigma Associated with Disability Within Diverse Communities

School leaders need to understand that culture and associated beliefs and stigma are a factor in some socioculturally diverse families' understanding, accepting, and navigating of a disability. Culture and belief can impact and delay the identification of disability and access to early intervention and special education services.[24] Be aware that families can experience social stigma, shame, denial, grief, loss, and shock when learning their child has a lifelong disability.[25] Sociocultural misconceptions of the disability's etiology—such as the belief that this is God's or Allah's will, superstitions, supernatural causes (e.g., curse, possession), or vaccine misconceptions—can delay help-seeking behaviors.[26] Autism carries a stigma that can make it difficult to participate inclusively in communities, such as the Somali community.[27] Thus, families, like the Abdis, might delay seeking services and sharing information as they fear social isolation and difficulty navigating community assumptions.[28] Families report community rejection in the form of staring, judgmental looks, isolation, and unsolicited advice to keep the child at home.[29] Research investigating Somali family involvement in school-based interventions reports that these factors contribute to parents not seeking, consenting to, or rejecting special education services, as well as late identification that results in children with autism not getting needed school services.[30] Some sociocultural communities are informed by and connected to traditional or spiritual healing methods and prefer seeking help through religious support before obtaining professional services.[31]

Provide Access to Socioculturally Relevant Educational Resources

School leaders should provide access to socioculturally relevant educational resources. These resources are essential, as families' perceptions of autism have been found to be influenced by a lack of or limited access to resources in their language.[32] Providing resources that help ease the difficulty of navigating educational systems—and ensure the provision of information about available services, eligibility criteria, and how to access support—can help families access timely identification and interventions.[33] Families express frustration and a lack of knowledge about how to access the federally mandated disability identification process, Child Find, that is designed to identify delays and disabilities.[34] Parents explain that they do not know where to go for services and that school staff do not provide special education resources.[35]

Discussion Questions

- How might an educational leader work to avoid the barriers created by a family's sociocultural identity to a child being identified with a disability and receiving special education services?

- How could a school leader work to increase knowledge that impacts the perceptions of disability and special education in socioculturally diverse communities?
- What are ways educational leaders can address challenges for socioculturally diverse families so schools can better meet the needs of children in special education?

Teacher Activities

Addressing challenges that families face requires socioculturally relevant and responsive approaches.

Activity A. Brainstorm Practical Strategies

Referencing the case narrative, brainstorm strategies for addressing socioculturally diverse families' challenges as they navigate disability identification and special education systems.

Jigsaw and Gallery Walk Option: Split students into four groups to capture strategies in one area. Post ideas and have students view all brainstormed strategies.

1. Utilize socioculturally competent communication
2. Increase knowledge and awareness of disability and special education system
3. Address sociocultural stigma associated with disability within diverse communities
4. Provide access to socioculturally relevant educational resources

Activity B. Summarize Learning and Conduct Formative Assessment

Improving communication, increasing knowledge of disability and special education, removing sociocultural stigma, and providing accessible educational resources are crucial steps toward improving identification and services for socioculturally diverse children with disabilities.

One Minute Paper: Describe something you want to learn more about as a school leader charged with meeting the needs of socioculturally diverse families and providing an opportunity for all students to receive an equitable education.

RESOURCES

Resources focused on the Somali and autism communities include the following:

- Somali Translated Materials, PACER Center, https://www.pacer.org/somali/.
- "First Steps: Pathway to Playing, Learning and Growing," https://edocs.dhs.state.mn.us/lfserver/Public/DHS-6751L-ENG. Pathway to Services and Supports includes resources for increasing awareness and expanding access to services and supports for autism in multiple languages.

CHAPTER 3

It's Not About Silos!

School Leadership to Address the Learning Needs of All and Include Immigrant and Refugee Students

AMIE B. CIEMINSKI, ANNE O. DAVIDSON, AND KATRINE S. GOSSELIN

University of Northern Colorado

ABSTRACT

This teaching case focuses on challenges that an elementary school team faced on receiving an influx of refugees from Central and South America. Dr. Mora, a second-year principal, must navigate growing tensions among her staff while responding to the needs of newcomer and refugee students. Many of these students have experienced trauma and limited or interrupted education, contributing to the complexities of the case. As educators work to meet the students' diverse academic, linguistic, and social-emotional needs, siloed practices such as pull-out instruction for multilingual learners (MLs) come under scrutiny for their potential to undermine student success. The narrative captures a critical moment during a third-grade data team meeting where staff frustrations, limited resources, and differing perspectives on inclusion and instructional support collide, prompting participants to consider Dr. Mora's next steps. The case challenges aspiring and current school leaders to explore inclusive, equitable, and collaborative approaches to serving MLs through professional collaboration, evidence-based service delivery models, and integrated, responsive systems of support. The teaching notes emphasize the legal and ethical responsibilities involved in serving MLs, outline distinctions among immigrant populations, and present evidence-based models for

English-language development, emphasizing professional collaboration and capacity building across staff roles.

The associated learning activities help leaders strengthen skills in setting priorities, analyzing team dynamics, assessing needs, planning, engaging stakeholder perspectives, reviewing policy with an equity lens, and mapping community resources. Each activity is designed to support school leaders in building inclusive, just schools for all.

CASE NARRATIVE

Dr. Mora is a second-year principal at Lincoln Elementary School. Forty percent of the school's students have a Latinx background, many of whom speak Spanish at home, participate in regular classrooms most of the day, and are identified with limited English proficiency (LEP). This year, Lincoln received an influx of refugees and newcomers, and Dr. Mora's staff are overwhelmed by the newest students' diverse needs. Many new students are from Venezuela and have migrated over recent years without receiving any formal schooling. During her first year as principal, Dr. Mora focused on establishing positive relationships with the staff and understanding the school data. She is now faced with additional challenges surrounding systems and practices to meet the needs of all students and create an inclusive school culture.

Today, the third-grade team is meeting to review students' performance data. The meeting includes Ms. Rivera, a special education teacher; Mr. Heinzman, an experienced educator; Ms. Bluski, a novice English-Language Development (ELD) teacher; and two other third-grade teachers.

Mr. Heinzman looks visibly frustrated as he reviews the data showing low student performance. "I'm struggling to manage the growing number of students with such varied needs. It feels like no matter what I do, their performance keeps declining," he says.

"It's impossible to give each student the attention they need," Ms. Rivera, clearly exhausted, chimes in. "I'm pulling students out all day for interventions. Despite my best efforts, their data isn't improving. I don't have time to collaborate with most grade-level teams. I'm overwhelmed and don't even have a chance to catch my breath." She gestures toward a stack of paperwork that she needs to finish.

Ms. Bluski, who has been listening quietly, finally speaks up, "We could work together to support students in your classrooms. The research says students' access to English development and content learning increases when students with diverse needs are included instead of pulled out." She continues hesitantly, "Aside from our teaching, many of our newcomer students are experiencing severe trauma and lack necessities. We can't expect students to show growth or meet benchmarks if their basic needs aren't met. But I don't know how to get them support outside school."

The conversation grows heated as staff members start blaming one another. "I need more support in the classroom! It feels like I'm alone in there and not getting enough help from the special education or ELD teams," Mr. Heinzman blurts out, holding his head in his hands.

To that, Ms. Rivera retorts: "Heinzman, I'm swamped! I barely have time to provide any support for the kids on my caseload, and I'm working with multiple grades. I don't get lunch breaks anymore. The paraeducators are overwhelmed. I don't know what to do anymore!"

"If we collaborate more to keep students in your classrooms effectively, instead of pulling them out, we could support each other's efforts. Then we *should* see more student improvement," Miss Bluski shares meekly.

Frustrated, Mr. Heinzman interrupts, voice raised, "End pull-out support? To keep students in the classroom, won't we need more meetings to plan together? How will students catch up if they aren't receiving direct support? We need additional staff and resources. The kids need more one-to-one support. Paraeducators need to take them out after my instruction."

Dr. Mora hears raised voices as she walks down the hallway. When she enters, Mr. Heinzman is looking to other third-grade teachers for support. One is looking down, and the other nods enthusiastically, adding, "You can't end pull-out! You need to take your kids so the other third-graders can learn."

Gathering some courage, Miss Bluski adds, "Right now, we're reacting to learning challenges instead of addressing the source of learning problems.

Do we even know who needs social-emotional or mental health supports, or help accessing food and housing? Without these, ELD instruction alone will not make a difference."

Ms. Rivera nods, "I would love to collaborate, but when? I have no time! Two paraeducators are threatening to quit, which will make the situation worse! Not only that, where is our school counselor? What days is he even here? He needs to help with trauma and mental health."

Disappointed, Ms. Bluski sighs, "I just don't think pull-out is working. Aligning our instruction would make learning more meaningful for the kids, right?"

The volume in the room has now increased significantly. Accusing glares are being exchanged among staff members. Dr. Mora realizes the discussion has spiraled out of control, and she is concerned about the team's productivity. She knows she needs to act, but the complexity of the situation and the competing demands of her staff are overwhelming. She believes in inclusion and knows the siloed approach to student support must end for Lincoln to be an equitable, inclusive, and just school. The lack of consensus and escalating frustration among the team leave her contemplating the best course of action.

She chimes in firmly, "Okay, let's take a step back! I hear your passion and know you want to support *our* students. Instructional supports will not end. We don't have unlimited resources, so we need to figure out what we can improve for students today and what long-term plans we need to develop to best serve all our students' unique needs. Unfortunately, planning time is over, so let's all bring ideas to next week's meeting." Staff members leave the room with unease hanging in the air. Dr. Mora is left with a pressing need to find a way to address her staff's concerns while managing her students' complex needs.

TEACHING NOTES

Refugees, Asylum Seekers, and Migrants

The number of people worldwide forcibly displaced due to persecution, conflict, violence, and human rights violations was estimated by the

United Nations High Commissioner for Refugees to exceed 120 million by the end of April 2024, with 49 million of those leaving their home country.[1] The United States has since its inception been a destination for people seeking refuge from persecution, conflict, or violence, and today, it remains a country that accepts refugees, asylum seekers, and migrants from all over the world. These groups have similar experiences, having left their home countries to seek a safer, better life, though their situations and rights vary. In 1982, the US Supreme Court in *Plyler v. DOE* established that children have the right to a free, appropriate public education within the United States, regardless of their parents' immigration status.[2] In addition, the Every Student Succeeds Act (2015) requires instructional programs to include appropriate support to develop English proficiency.[3]

The 2021 Census documented 45 million foreign-born residents, approximately 13.6 percent of the US population, of whom just over half (50.1 percent) are from Latin America.[4] The number of people with Latine backgrounds and multilingual learners are growing in the United States, with implications for our schools, yet not all Latines in the United States are multilingual.

Program Requirements and Models for MLs

Schools must provide evidence-based language instruction education programs to support MLs' access to English for academic and social development. Federal regulations require schools to identify MLs, provide instruction, and monitor progress for students with limited English proficiency. New students who are not yet proficient in engaging the world through English have the challenge of learning English while also navigating social and academic opportunities for development. Schools are obligated to provide access to grade-level or content while supporting language development and monitoring students' progress in both language and academic development. School leaders must ensure MLs have equitable access to opportunities. At the same time, developing fluency in English as an additional language requires up to ten years.[5]

Therefore, professional learning is essential to increasing schoolwide capacity to provide MLs with equitable access to high-quality instruction and foster collaborative family partnerships. Professional development should build capacity among all school personnel to include these students in school opportunities. There are a range of evidence-based English-Language Development program models, including push-in or pull-out English as a Second Language (ESL) or ELD, dual language or two-way immersion, transitional or early-exit bilingual education, content classes with integrated ESL support, and newcomer programs that provide intensive English-language development and acculturation education for short periods of time until students are integrated into typical classrooms with other ELD supports.[6] Every program model has pros and cons. For example, pull-out ESL may be tailored to students' English proficiency level but may focus on discrete skills and be disconnected from learning in other content areas. Students may also miss grade-level instruction, fall further behind on academic skills, and miss productive interactions with language role models and grade-level peers that can accelerate learning and promote a sense of belonging. On the other hand, co-teaching allows two or more educators to help meet the linguistic and academic needs of diverse learners; students with varying needs learn alongside their grade-level peers rather than in separate or segregated programs. While co-teaching traditionally has been used to support students with disabilities, co-teachers may be ELD teachers, reading specialists, or other educators with specific expertise. Co-teaching requires time for teacher teams to co-plan, co-teach, co-assess, and co-reflect to maximize the benefits of inclusion and accelerated learning.

While many children in the United States also speak primary or home languages other than English, they may not experience the additional challenges that arise for newcomers. For newcomer MLs, additional sociocultural issues can arise based on their country of origin, prior languages, cultural backgrounds, and previous education experiences.[7] Many students have experienced limited access to education in their home countries, due to educational norms and costs like books or uniforms, which may starkly contrast with US compulsory attendance laws and free public education. Newcomer immigrants and refugees may have additional trauma experiences from dangerous journeys, separation from home and family, or exposure to violence or war. They may also have received interrupted, limited, or no formal schooling because of conditions in their home country, like the millions of people who fled Venezuela, or the lived experiences of immigrant or refugee journeys.[8]

Social Justice Leadership

Current US standards for educational leaders emphasize responsibilities for equity, diversity, and inclusion. Federal policy has used two paradigms to approach improvement for students from minoritized groups: the equity paradigm (e.g., Title IX, Individuals with Disabilities Act) and the accountability paradigm (e.g., high-stakes assessments, No Child Left Behind). Neither approach has successfully closed opportunity gaps evident in disparate achievement and graduation rates, instead resulting in siloed service models for MLs, students with disabilities, and students living in poverty. Social justice leaders make "issues of race, class, gender, disability, sexual orientation, and other historically and currently marginalizing conditions in the United States central to their advocacy, leadership practice, and vision."[9] They promote inclusion, work to end segregating conditions like pull-out programs, and align instruction to ensure all students receive high-quality teaching. Social justice leaders provide professional development to facilitate effective strategies and models for diverse learners, culturally responsive pedagogy, and high-leverage practices for fostering inclusive, equitable schools.[10]

Meaningful Inclusion

Meaningful inclusion involves adapting daily practices and routines beyond superficial efforts to ensure every student has access to learning opportunities.[11] Yet the US Department of Education reports that more than one million students still lack access to inclusive education (e.g., students with disabilities, MLs). An inclusive approach fosters universal respect for differences, patience with diverse learning styles and needs, and opportunities for students to challenge and support each other's understanding.[12] Inclusion is rooted in providing quality education for all. Staff engage in professional collaboration to ensure every student receives the support they need for access to meaningful participation in all aspects of education.

Collaborative Teaming and Co-Teaching

To meet the needs of students, schools use numerous collaborative planning and problem-solving teams (e.g., multitiered system of support (MTSS) teams, content or grade-level teams, professional learning communities, individualized education program (IEP) teams, co-teaching teams). These collaborative teams usually capitalize on the specialized knowledge and skills of the team members and generate shared, creative solutions to perplexing challenges. Villa and Thousand define effective collaborative teams as those whose members share a common goal, take on different roles (such as teacher, learner, expert, or supporter) within the team depending on the task, distribute leadership, and use a cooperative process to complete their work.[13]

Co-teaching teams are unique types of collaborative teams in which two or more members of the school community distribute planning, instructional, and assessment responsibilities in a mixed ability classroom. Co-teaching is a vital framework providing teachers with strategies and resources with which to respond to diverse needs within heterogeneous classrooms and provide students with fuller access to appropriate, effective instruction.[14] It also grants educators the opportunity to learn from one another, leveraging collegial partnerships and collaborative practices to expand their skills.[15] A transition from siloed services and programs to collaborative delivery models is a process of change that requires educators' commitment to collaboration. As educators learn to engage in these collaborative processes, school leaders should consider how best to structure educator collaboration to sustain co-planning, co-teaching, co-assessing, and co-reflecting.[16]

Discussion Questions

Activity A. Reflective Discussion

- If you were Dr. Mora, what top concerns would you prioritize at the next meeting?
- What actions would you take before next week's meeting?
- How could you alleviate the tension among the teachers on this team?
- Identify your concerns about ending or refusing to end pull-out services.
- How could the influx of immigrant, refugee, and multilingual students impact teachers who are not prepared to provide inclusive instruction for these students?
- Which evidence-based ELD program models could be implemented to support MLs and classroom teachers while phasing out the pull-out ELD model? For more explanation of evidence-based program models for MLs, see resources hosted by the National Clearinghouse for English Language Acquisition.[17]

Activity B. Needs and Options Brainstorm and Responsive Action Plan

School leaders address complex challenges with diverse stakeholders, various perspectives, and policy, legal, and resource constraints. First, brainstorm as many needs demonstrated by students, families, teachers, and staff as your group can think of. Consider the needs of MLs beyond language and MLs who have experienced significantly limited or interrupted schooling. Next, create a T-chart labeled "Immediate/Short-Term" on one side and "Planned/Long-Term" on the other, and categorize needs that require immediate action versus those that demand planned support. Then, generate as many options as possible to support the needs of students, families, teachers, and staff. Finally, develop an action plan with a logical sequence of actions to be implemented, timelines, and persons responsible. Consider the following parameters:

(1) urgent needs and resources already available
(2) extended needs, resources, and actions that require time to plan
(3) sustainable actions to implement over time to nurture an inclusive, equitable, and socially just school community.

Activity C. Role-Play

This activity can be done in various structures appropriate for the context and number of participants. Each participant takes on the perspective of a character to engage in the meetings proposed below.

Option 1: Site-based meeting. Fishbowl: Up to seven volunteers each take on a participant role from the case and continue next week's meeting while other students observe with back-channel discussion. The central focus of the meeting should be how Dr. Mora could help this team resolve their conflicts and move forward.

Option 2: School leadership team meeting. School leaders are meeting to devise a school action plan to move toward an inclusive ELD program. Meeting participants (i.e., principal, ELD and special education providers, school counselor, grade-level team leader) are trying to answer two big questions:

- What are the needs of students and families and of teachers and staff?
- How can the school support the range of evident needs in ways that are equitable and just?

Option 3: Districtwide principals' meeting. Principals from different schools and district leaders are meeting to discuss the challenges experienced by MLs and personnel, the resources available for support, and the constraints leaders have. Consider these questions:

- What needs are currently unmet?
- What are the district's legal obligations?
- How can students' learning and teachers' needs be supported while transitioning toward a just, inclusive, evidence-based ELD program that keeps students in their general education classrooms?
- How can leaders build a sense of belonging in the school community for students and families?

Activity D. Policy Review

Gather the policies implemented at the school, district, or state level. Review the policies and consider whether they are sensitive to the needs of students who are immigrants or refugees, or have experienced other barriers to equitable access, such as trauma or poverty. How could the policies, such as those regarding the issues listed below, be revised to better support students' needs?

- attendance and tardiness
- dress code
- fees, materials, and co-curriculars
- classroom expectations
- multitiered systemic student support
- grading, late work, and homework
- behavior and discipline

Activity E. Resource Scavenger Hunt

Review the resources provided:

- Sheltered Instruction Observation Protocol (SIOP), Center for Applied Linguistics (CAL), www.cal.org/siop
- World-Class Instruction Design and Assessment (WIDA), wida.wisc.edu
- National Center for Homeless Education, The McKinney-Vento Homeless Assistance Act, nche.ed.gov/legislation/mckinney-vento
- U.S. Citizenship and Immigration Services, www.uscis.gov
- U.S. Committee for Refugees and Immigrants, refugees.org
- International Rescue Committee, www.rescue.org
- Intercambio, Uniting Communities, intercambio.org
- Empowering Communities Globally, empoweringcommunitiesglobally.org
- Soccer without Borders, www.soccerwithoutborders.org

Generate a Resource Toolbox by gathering the following types of additional support resources available in the school's surrounding community:

- financial support resources
- refugee resettlement services
- basic needs
- technology access
- legal services
- community-based organizations
- mental health

CHAPTER 4

Changing Times

Exploring the Role of Culturally Responsive Leaders in New Immigrant Destinations

KRISTINA F. BREZICHA AND HONGJIE GUAN
Georgia State University

ABSTRACT

This case takes place in a new immigrant destination (NID) that has experienced rapid growth in its immigrant student population over the past twenty years. While in some communities this growth has been contentious, this NID district has managed to support the integration of their immigrant students by partnering with various community organizations and their state's Department of Education. These partnerships have helped this small community see their new immigrant neighbors as welcomed and valued community members rather than economic threats or drains on the community's resources.

This case focuses on the role of the partnership between the local educational agency (LEA) and state educational agency (SEA) and how the SEA can support school leaders working with their growing immigrant student population. It draws specifically on the notion of the nested context of reception, policy design framework, and culturally responsive school leadership to explore how school leaders can help shape the types of experiences immigrant students encounter. The teaching notes will first unpack what these concepts are and how school leaders can deploy them in their work with their schools, districts, and state partners. The chapter concludes with several possible teaching questions for aspiring school leaders.

CASE NARRATIVE

Dr. Kimberly Ballard recently joined the Newtown County School District's (NCSD) team as the director of multilingual programs. Dr. Ballard brings extensive experience as an English as a Second Language (ESL) teacher, a dual language (DL) teacher, a DL program coordinator in her district, and director of emergent bilingual support at the Texas Education Agency (TEA). While Texas has long had a large population of immigrant students, Dr. Ballard moved to Newtown County specifically because it was a new immigrant destination in a new immigrant state,[1] and she was looking for a new challenge.[2] Superintendent Bristol had recruited Dr. Ballard after hearing her presentation at a leadership conference on her TEA work organizing and supporting districts' efforts with immigrant students and DL programs.

When Dr. Ballard arrived in Newtown, it had experienced about twenty years of growth in its immigrant population. For the first decade, the arriving immigrants received a warm welcome from longtime residents. However, as the national political rhetoric heated up on immigration, local politicians began sounding the alarm about the "invasion of illegal immigrants." Coupled with a murder initially blamed on an undocumented immigrant who was eventually cleared of the charges, the residents' once welcoming stance devolved into tensions and bitter accusations between those who sought to limit immigrant arrivals in the community and those who sought to preserve the community's welcoming stance. Ballard knew this history because she had several frank conversations with Superintendent Bristol before she accepted her position. Part of these conversations revealed that NCSD had few institutional supports for its newcomers. Data from local and state assessments showed that these students often lagged behind their peers. Bristol shared her struggles with getting members of the school board and community to accept these children's right to an education. Dr. Bristol also highlighted that some community members worked hard to build bridges between the longtime, predominantly white residents and the newcomers, including opening a community center that focused on creating a space of integration. This center had developed programs to support newcomer youths, including after-school tutoring and English classes for the students and their families. Thus, Superintendent Bristol sought Dr. Ballard's help in developing a plan to support these students and the teachers and leaders who worked with them.

Dr. Ballard realized that to help the students, she needed first to reach out to the schools' leaders and get to know the different schools and their needs. As she met with the elementary and middle school principals, she found many receptive leaders open to Dr. Ballard's ideas for working with their increasingly diverse learners. Her meeting with the sole high school leader, however, raised red flags. She found Principal Ford using coded language to refer to immigrant and refugee students. Ford also did not think that his teachers' and staff's practices needed to change to support newcomer youths. Moreover, Dr. Ballard suspected that most immigrant and refugee students were being shuttled into the high school's vocational program rather than being appropriately placed into the school tracks that matched their interests. Importantly, though, Dr. Ballard noted that across all leadership teams, many expressed outdated understandings of how children learn language and a limited understanding of students' cultural backgrounds. Principal Ford even stated that, to learn English, "the kids just need to speak English."

Following her meetings with leaders, Ballard met with ESL teachers and with newcomer students. The meeting with teachers revealed that most felt isolated in their schools, and their skills and expertise were not being used. Ballard then met with upper elementary, middle, and high school students. These meetings highlighted how many students felt neglected and sometimes openly discriminated against. Many in the high school noted that there was a stark divide between immigrant and refugee students and other students both academically and socially. One remarked, "You would never see an immigrant kid in an advanced placement course." Another noted that the white kids stick to themselves, and the immigrant kids stick to themselves.

Considering all that she learned, Ballard knew she would need to implement professional development for leaders and teachers. In speaking to the state's ESL and Title IIIA program manager, Mr. Dawson, Ballard learned that the state had recently recognized bilingual education as a possible language-learning model for ESL students. Mr. Dawson offered to partner with her as he built the state's support for their immigrant students. Ballard started to brainstorm ways to support the students holistically. She also recognized that bringing the schools and community together would be important. As the fall semester wrapped up, Superintendent Bristol asked Dr. Ballard for an update on her plans for developing the schools' and district's responses to their newcomer students.

TEACHING NOTES

Dr. Ballard's experiences in NCSD reflect a distinct *context of reception* (COR) where many newcomer students attend schools with teachers and leaders who are woefully underprepared to meet their needs. Contexts of reception refer to the political, structural, and normative characteristics of immigrants' new communities that introduce them to their new societies and shape their opportunities for successful integration.[3] Scholars have recently begun arguing that the context of reception often focuses on the macro conditions found at the federal and state levels while not recognizing that local communities are often unique sites of reception that include entwining influences from across levels of governance.[4] Thus, to understand how immigrants experience their new communities, scholars and educators must consider their unique community contexts, including the local districts' and schools' responses to their immigrant students. While the state had recently taken several steps to support their immigrant and refugee students more holistically, Dr. Ballard still needed to contend with the tense local community environment. Moreover, the conflictual community context was reflected in the students' experiences in their schools, as many immigrant students reported feeling disconnected and isolated. Therefore, Dr. Ballard knew that to respond to Dr. Bristol's update request, she would need to consider how to draw on Mr. Dawson's expertise at the state level and connect the school leaders with experts who could help support their development of a more culturally responsive stance toward their immigrant students.

To help move the schools toward greater inclusivity, Dr. Ballard thought about the work of Muhammed Khalifa and others who proposed the notion of culturally responsive leadership (CRL).[5] Dr. Ballard's initial contact with students, teachers, and leaders in NCSD showcases the urgency of developing leaders' capacity to be culturally responsive. CRL has emerged from decades of pedagogical efforts to empower students of color, newcomer students, English-language learners (ELLs), and other underrepresented students by validating their ways of knowing and situating their academic success within their cultural experiences and perspectives.[6] Creating a school culture that responds to students' cultural backgrounds and unique pedagogical needs is impossible without support from leaders.[7] To do so, district and school leaders should openly affirm and welcome these students, thereby setting a tone of inclusivity for the students. Other possible actions that leaders can take include encouraging the use of students' heritage and native languages beyond ESL and DL classrooms and providing translated school documents as well as translators so that families and educators can communicate with one another. School policies, such as the dress code, could be modified to be culturally responsive to newcomer students. Leaders also need to identify and support teachers who hold deficit views of newcomer students' academic capacities or feel overwhelmed supporting newcomer students.[8] For example, ESL teachers in Newtown who reported feeling marginalized could also feel overwhelmed supporting an increasing number of newcomer students amid the instructional changes involved in shifting from ESL to DL programs. Dr. Ballard could provide both emotional and professional support for ESL educators by organizing district-level professional development and impact review sessions in which ESL educators would be encouraged to raise their concerns, share their expertise, and support one another.

Principals and administrators should recognize that they are responsible for challenging the exclusionary state- and district-level discourses and implementing school policies that support immigrant students. Not contesting deficit discourses will automatically lead to the reproduction of marginalization and oppression at school.[9] As discussed earlier, some in NCSD even embraced veiled and xenophobic discourses about immigrants and refugees. These discourses affect students' integration into the cultural and academic fabric of the school, which in the longer term will shape their sense of belonging and civic participation in the United States.[10] One way of contesting deficit discourses in NCSD is to set high academic expectations for newcomer students and their teachers, rather than shuttling them into vocational programs.[11]

CRL asks leaders to be mindful of possible educational knowledge differences held by themselves and the newcomer communities they serve, knowledge differences often informed by lived experiences and histories.[12] School leaders, especially those who do not share community histories with their newcomer students, can seek out trade and academic journal articles, conversations with community members, and other possible venues to learn about their knowledge differences and, more important, to consider those knowledge differences in designing and implementing school policies.[13] Critically examining differences in groups' histories and lived experiences enables leaders to understand how immigrant students position themselves in the school and how their parents perceive their roles in children's education.[14] It also encourages leaders to acknowledge the privileges they may enjoy as members of a specific community, and how these privileges shape their educational experiences and perceptions and affect their involvement in the schooling contexts of oppression.[15] Educational leaders should ask themselves: To what extent do I acknowledge the presence of newcomer students and their knowledge, languages, and cultures? Where does my knowledge of newcomer youths come from? Specifically, to what extent do newcomer communities contribute to my knowledge of them?

Immigrant communities in Newtown are framed as having criminal tendencies and illegal residency status that threaten to overrun the local community and rob longtime white residents of resources. Immigrant students are depicted as needing remediation for their linguistic deficiency and academic incompetence. Such depictions are devoid of both the voices of immigrant communities and any supportive local context. Specifically, immigrant students in NCSD are categorized as ELLs in district and school policies. This approach is counter to CRL as it frames immigrants as a monolithic group regardless of their diverse cultural backgrounds and normalizes immigrant students' linguistic identities as deficient. Principal Ford's stance reflected an English-only approach that silenced immigrant students' heritage languages in their classrooms. As a dual language educator and advocate, Dr. Ballard would need to challenge Principal Ford's deficit-oriented knowledge of immigrant communities and English-only ideology. In designing her training programs in Newtown, Dr. Ballard should invite educational leaders and teachers to reflect on how they came to their beliefs about newcomer students. By collaborating with Mr. Dawson from the state Department of Education, Dr. Ballard could also incorporate research into trainings that educate leaders, teachers, students, and immigrant communities about DL as a form of bilingual education, in which English acquisition and native or heritage language maintenance could work together to support newcomer students' academic success.[16]

The term *responsive* in *culturally responsive leadership* requires school leaders not just to teach immigrant students the dominant language (English) and curriculum in their languages but also to consider how our education system should develop to integrate our students' cultural-linguistic realities.[17] This shift of educational systems stands in tension with those that would rather just have the students assimilate into the educational system, a perspective Principal Ford, among others in NCSD, holds. For example, Dr. Ballard could collaborate with school leaders and step into classrooms, documenting teachers' sense-making practices of implementing school-level language policies. She could identify and support teachers' practices that cater to newcomer students' specific needs, such as code-switching between English and students' native or heritage languages. She could also work with social studies curriculum and other content subject matter experts to examine and modify and, if necessary, revise the curriculum to reflect and include the accurate histories of newcomer communities. Notably, Dr. Ballard understands community as a central tenet of CRL.[18] Immigrant newcomers in NCSD are vulnerable to multiple layers of minoritization, including xenophobic national and local political narratives, English-only policies that devalue bilingualism, within-school segregation, and school leaders' inadequate understanding of students' strengths and needs.[19] As a culturally responsive leader, Dr. Ballard should work closely with community members and advocate for community-based issues, such as limited job opportunities for newcomer adults due to the restrictive context of reception in the district. One such example comes from a school that hired students' family members as translators and staff in a variety of positions.[20] Bringing the students' families into this school immediately communicated the value the school placed on the students' families and communities. Although schools are important sites for newcomer integration, community experiences constitute a significant part of newcomer youths' realities and are central to their sense of belonging.[21]

CRL seeks to empower newcomer communities to craft and achieve their own goals.[22] Community members should be invited to participate in the training programs for school professionals as tutors and consultants. To challenge Principal Ford's deficit-oriented knowledge, Ballard should encourage him to take opportunities, such as home visits and report card delivery, to establish rapport with newcomer families. Ballard also knew that she should participate in community-based issues beyond school contexts and enact her district leadership role to attract resources to assist newcomer families in leveraging their social capital and forming relationships with one another.[23] Collaborations could be established with the local school board, councils, and employers to design bilingual and other programs for adults that recognize and develop newcomers' skills and expertise and prepare newcomers to participate in local policy making through petition writing and the like. In this collaborative way, Dr. Ballard could help lesson social fracturing and create a more welcoming community that allows for all students to flourish.

Discussion Questions

The questions below are designed to get you thinking about all that you read in this case and apply it to your community context. We hope that they spark reflective moments and powerful conversations.

1. Compared to NCSD, what are the contexts of reception in your school district? What resources in your district inform your understanding of CORs?
2. As educational leaders, how could you affect the current COR in your school district?
3. If you were Dr. Ballard, how would you respond to Principal Ford and other school leaders who are resistant to listening to community voices and combating existing oppression of newcomer students?
4. In what ways have you brought voices to the table that represented newcomer families and communities in school policy planning and implementation? What factors or circumstances led to the success, or the failure, to do so? Which voices representing newcomer families and communities have you already brought to the table? If none, who could you invite as a starting conversation partner?

Teacher Activities

1. Discuss with your leadership team and faculty the challenges of supporting newcomer students and communities. Working with your team (both leaders and faculty), conduct a mapping activity of groups and individuals in the school, district, and state that have expertise in the community and your particular population of students. Identify different actors who could be resources both within the school and in the broader community. Once you have identified these actors, consider how your school can develop relationships with these individuals and groups that will help provide insights into your students' cultural and linguistic backgrounds. You should also consider how these individuals may be able to help address specific challenges or barriers. Draft an action plan for reaching out to identified actors for collaboration.
2. *Shadowing* refers to a research methodology involving "observation on the move," in which the researcher follows a participant for an extended period of time as a nonparticipant observer.[24] Immigrant newcomers have various pre- and post-immigration experiences. Shadowing can enable leaders to learn about COR from newcomer

youths' perspectives through detailed observation. It can also assist educational leaders in critical reflections. After obtaining both the student's and their family's consent, identify and shadow a newcomer student throughout a school day. Take observational notes whenever you feel struck. Conduct reflections at the end of the day: What have you learned about the student, their family, and community that you didn't know before? How can you help the student with their integration and academic success? Form a small group with other leaders in your district. Meet with them to discuss your shadowing experiences.

RESOURCES

- "Partnering with Immigrant Families to Promote Student Success," Carnegie Corporation of New York, 2023, https://www.carnegie.org/our-work/article/partnering-with-immigrant-families-to-promote-student-success/.
- "Supporting Newcomer Students: Resource Gallery," Colorín Colorado, 2023, https://www.colorincolorado.org/ell-newcomer-resources.
- "Supporting Immigrant Students in Schools Video Series," Initiative on Immigration and Education, City University of Newy York, 2024, https://www.cuny-iie.org/sis-videos.
- M. Mavrogordato, C. Bartlett, R. Callahan, D. DeMatthews, and E. Izquierdo, "Supports for Multilingual Students Who Are Classified as English Learners: Overview Brief," EdResearch for Action, update September 2024, https://edresearchforaction.org/research-briefs/supports-for-multilingual-students-who-are-classified-as-english-learners/.

SECTION 2

Within-School and Classroom Considerations

The chapters in Section 2 consider how newcomer students and families first experience US schooling norms, processes, and classrooms. The case narratives engage leaders with regard to designing safe, welcoming, and inclusive school spaces that facilitate newcomer students' access to schooling and full participation in it. The chapters take on a variety of timely topics, from reconceptualizing welcoming schools to exploring the complexities of school enrollment processes and documentation practices for refugees and asylees (chapter 5, by Okilwa and Gutierrez). Bogotch (chapter 6) critically examines what democratic school leadership practices with newcomers mean, raising both questions and possibilities for increased participation, power sharing, cooperation, and communication among leaders and newcomer populations. Hammouda, Bittel, and Mann (chapter 7) examine how theories of "place attachment" can be used to foster newcomers' integration and belonging in schools. Hamidy and Belkin (chapter 8) take readers through a real-life journey (based in London but applicable to the US context) of a leader and her team as they learn and grow from their experiences working with displaced individuals from Afghanistan, in the process developing more culturally relevant and responsive practices. In chapter 9, Bittel and Bittel situate their work in the science education classroom. They challenge readers to think about how equity is central to creating inclusive classroom environments, which entails educators ensuring that newcomers' cultural backgrounds and experiences are recognized and honored. The authors offer ways for educators to incorporate students' cultural and experiential resources into the curriculum to enhance students' meaningful engagement and learning. Alvarez and Tran (chapter 10) show how summer programming can close gaps in newcomers' English language acquisition and bolster teacher professional development to work with multilingual learners.

CHAPTER 5

What's Your Birthday?

The Birthday Mystery and the Enrollment Conundrum

NATHERN OKILWA
Baylor University

DAMARIS GUTIERREZ
Northside Independent School District

ABSTRACT

Enrolling in school in the United States requires identifying documents. Our local school district, for instance, requires newly registering students to provide an original certified copy of the child's birth certificate, an up-to-date immunization record, and proof of residency such as the current or the prior month's utility bill; or a sales, lease, or rental contract; or a notarized Affidavit of Residence (AOR) form. For most Americans, these documents are readily available. However, for newcomer families, especially refugees and asylees, these document requirements add to the anxiety of transitioning and settling in their newly adopted home country. This chapter teases out the nuances embedded in school enrollment for refugee and asylee students by describing three vignettes. Vignette 1: In a class of refugee students from a variety of countries, including Republic of the Congo, Democratic Republic of the Congo, Eritrea, Uganda, Afghanistan, Thailand, Myanmar, Nepal, and Malaysia, a teacher's activity to celebrate a birthday revealed something unique: the majority of the students had a January 1 birthday. Vignette 2: An Afghan family of six children, from rural Kunar province, sought the help of Mr. Mendez to fill out the intimidating forms necessary to apply for free or reduced lunch. To Mr. Mendez's surprise, all of the children had a

November 17 birthday. Vignette 3: A "ten-year-old" (on paper) Iraqi student who was enrolled in the fourth grade seemed much older than his classmates and even some fifth graders. In the initial conversation with the teacher, the father insisted that his son's age was correct and that his son had attended advanced academics in Iraq. Later in the year, the father advocated for the son to be advanced to middle school. After several parent-teacher meetings, the father finally acknowledged that his son was twelve years old.

CASE NARRATIVE

Central City Independent School District (CCISD) is located in a southern US city of 1.5 million people. Overall, Central City is attractive to many immigrants because it is diverse and offers better economic opportunities than some other places. CCISD has a student population of about 102,000, of whom 7 percent are Black or African American, 68 percent are Hispanic, 17 percent white, 4 percent Asian, and 4 percent other. Fifty-four percent of the students are considered economically disadvantaged, and "emerging bilinguals" make up 12 percent of the student population.

Most school districts in the United States require official identification documents to enroll in school. For instance, CCISD indicates on its website that newly registering students are required to provide an original certified copy of the child's birth certificate, an up-to-date immunization record, and proof of residency such as the current or prior month's utility bill; or a sales, lease, or rental contract; or a notarized Affidavit of Residence (AOR) form. Most Americans can readily obtain these documents. However, for newcomer families, especially refugees, asylees, and undocumented families, these requirements add a level of anxiety and frustration in the process of transitioning and settling in the United States, as the three vignettes below indicate. Out of precaution, most resettlement agencies and school districts still adhere to contact-free practices adopted during the COVID-19 pandemic; hence, new enrollment or registration is all online. The online registration forms are not available in languages other than English and Spanish, and that can add another barrier. The purpose of this chapter is to present educators with an opportunity to troubleshoot the multiple dimensions of proper documentation requirements for refugees as presented in the following three vignettes. Also, we present brief teaching notes, discussion questions (or teaching activities), and helpful resources.

Vignette 1: Birthday Anchor Chart

Gina Watson was a teacher at Highland Elementary School for a combined third- and fourth-grade self-contained class of newcomer refugee students from countries around the world, including Afghanistan, Republic of the Congo, Democratic Republic of the Congo, Eritrea, Iraq, Malaysia, Myanmar, Thailand, and Uganda. The students spoke eleven different languages and were emergent bilinguals. Each child had different educational experiences ranging from no prior schooling to interrupted formal schooling. Each lesson was designed to support the students' grade-level content knowledge and English-language development. Ms. Watson planned interactive learning tasks that engaged students with visuals, manipulatives, and relevant content. One day, the task's learning intention was that students develop a pictograph to order and compare birthdays of their classmates. In preparation, Ms. Watson noticed that many of her students had a January 1 birthday, but she did not spend time investigating this finding. During the lesson, each student had their birthday cupcake paper cutout with their birthday written on it. She had students talk with their peers about their birthday, and each student brought it up to the board and shared. Once all the birthdays were posted on the pictograph chart, Ms. Watson asked the students to tell her how to order the birthdays for each month. Ms. Watson started with January and when she spoke aloud to the class, she said, "Hmm, I am noticing that many of you have a January 1 birthday." The students agreed and many were eager to share about their birthdays. Mohammed from Eritrea said, "This is not my real birthday; I have a different one." Mohammed did not share his real birthday but said that he was nine years old. Most of the children claimed to know their ages but not their birth date. In her head, Ms. Watson wondered about the accuracy of the birthdate and age data she was getting from the students. The room exploded with many children sharing their personal stories of birthdays and age. Some students noted that at the resettlement camp where their refugee paperwork was processed, their parents gave January 1 as the birthdate for all the children in the family. The students' stories left Ms. Watson bewildered, and the following week she decided to share with her principal, Ms. Johnson, what she had learned from the students. Ms. Johnson listened attentively and was left in wonder as well; this was new and "strange" information to her, and she did not have an immediate next step to suggest to Ms. Watson. The principal promised to look into the matter and get back to her soon. Ms. Johnson was in her second year as principal and was new to this school community, though she had served as a teacher and assistant principal (AP) for ten years in the district. The demands and responsibilities of the principal's position at Highland Elementary, a high-needs school, were formidable. And given that Highland did not meet the enrollment threshold to qualify for two administrators (i.e., a principal and AP), Ms. Johnson did not have an AP. Needless to say, the semester ended without Ms. Johnson getting back to Ms. Watson with a response concerning the coinciding birthdays.

Vignette 2: Siblings with Same Birthday

Daniel Mendez had recently been appointed as one of the three assistant principals at Eastside Middle School (MS), where he had served as an English as a Second Language teacher and the ESL program coordinator for the past fifteen years. Eastside MS consisted of families from different socioeconomic statuses, and 30 percent received free or reduced-price lunch. To qualify for this service, families had to complete the free or reduced lunch (FRL) online or paper application. The application was offered by the district only in English and Spanish. As a teacher and program coordinator, Mr. Mendez always worked in partnership with different campus personnel to support families with registration, enrollment in their middle school courses, immunization, and FRL application. Mr. Mendez loved supporting these families and students as it allowed him to build community in the school and with families.

One afternoon, Mr. Mendez encountered Rezwanullah, an older brother of Abdullah, a seventh-grader in the ESL program. Rezwanullah came to the school one day to give Abdullah money for lunch because the cafeteria manager, Regina Martinez, told him he owed money for his lunch. Mr. Mendez investigated the situation by inquiring with Ms. Martinez, who told him that the family had not applied for FRL, so it was charged each time Abdullah and his sister, Farishta, ate lunch from the cafeteria. Mr. Mendez informed Rezwanullah about the FRL program and offered to help him with the online application if necessary. Rezwanullah's parents spoke only Pashto and felt unequipped to fully support their children with school-related tasks and responsibilities. Rezwanullah, who was bilingual, served as liaison between his family and the school. Rezwanullah shared with Mr. Mendez that his computer skills were limited because when he was in Afghanistan he did not have access to computers. He was having a hard time adjusting and navigating US society, which relies heavily on technology. In the process of helping Rezwanullah fill out the FRL application for all his siblings enrolled in district schools, Mr. Mendez noticed something: All the siblings had a November 17 birth date: Bilal, a ninth-grader was born November 17, 2010; Abdullah, the child in middle school, was born November 17, 2011; and Farishta's birthday was November 17, 2012. Mr. Mendez asked Rezwanullah if all the children had the same birthday. Rezwanullah was quiet for a couple minutes and finally responded, yes, "except me." Mr. Mendez was puzzled but proceeded to help Rezwanullah complete the FRL application. This was Mr. Mendez's first encounter with this distinctive siblings' birth date situation, and out of curiosity, he asked Rezwanullah about it. The children had not been born in a hospital, Rezwanullah replied, nor did they have access to state-issued birth documentation. Therefore, while filling out their refugee paperwork to migrate to the United States, they chose November 17. Rezwanullah also noted that his family did not celebrate birthdays because it was considered a taboo in the region of Afghanistan where they originated. Mr. Mendez talked to the principal, Mr. Keeling, about the birthdate situation. Mr. Keeling was approaching retirement—one more year to go—and he simply told Mr. Mendez, "That is a can of worms not worth opening."

Vignette 3: My Child's Age Is Incorrect

Grace Robinson was a fourth-grade ESL teacher at Lindahl Elementary School whose students included newcomer refugees mostly from Iraq, Nepal, and Thailand. The ESL program at her campus was expanding because more students from Iraq were arriving as the war in Iraq ended. Many of the Iraqi families were from the middle and upper classes, and the children had had educational experiences in their country prior to the war. The children were literate in Arabic and acquired English at an accelerated pace.

Ms. Robinson met with families to discuss their children's educational progress and inquired about variability in developmentally age-appropriate behaviors she had observed. Prior to the meetings, multiple students had confided to Ms. Robinson that their birthdays and ages were incorrect. Ms. Robinson mentioned these student revelations to the principal, Ms. Comfort. Ms. Robinson was particularly curious about Yusef's age because he conducted himself more maturely and seemed developmentally more advanced than his fourth-grade peers. She spoke to Yusef's father to inquire about his age and potential grade misplacement. Yusef's dad, Khalid Ahmed, who had served as an interpreter for the US military, was adamant that Yusef's age was correct and he should be in the fourth grade.

The following year, however, when Yusef went to the fifth grade with Agnes Aguilar (who taught in the classroom next Ms. Robinson's), Mr. Ahmed requested a meeting with Ms. Aguilar and Ms. Comfort, the principal, to discuss his son's grade placement. During the meeting, Mr. Ahmed disclosed that Yusef was actually twelve years old and should be moved to middle school. Over the summer, Yusef's cousins had relocated to town, and his age-mates among these family members were in middle school. Consequently, Mr. Ahmed wanted Yusef to be in the middle school so that he could be with his cousins and participate in advanced studies. Ms. Comfort asked Mr. Ahmed to come back next week for a meeting that would involve the school counselor and psychologist. In scheduling this meeting for the following week, Ms. Comfort gave herself time to seek insight on how best to handle Mr. Ahmed's request. However, before the meeting could take place, somehow word reached the Parent-Teacher

Organization (PTO) president, Jen Whitmann, about the age situation with Yusef. She spread word in the community about refugee families trying to "game" the system. Some members of the community were riled, particularly those who felt refugee students were significantly changing the demographics of their school for the worst.

TEACHING NOTES

As long as political and economic instability, constant sectorial violence, religious persecution, and natural disasters continue to plague nations around the world, migration and resettlement of people will continue to be necessary. The current Russia-Ukraine and Israel-Hamas wars, as well as the political instability in Afghanistan, South Sudan, and Haiti, to mention only a few, are painful reminders of the destabilizing conditions that people find themselves in that prompt many to flee their homelands. Furthermore, recently the United States has experienced an unprecedented number of migrants crossing through the southern border, seeking better economic opportunities.[1] Given the circumstances under which most of these refugees leave their countries, it is not surprising that many of them lack basic legal documents such as a birth certificate or passport.

Proper Legal Documentation

According to the United Nations High Commissioner for Refugees, at the end of 2023, "an estimated 117.3 million people worldwide were forcibly displaced due to persecution, conflict, violence, human rights violations and events seriously disturbing the public order." Of this refugee population, an estimated 40 percent are school-age children, and displacement often means an interruption in their education.[2] When these children are resettled in the United States, they are entitled to free and appropriate education. In the new homeland, these students confront many hurdles, some of which emerge from experiences in their country of origin while others are related to adapting to the new homeland. Existing evidence suggests that refugee students arrive in the United States with an array of psychosocial, cultural, socioeconomic, and academic challenges. In addition, some refugee families deal with misplaced or lost identification documents. The International Organization for Migration (IOM) estimates that there are "one billion people in the world without access to legal identity (birth, marriage and death certificates, identity cards, among others)."[3] A person without properly registered identification documents, particularly if they are attempting to resettle in the United States, faces challenges from the agencies and organizations involved in the resettlement process. Families have to delay enrollment in school until they can resolve any document-related issues. The IOM suggests four potential proactive approaches to accessing legal identity and documentation for migrants: (1) develop consular services for the issuance of civil registration, citizenship certificates, and identity and travel documents; (2) institute effective national civil registration and identity management systems to facilitate migration and mobility; (3) highlight the relationship between migration, displacement, and legal identity, including the impact of legal identity on the protection of migrants; (4) to avoid further exploitation and trauma, coordinate assistance as necessary to provide documentation services, proof of nationality or travel, regularization of residency status, or support for migrants to register their identity information in the host country's legal identity system.[4]

The Principal's Role

Increasing diversity in terms of students' abilities, social class, culture, language, race and ethnicity, and nativity is challenging, particularly for schools that have typically served a homogenous student population or have used mainstream philosophies of teaching and learning.[5] Efforts to reenvision educational practices require the leadership of the principal to foster an innovative and inclusive educational environment.[6] The reenvisioning could entail reconsidering the age-centric grade placement or the normative grade configuration practices.[7] Research indicates that successful school leaders in these diverse environments demonstrate a common set of understandings, dispositions, and practices.[8] For instance, Howard has suggested that effective principals in diverse contexts adhere to five phases: building trust, engaging personal culture, confronting issues of social dominance and social justice, transforming instructional practices, and engaging the entire school community.[9] Refugee students and their families are particularly overwhelmed trying to navigate the norms of their new homeland. Knowing that they can trust educators and lean on them to help negotiate the complex US education system is important. Furthermore, Riehl, after analyzing a vast scholarship about the principal's role in creating inclusive schools for diverse students, identified three critical administrator tasks or practices: fostering new meanings about diversity, promoting inclusive school cultures and instructional programs, and building relationships between schools and communities.[10] And Khalifa has established that a school leader who seeks to establish a healthy relationship (e.g., trust and rapport) between the school and the community needs to assume the role of a community leader—including high principal visibility in the community and advocacy for community causes.[11] On aggregate, then, successful leaders in diverse settings are critically self-reflective, cognizant of the internal and external school contexts, and centered on improving student educational experience.

Building Capacity

Effective principals acknowledge that the ever increasing demands of leading diverse schools cannot be met single-handedly. Given that teachers matter most among school-related factors in improving student outcomes and that they form a significant part of the team, the job of recruiting, hiring, and retaining a cadre of teachers to support refugee students is imperative.[12] Principals must ensure that newly hired teachers, especially those working with refugee students, receive, at a minimum, high-quality mentoring, common planning time with peers, continued professional development, and routine feedback.[13] Darling-Hammond has argued that "the number one reason for teachers' decisions about whether to stay in a school is the quality of administrative support—and it is the leader who must develop this organization."[14] These supports, coupled with empowering teachers through distributed leadership, are greatly needed in diverse contexts.[15]

Core to teachers' responsibilities is delivering curriculum and instruction. However, in working with refugee students, much more is expected of teachers, such as assuming the responsibility of cultural brokers. Teachers can become cultural brokers for refugee students and their families by (a) seeking an understanding of different cultural groups, (b) having firsthand experiences in classrooms and communities with different people groups, and (c) building cross-cultural awareness that understands the needs of students from culturally and linguistically diverse (CLD) backgrounds.[16] As cultural brokers, teachers help CLD students and their parents navigate the language, customs, and norms of the school and school system while simultaneously affirming students' own culture. Brokering understanding should be two-way: schools understanding refugee families and vice versa. For instance, understanding and acknowledging that some cultures do not celebrate birthdays or do not eat pork. As Gay posited, an important element of an effective cultural broker is being cross-culturally competent, which means recognizing, interpreting, and understanding cultural elements that contrast with one's own behaviors, values, and beliefs.[17] As Moll and colleagues observe, funds of knowledge recognize that the cumulatively acquired and developed bodies of knowledge and skills are essential for individual functioning and well-being.[18] Teachers need to extend this understanding to refugee students because they, too, bring to class funds of knowledge that can be tapped to enrich their learning experience. In terms of pedagogy for CLD students, Gay has proposed a culturally responsive teaching (CRT) approach that acknowledges diverse student backgrounds and ways of knowing. According to Gay, CRT is geared toward "understanding students' prior experiences and learning styles, as well as [using] cultural knowledge to ensure that learning is appropriate to culturally diverse learners."[19] In a classroom where CRT tenets are espoused, students connect with the content (or find content relevant), and they are more likely to be fully engaged in the learning process and to feel empowered intellectually, socially, emotionally, and politically.

Discussion Questions

Vignette 1

(1) If you were Ms. Watson, how would you approach the January 1 birthday phenomenon with your students and their families?

(2) As a school leader, how would you respond to the findings shared by Ms. Watson about her students' birthdays?

Vignette 2

(1) What leadership qualities did Mr. Mendez demonstrate in his interactions with Rezwanullah and the ESL students?

(2) How does Mr. Mendez's background and experience as an ESL teacher inform his approach to his new role as an AP?

Vignette 3

(1) What leadership qualities did Ms. Robinson demonstrate in her interactions with Yusef and his family?

(2) As a school leader, how would you address the concerns raised by the PTO president and the community regarding the refugee students?

General Discussion

(1) How can the school leader foster a culturally sensitive and inclusive environment for students from diverse backgrounds?

(2) What are the potential implications of the birthday inaccuracy phenomenon for the school system?

(3) How can school leaders balance the need for accurate data with respect for students' personal stories and experiences?

(4) How can school leaders ensure that the privacy and dignity of refugee students and their families are respected?

(5) What ethical considerations should be taken into account when handling sensitive information about students' backgrounds?

(6) How can the school develop policies to address the unique needs of students with uncertain or incorrect birthdates and ages?

Beyond the Birthdate Conundrum

(1) Considering your specific context, how can the school involve parents and the broader community in addressing the needs of newcomer refugee students and families?

(2) What role can civic and government agencies and organizations play in supporting the school's efforts to provide a supportive learning environment for refugee students?

RESOURCES

Cultural Orientation Resource Exchange (CORE), https://www.coresourceexchange.org/.

InterAction, https://www.interaction.org/.

Migration Policy Institute (MPI), https://www.migrationpolicy.org/.

Office of Refugee Resettlement, US Department of Health and Human Services. https://www.acf.hhs.gov/orr.

Refugee Council USA, https://rcusa.org/.

US Refugee Admissions Program, https://www.state.gov/refugee-admissions/.

Resettlement Agencies

Bethany Christian Services, https://bethany.org/.

Church World Service (CWS), https://cwsglobal.org/.

Episcopal Migration Ministries (EMM), http://www.episcopalchurch.org/emm/.

Ethiopian Community Development Council (ECDC), http://www.ecdcus.org/.

Hebrew Immigrant Aid Society (HIAS), http://www.hias.org/.

International Rescue Committee (IRC), http://www.rescue.org/.

Lutheran Immigration and Refugee Services (LIRS), http://www.lirs.org/.

United States Conference of Catholic Bishops (USCCB), http://www.usccb.org/.

US Committee for Refugees and Immigrants (USCRI), http://www.refugees.org/.

World Relief Corporation (WR), http://worldrelief.org/.

CHAPTER 6

School Leadership Democratic Practices

Welcoming and Integrating Newcomers

IRA BOGOTCH
Florida Atlantic University

ABSTRACT

The school leader highlighted in this case story did not deliberately set out to teach democratic practices to newcomer students or their families. Yet, every day, Principal Margaret Court faced having to peacefully resolve conflicts and disagreements directly related to the journey of newcomers. She was determined to ensure that newcomer students and their families felt welcomed and part of the school community and her native-neighborhood students prospered. She viewed newcomers as assets who brought gifts to the neighborhood; the least she could do was reciprocate. In other words, she learned that including others respectfully in her decisions worked for the school as a whole. There was very little of the get-it-done-efficiently kind of leadership. Rather, Principal Margaret's leadership took the long view regarding welcoming and integrating newcomers. Therefore, in this chapter, democratic school leadership practices are framed as understanding participation, power sharing, cooperating, and communicating with and across political disagreements and conflicts among children and adults to create a democratic school culture.

CASE NARRATIVE

Setting the Table: Welcoming Newcomer Students and Parents

When I met Margaret Court, principal of Tanglewood Elementary School, both she and her staff had years of experience with the many newcomer students who enrolled each year in the school district.[1] They understood that the newcomers, from families who spoke more than fifteen different languages, often came to her school with the most traumatic experiences, from civil war and famine to poverty. What these families all had in common, however, was the need to survive and find a better life, especially for their school-age children. Some newcomer students had gaps of up to five years in their formal education; others had no formal schooling. Other students came from upper-middle-class homes that they had been forced to leave. Every newcomer student and family is unique; therefore, keeping an open mind and interrogating biases are fundamental to practicing democracy.

Welcoming and integrating, like the practices of democracy itself, encompass growth and development; they are always in process and unfinished. There is always more to learn and more to do. At the same time, the pace of a school leader's life in school is not conducive to careful study and reflection. Events happen one right after another, overlapping and unresolved. It is within these continuous leadership contexts that the tasks of welcoming and integrating newcomer students can challenge the democratic practices embedded in decision making and conflict resolution. What might appear ordinary to long-term residents can feel unfamiliar to refugee and newcomer students and their families. These individuals are navigating entirely new social, cultural, and political landscapes—containing complexities that lifelong US community members often take for granted. If all a newcomer student and family has ever experienced has been autocratic and dictatorial authorities, then the values and beliefs of democracy can be new and confusing. How does a school leader create a sense of belonging for children and adults who were forcibly displaced from their homes? Principal Margaret knew from her years of experience that her leadership responsibilities extended beyond teaching English as a second language and beyond mastering academic subject matter content. Creating a welcoming and integrated school community grounded in cooperation, respect, and dignity required her, as a school leader, to assist others—newcomer students, their families, and school teachers and staff—in accepting greater responsibilities and participating more actively in decision making. How would she do this without appearing weak and indecisive as a leader?

A Day with Principal Margaret Court

As the school year was just beginning, Principal Margaret wanted to do something special for the most recent newcomer students and their families from Syria. She asked her leadership team for ideas about welcoming and integrating. Someone suggested having a pancake breakfast. The idea was to hold the breakfast for these newcomers only on the first or second day of the school year. But Margaret quickly changed her mind as she listened carefully to other team members, parents, and teachers. "Everyone likes pancakes," she said, "and if this breakfast idea was to build school spirit, then maybe everyone should be invited. I want to make sure that it's for all my students; I don't want something to be for just newcomers because we have lots of children from everywhere who like pancakes, and we don't want any division."

At the same time, Margaret, her staff, and all the newcomer families were keenly aware of how the government and district policies kept changing with each new wave of new arrivals. She knew this caused resentment not only among the different immigrant groups, which included Iraqis, Filipinos, Indians, and Chinese, but also among her neighborhood families. Everyone could be happy eating pancakes at least.

Moments later, she heard on her walky-talky that a fight had just broken out between two of her fifth-grade students, one a local, the other a Syrian newcomer. While fighting was not a common occurrence at Tanglewood, Margaret had confidence in her rapid response team. She knew that even before she arrived on the scene, the fight would be over, and the children would be waiting in the hallway outside the behavioral interventionist's office. So that's where she headed.

Because the school year had just begun, Margaret hadn't been to Ms. Snyder's office. She saw the two children sitting outside but just walked past them. It was her practice to let her trained staff have direct control over such situations. There was usually no need for Margaret, the principal, to interfere. Margaret entered Ms. Snyder's office and immediately noticed that a gym mat was hanging on the far wall opposite Ms. Snyder's desk.

"What's this?" she asked, pointing to the gym mat.

A smile appeared on Ms. Snyder's face. "Oh, you noticed," she replied.

> Last year, I was dealing with conflicts all day long. There was lots of fighting. So, I thought that after I brought the students in and we talked for a while, if their anger hadn't subsided, maybe by them hitting the mat, it might help. I tell them, "Punch as hard as you can. No one will get hurt this way." Since Tanglewood became a magnet school for newcomers, the stories the children tell me are heartbreaking. These little ones have so much anger from what they have seen and experienced before coming to us. The horrors—landmines and family members being killed in front of them. I knew they needed an outlet. Instead of hitting another student, what if I let them hit the gym mat in my office? And when I asked how they felt afterward, they all said "better."
>
> Now, some of them just knock on my door, and if no one is in my office, I let them hit the gym mat. I was going to speak to you about maybe ordering a couple of stationary bicycles which also might relieve their stress. They could peddle as hard and as fast for however long it takes for them to calm down. What do you think?

Ms. Snyder's request to order stationary bikes cost money, and money was always an issue. Principal Margaret was certainly open to innovative ideas to de-escalate conflicts and address the emotional trauma and cultural differences her many newcomers had experienced. No matter how many school leader–parent meetings, conversation circles, moms' or dads' clubs, afterschool picnics, or soccer games it took, her students needed to learn how to disagree peacefully without fighting as their first response. Margaret was proud of how most of her staff and teachers handled difficult and stressful situations. Her job was to make their lives less stressful.

Margaret Court relied heavily on her leadership team. What she liked best was the different perspectives they brought to complicated problems. Among the themes continuously brought up were student behavioral issues and, occasionally, the behaviors of parents. At one meeting, the assistant principal (AP) had suggested creating a checklist of behaviors to avoid that could be handed out to newcomers during orientation each year.

"Wouldn't this be viewed as being culturally insensitive?" she asked.

The AP countered, "What do you mean by culturally insensitive?" Every summer, the district offered many professional development workshops on being culturally sensitive. Margaret trusted how her leadership team incorporated the new ideas into their practices. Yet she also knew that every so often members of her team looked for the most efficient administrative response to complicated issues like cultural understanding. Nevertheless, as the school's leader, she could not ignore the persistently strong views voiced by leadership team members. It was not just efficiency that drove leadership discussions; some staff were more concerned about academics rather than about cultural differences and the conflicts that resulted. Principal Court informed AP Roberts to draft a checklist, and the team would review it at their meeting next week. Immediately, she wondered whether she had acted too quickly in agreeing to the checklist idea.

Just then, one of her fourth-grade teachers walked into her office with a child in each hand. One was Ahmed, an Iraqi newcomer, and the other was Liam, a native-born student. The teacher was upset and in a hurry to get back to her classroom. She said the students would explain why they were there and did a quick about-face out of the office. Principal Margaret asked them politely to take seats. Neither child looked up, but she could sense they were still very angry.

MARGARET: Ahmed? Would you like me to call in an Arabic interpreter, or are you comfortable talking to me in English?

AHMED: I can talk to you.

MARGARET: Okay. Who wants to tell me what happened?

AHMED: Liam said mean things about my mother.

LIAM QUICKLY SHOUTED BACK: "*I did not!* I don't even know his mother."

MARGARET THEN ASKED LIAM: "You didn't say anything mean to Ahmed?"

LIAM: "I said his answer to the teacher's question was stupid. He didn't understand her. I don't know why he goes to our school. He can't even speak English."

Principal Margaret knew how some of the local children's parents talked about the newcomers at home, often in unwelcoming ways. Still, it was her mission to make Tanglewood Elementary a model of diversity and inclusion. If she could win over the students, then it didn't matter what some of the parents said. It was not enough for her to just listen, as important as listening is for leadership. Could she find a way for Ahmed and Liam to reconcile and then get to know each other better? Maybe work together?

She knew from experience that her newcomer students needed to learn that when they didn't understand what another child was saying in English, it didn't mean they were talking badly about them or any family member. Margaret knew there was a lot of misunderstanding in the cross-cultural transitions and that it would take time for Ahmed and other newcomers to make friends and feel like they belonged at Tanglewood.

It was also important that her native-born students, such as Liam, learn how to see newcomer students as she did, as students who were motivated to learn and could be good neighbors and friends. This isn't easy with more than fifteen different native languages spoken by the families at Tanglewood. But if the entire student body can be given opportunities in class or after school, there might be more understanding and respect and fewer conflicts.

MARGARET ADDRESSED AHMED: You are a smart young man. You are learning English, right? And Liam did not make fun of your mother.

AHMED: My mother stays home all day, and she doesn't know any English. And I asked the teacher to repeat the question she asked me.

MARGARET THEN TURNED TO LIAM: Liam, Did you talk about Ahmed's mother?

LIAM: At dismissal, I always hear his mother talking in some foreign language, but that's not what I said. He didn't understand me, and he didn't understand the teacher.

MARGARET STILL LOOKED AT LIAM: How does that make you feel when you hear Ahmed and his mother talking in Arabic? That's the language they speak at home, and that is the language they have back in Iraq, where they came from. That's how they talk to one another.

LIAM: Why can't they speak English? My mom says that everyone should speak English in this country.

MARGARET: Well, Liam, Ahmed is at Tanglewood to learn English better. We're all here at Tanglewood to learn. Does that make sense to you?

LIAM: I guess.

Looking back at Ahmed, she paused, knowing from her years of experiences working with newcomer students that if she didn't punish Liam, Ahmed would remain angry. And that was exactly what she heard next.

AHMED: I want you to punish Liam. If this was Iraq, my principal would punish him.

MARGARET HESITATED: Ahmed, I think this was just a misunderstanding, and when we have misunderstandings in Tanglewood, we always talk about them. We don't punish first. I know this is different from how you think a principal should act, but here at Tanglewood, we settle arguments by talking and then making up. For now, I need you both to return to class. I don't want you to miss any more of the class. Can you both shake hands?

That same afternoon, the AP who had volunteered to draft a newcomer student and parent checklist for next week's leadership meeting came into Margaret's office and handed her two sheets of paper. It was a draft titled "Do's and Don'ts": One sheet was for newcomer students, and other for newcomer families. Margaret looked at the lists. As she read, she became angry, more at herself than at her AP: Why had she so quickly given this idea the go-ahead? She knew that (1) she would never approve all the items on this list but also that (2) she had put herself and her leadership team in a difficult situation. Yes, at Tanglewood, the children's safety would always be a top priority. Most items on the list seemed fine, like waiting with your child at the bus stop, wearing seatbelts when driving in a car, following the teachers' instructions during a fire drill, and crossing the street at corners in the crosswalks. These were all essential guidelines and rules, but when it came to how parents disciplined their children at home or how to deal with some of the men who had been urinating in the bushes behind the school while waiting for dismissal, the checklist just didn't seem to be the most culturally sensitive approach to solving problems. She continued reading, but she did not want her face to show any of her feelings at this particular time.

TEACHING NOTES

In this case narrative, democracy is grounded in specific school leadership practices, such as promoting participation, power-sharing relations, and the capacity to be flexible. When practicing democracy, cooperation and communication with others—both adults and children—emerge when school leaders are confronted with misperceptions, disagreements, or conflicts. This narrative is filled with democratic values and decisions as central to Principal Margaret's everyday practices. Ruitenberg has argued that teaching democracy "must include opportunities for students to enact and practice their equal capacity as speaking beings outside the classroom—in the larger school community."[2] Yet a democratic ethic also challenges the orderliness of school rules, disciplinary measures, compliance, and conformity. Newcomers bring multiple cultural values, many of which are considered different from the dominant culture. Biesta has emphasized how "citizenship is actually learned in and through processes and practices that make up the everyday lives of children, young people, and adults."[3] Hence, as conflicts inevitably arise, educators rely on discussions and dialogues to resolve disputes. Schools in a country foreign to newcomers often provide them with "alternative world views."[4] This does not mean that educators put their personal political thoughts into declarative statements in response to their students. Rather, democratic values are simply initiated through listening and talking.[5] The keywords here are *pluralism*, *participation*, *deliberation*, and *communication*. In a general sense, democracy is a value-oriented political literacy that necessarily toggles between assimilation or socialization and freedom of expression. However, toggling too far in either direction may lead to either indoctrination or chaos.

As you may have observed in the case, cross-cultural misunderstandings triggered opportunities for Principal Margaret and her staff to practice democracy. In other words, democracy did not emerge from avoiding conflicts or disagreements. As principal, Margaret quickly learned to appreciate the unique talents of her staff and faculty without imposing on those at her school who were not yet ready to engage in welcoming and integrating. Specifically, Margaret learned to trust her specialists: the social workers, counselors, community settlement workers, and behavior interventionists. For example, the social worker at Tanglewood remarked: "I talk all the time with teachers about what they are seeing and feeling. Sometimes, all I hear back from them is that 'literacy and numeracy are the goals,' but here is my question: How is it that if a child is not able to learn because she has been traumatized, why do we give a shit about literacy and numeracy? If a child is unavailable to learn, I don't care what tools or strategies, cute little tests and assessments you come up with for literacy and numeracy: What's the point?"

Principal Margaret understood what her social worker was saying, but she also knew that she had to balance the other academic priorities in her school. She had to be empathetic and understand strongly held, diverse points of view. By learning which members of the school community had the right dispositions to engage in this work, she could both promote common values and respect differences. The systemic tasks of welcoming newcomer students and families call for democratic leadership, as it brings forth new and different challenges to both schools and school systems. The most successful school systems do this work deliberately and intentionally. For example, highly trained and dedicated staff (e.g., teachers of English learner students, paraprofessionals, translators, interpreters, community and settlement workers) are assigned these welcoming and integrating roles. Not every member of a school's faculty and staff wants to or can do this specialized work. Success is not simply a matter of tweaking existing rules and regulations: When immigration numbers increase a school's enrollment, the school system responds as a whole, acknowledging the need to be flexible. For example, where there are teacher unions, they may have to reassess their seniority rules, and central district offices may have to reallocate discretionary funds in order to hire additional staff where they can target the need. Again, systemically welcoming and integrating is not business as usual, nor is it a matter of fitting these tasks onto regular and already busy assignments.

Discussion Questions

1. In the vignette on the pancake breakfast, Margaret at first wanted the event to welcome the school's newest arrivals. But, after listening to members of her leadership team, staff, and parents, she changed her mind.
   a. Are there any unintended consequences when a school leader publicly changes their mind and reverses a previous decision?
   b. If keeping an open mind and listening are fundamental to democratic leadership, how might those values be perceived by newcomers who come from different cultural and political backgrounds?
2. Principal Margaret had not known about the innovation (i.e., the hanging gym mat) used by her behavior specialist to handle newcomer trauma (e.g., anger and frustration).
   a. What factors should a school leader consider in deciding whether to extend trust to members of their staff?
      i. Do you think the principal should have known about this innovation before it was implemented?
   b. Regarding trust, to what extent should it be a value extended by a school leader to all or have to be earned?
3. In your opinion, to what extent did Margaret Court and staff members treat newcomer students and their families as unique human beings?

   a. Were there times when the pressures and tensions of being a school leader resulted in either the school leader or her staff relying solely on their past experiences and not treating situations and people as unique?
   b. Checklists and rubrics have become commonplace in school administration practice. In your opinion, are checklists appropriate for implementing cultural "Dos and Don'ts"?
      i. What are other, more culturally sensitive approaches to implementing school policies?
      ii. What was your reaction to reading the cultural checklist?
4. In groups of three, role-play the scenario between Principal Margaret and the two fourth-graders, Liam and Ahmed.
   a. As you do so, try to name different leadership theories at play here that you have been learning in your preparation program.
   b. Would you have handled the situation between Liam and Ahmed differently? How so?

CHAPTER 7

Creating Schools That Are Inclusive Places for Newcomer and Refugee Students

DANIAH HAMMOUDA, MEREDITH BITTEL, AND BRYAN MANN

University of Kansas

ABSTRACT

Recent work emphasizes the need for newcomers' host societies to enact a framework of "radical hospitality." Creating welcoming schools is crucial to this enactment. However, scholarly literature and advocacy work have neglected the intersection of critical geography and newcomer experiences in schools. Without a clear understanding of how newcomer students experience schools as places, educators may inadvertently create environments that hinder newcomer student development rather than support it. Children who experience places that are unsafe, unwelcoming, or distressing struggle to learn, grow, and become integrated in society.

This chapter considers research on placemaking and place attachment and applies it to schools hosting newcomer and refugee students. This chapter assumes that places exist at the intersection of physical space and social relationships, thus providing a way to think about designing schools as welcoming places along this intersection. The chapter then provides a scenario featuring a school that is welcoming to newcomer and refugee students and what this school is doing to offer a welcoming place. It also considers a school that is unwelcoming and what school leaders can change to make it more welcoming. The primary takeaway from this chapter for school leaders is to acquire theoretical tools about place and explain how to apply them in practice. These applications can help leaders intentionally create schools that are welcoming places.

CASE NARRATIVE

It is Monday morning and Yusuf has been anxiously anticipating his first day of high school in the United States. He is unsure of what to expect—were American schools like what he had seen on TV in his childhood home in Syria? Did they have state-of-the-art libraries, science labs, and gymnasiums?

Due to the ongoing war, the COVID-19 pandemic, and the 2022 earthquake, the last few years of Yusuf's schooling occurred in a makeshift community school. His school was one of the thousands of schools that the bombings damaged or demolished. After being damaged, their school was repaired and repurposed as a shelter for the displaced. His school location constantly shifted, and lessons would depend on whether teachers and a space to hold the lessons could be found.

Attending a public school was far removed from Yusuf's reality in Syria. There, he knew all his classmates—their families, fears, and ambitions. They played soccer together, shared meals together, and prayed together. Classmates and teachers felt like family, and the challenging circumstances brought them even closer.

His new school, Fairview West High, is a two thousand–student suburban facility. The school district is the fifth largest in the state with twenty-six thousand students. The district has a 10 percent English language learner population and 0.2 percent migrant population. The district has much to improve on, including its relationship with the local Refugee Student Support Network and general accommodation of the needs of different learners.

Yusuf's first day was a whirlwind. There were too many new teachers, students, and staff to remember. He frequently got lost in the large building. The language barrier made him feel uncomfortable asking for help, especially since he did not know whom he could trust. Yusuf also noticed small details that added to his discomfort, from the murals in the hallway to the posters in the classrooms. He had questions about them but suppressed them as he preferred to have a low-key, unassuming, nonchalant presence to detract from his "outsider" identity. The bulletin board in his math classroom, for example, struck him as curious. The board depicted people who "invented math." Although his education in Syria had been intermittent, he still remembers learning about Al-Khwarizmi and Al-Battani and how much they contributed to algebra and trigonometry. He wondered if there was a reason their pictures were absent.

Yusuf prays five times a day, as prescribed by his Islamic faith. In Syria, he and his classmates always prayed together in one space. It suddenly occurred to him that he did not know where to pray. He felt guilty when he missed his first prayer. Finally, he overcame his anxiety and approached his history teacher, Mr. Johnston, to ask if he could pray in his classroom. "Pray? How long will it take?" Mr. Johnston responded nervously. Yusuf assured him it wouldn't take long. Mr. Johnston worried about losing his job for allowing religious practice in his classroom. In addition, he adhered to the common misconceptions about the Islamic faith that they support terrorism and oppress their women.

After some thought, Mr. Johnston suggested to Yusuf that he pray behind the stairs in the hallway. Yusuf found cleaning supplies stored in that space. In the space between a mop and bucket, he finally prayed. However, as he was praying, he noticed students passing by and whispering comments. "What is he doing?" "Do you think he is going to blow the place up?" "Does he have a bomb in his backpack?" "Why does he have to do that here?" Not only that, but when he stood up after praying, he noticed his pants were soaked with foul-smelling water from the bucket.

After a few days of praying behind the stairs, Yusuf decided to approach the librarian about praying in the library. The librarian rolled her eyes and in a loud and slow tone of voice made a remark about how he should pray to "his God" at home because this is a secular space. But Yusuf could not wait; each prayer has a prescribed time.

Finally, Yusuf decided to approach one of the principals with whom he was building a positive relationship, Ms. Kendrick. She listened empathetically and told Yusuf that she had a place where he could pray. Thrilled, Yusuf thanked her. Mrs. Kendrick recalled someone from the Refugee Student Support Network a few years back talking about prayer rooms. The next day, Yusuf discovered that the room she let him pray in was away from all the classrooms. When he opened the door, he saw a small, dimly lit storage room with poor ventilation and copious amounts of dust that made it hard to breathe. Better than nothing, he thought. After he prayed, he immediately headed to science class. When he walked in, the teacher glared at him with disdain. "Look who finally decided to show up," the teacher stated. "Just because you're used to doing things your way from wherever you came from doesn't mean you get to ignore our rules here. This is America. Here, we follow the rules and show respect for how things are done." Yusuf was humiliated and disillusioned by his experiences at his new school. He had not thought it would be this difficult to complete simple routines.

FROM THEORY TO PRACTICE: PLACE AND NEWCOMER STUDENTS

The preceding scenario highlights the spatial and place-based challenges of leading a school with newcomer students. These challenges are rooted in broader societal shifts in which the relationship between society and newcomers has maintained a hostile host-hostage rather than a host-guest dynamic, reflected in both rhetoric and policy.[1] These societal struggles permeate schools, making it crucial for leaders to consider how their schools serve as either welcoming or unwelcoming environments. Place is particularly significant for immigrants and refugees who must navigate the loss of familiar place surroundings and attachments while adapting to new ones.[2]

Nour Halabi calls for "radical hospitality" in discourse and immigration policy, a principle equally vital for schools.[3] This concept underscores the importance of creating hospitable practices across various domains in the educational environment. In this section, we focus on the space- and place-based domain, noting a significant gap in scholarly literature and advocacy work regarding the intersection of critical geography and newcomer experiences in schools. When children perceive places as unsafe, unwelcoming, or distressing, they are likely to struggle with learning, personal growth, and integration into society.

Theories of place from human geography and environmental psychology offer insights for school leaders who aim to create welcoming environments. This research emphasizes that places exist at the intersection of physical space and social relationships, requiring school leaders to focus not only on the design of spaces but also on the interactions that occur within them. Schools are not empty containers; their design, the way people navigate them, and the perceptions of staff and students all contribute to whether school spaces feel welcoming or unwelcoming.[4] For instance, scholarship on "carceral schools" highlights how features such as metal detectors and surveillance cameras can make schools resemble prisons, sending a message that students are viewed as part of a carceral system.[5]

The challenge lies in translating spatial theory into practical applications. Of the many spatial theories scholars have proposed, this chapter focuses on "place attachment," which describes the bond that individuals form with the spaces they use and inhabit.[6] Within place attachment, the "PPP framework" offers a useful organizing structure for examining this bond through three components: person, psychological process, and place.[7]

The PPP framework of place attachment begins with considering the *persons*, or the actors in a space: Who is attached, and to what extent is this attachment shaped by individually and collectively held meanings? Key goals related to the person include:

1. Cultural and historical recognition of groups
2. Individual care, personal development through experiences, and milestones for growth
3. Emphasis on not just the physical place itself but the experiences people have within it

The second dimension of the PPP framework is the *psychological process*: How are affect, cognition, and behavior manifested in attachment? Key goals related to the psychological process include:

1. Affect: fostering happiness, pride, and a love of place. How can this place become a source of pride for students?
2. Cognition: building memory, knowledge, schemas, and meaning. What do we want students to remember about their time in the place? How can we challenge preconceived schemas (place-related knowledge and beliefs) often associated with schools?
3. Behavior: Addressing feelings of displacement and homesickness by allowing individuals to reconstruct their sense of place. What place-related behaviors do we want to encourage, and how will we build this? How can we prevent the reconstruction of negative elements and ensure their safety?

The third dimension of the PPP framework focuses on the characteristics of the *place*: What is the attachment to, and what is the nature of, this place? Key goals related to place include:

1. Social symbols: incorporating elements like murals and religious acknowledgments that reflect the community's diversity
2. Inclusive and welcoming design: creating physical spaces that foster connection for newcomers and their families. How can these spaces be designed to promote inclusion and shared experiences?

While the theory helps delineate abstract concepts related to place, school leaders have the difficult task of connecting theory to practice. As leaders help craft their school environment, especially for those who have experienced massive disruptions of place, it is helpful to consider the students' backgrounds and what care looks like in their cultures; to interrogate experiences of place and foster positive ones; attend to the affective, cognitive, and behavioral dimensions of place; and design effective places using affirmative social symbols.

TEACHING NOTES

Yusuf's example helps to show common mistakes leaders make by limiting the number of inclusive places and hindering possibilities for place attachment. These experiences relate to each element of the PPP framework tied to place attachment. The school's practices detach newcomers like Yusuf from the school and reinforce their trauma.

The first violation of the PPP framework is failing to recognize the *person* element of Yusuf's placemaking that would foster place attachment. Before thoughtful development of place can occur, leaders must know their people as individuals so they can be mindful of positive placemaking. The members of the school community lacked a cultural awareness of Yusuf's identity. Some, such as the students and librarian, were openly hostile and did the opposite of taking individual care to consider his experiences. Stereotypes like these are inherently impersonal and make Yusuf feel not as an individual in a space but as part of a group that doesn't belong, which represents the antithesis of place attachment.

Instead of the impersonal approach the school took and the hostile interactions, school leaders should implement practices that personalize Yusuf's experience. Prior to his first day, leaders should have conversations with Yusuf to understand his personality, what he fears in this new place, and what would make him feel welcome. The school leaders should find student allies who can travel with Yusuf, show him the building, introduce him to peers, and connect with him on a personal level. Places are relational and school leaders must personalize Yusuf's experience so he can form positive bonds with it from the start.

The second violation of the PPP framework relates to fostering a negative *psychological process* of place. The lack of strong personal and relational bonds facilitates negative psychological processes. Yusuf's affective experience was corrupted with individuals mocking his religion and implying he is dangerous. This issue could be avoided if administration provided him a special pass that communicates to teachers that he may be a little late to class. In addition, his memory was questioned due to the differential representation of math and the thinkers that contributed to it. The place-related behaviors of Yusuf praying under the stairs while others gawked at him encourage negative and unsafe placemaking. Yusuf's social experience in the physical space reinforce his trauma, causing him to feel unwelcome in the space, and when he looks back on his time in this place, his psychological processes will cause him to reproduce gut-wrenching and emotionally fraught place memories.

Instead of the psychological processes that the school fostered, school leaders should help Yusuf develop a sense of shared ownership in the space. On understanding his needs as a person, leaders should facilitate positive psychological processes by having him identify a suitable location and help design the prayer room, learn of his best memories from home and try to re-create them, and provide programming alongside Yusuf to prompt positive experiences.

The third violation occurs through the obvious concrete constructions of the *place*. In particular, the bulletin boards and the prayer room in a closet provide symbolic, physical messaging to Yusuf that he does not belong in the space. Leaders should strive for physical symbols of inclusion rather than exclusion. These symbols include bulletin boards with diverse representations, a legitimate prayer room (designed by students), and spaces that promote cultural exchange and shared experiences. For example, the library can offer a display of prominent works from scholars around the world, enabling students to collectively create mutual discovery.

Discussion Questions

1. Reflect on the ways school leaders can better understand and respond to the cultural and religious needs of newcomer students. How might developing cultural competency among staff and students transform the school as a place? What strategies could leaders implement to ensure that newcomer students feel seen, heard, and valued in the school?
2. What steps can school leaders take to confront and dismantle biases and stereotypes in their school? How can school policies and practices be revised to create a more inclusive place for newcomer students?
3. Research shows that places are just as social as they are physical. What does this mean? How does the social element of place affect how people remember a place?

4. Discuss the impact of physical spaces, such as prayer rooms and bulletin boards, on students' sense of belonging and attachment to their school. How can school leaders ensure that the design and use of these spaces reflect the diverse identities and needs of the student body? What role can students play in creating and maintaining these inclusive spaces?
5. Using the PPP framework, analyze how school leaders can foster a sense of place attachment for newcomer students. What practical actions can be taken to build positive connections between students and the school? How can these efforts contribute to students' overall well-being and academic success?

Teacher Activities

1. *Reflection Room Space Design:* Design a conceptual layout for an inclusive, multifaith prayer space. Conduct research into different religious practices and design a room that caters to them. Consider location, privacy, accessibility, furnishings, and necessary items. Then, reflect on what steps you could take to apply this design to the context of your building.
2. *"Representation Matters" Plan:* Reflect on the imagery in your building. What voices are amplified? Which voices are not present? What historical, artistic, and cultural achievements are represented? Which are not? Draw out a visual of a plan for integrating diverse imagery throughout the school. This might include posters, signage, artwork, murals, or visual displays that reflect different races, cultures, and ethnicities. Then, reflect on why such representation matters for students.
3. *Multifaith Space Policy Development:* Write a policy that provides guidance on creating spaces for religious practices in schools. This policy could be at the building, district, or state level. Consider the following: allocation of space for prayer, space requirements, types of support for students using the space (i.e., accommodation of their individual schedules), inclusivity of multiple faiths, and

communication with families about the availability of the space. Then, reflect on what process is in place for the policy's implementation.

4. *First Day Plan:* Create a plan for the first day of school for a newcomer student. How would you make them feel welcome and attend to their personal, psychological, and place needs?

EDUCATOR RESOURCES FOR FURTHER LEARNING

1. "Transformative Placemaking at Brookings," Brookings Institution, accessed August 26, 2025, https://www.brookings.edu/projects/transformative-placemaking/.
2. Sarah Dryden-Peterson, *Right Where We Belong: How Refugee Teachers and Students Are Changing the Future of Education* (Harvard University Press, 2022).
3. Nour Halabi, *Radical Hospitality: American Policy, Media, and Immigration* (Rutgers University Press, 2022).
4. Mandy Manning, Ivonne Orozco Sahi, Leah Juelke, and Sarahí Monterrey, *Creating a Sense of Belonging for Immigrant and Refugee Students: Strategies for K–12 Educators* (Routledge, 2022).
5. Sun Young Rieh, *Creating a Sense of Place in School Environments: How Young Children Construct Place Attachment* (Routledge, 2020).
6. Lynda H. Schneekloth and Robert G. Shibley, *Placemaking: The Art and Practice of Building Communities* (Wiley, 1995).

CHAPTER 8

Welcome?

A Headteacher's Approach to Integrating Afghan Evacuee Children in a London Secondary School

AFSANA HAMIDY
King's College London

LILIANA BELKIN
University of Roehampton

ABSTRACT

This chapter presents the case of a London secondary-school leader's challenges and the actions she took to address the unexpected resettlement of Afghan families in the UK in August 2021.The case narrative is based on research conducted with public school leaders who were, in most cases, compelled by the national and local government to open their doors to newcomer Afghan children fleeing their homeland. Despite initiatives and policies at the national and local level purporting to support the schools in "welcoming" newcomer Afghan students, school leaders faced numerous obstacles in addressing the needs of these students and engaging with their families. The narrative highlights culture clashes that arose when Afghan students' needs and family expectations collided with the school's values and practices and staff preconceptions of "refugee" students. This case presents the leader's and school staff's actions that both enhanced and impeded the newcomer students in becoming part of their school community. This case illustrates the journey of the leader and her team, the assumptions that influenced their actions, and what they learned from their mistakes about developing a more culturally relevant and responsive practice. Drawing on community-based leadership and culturally relevant leadership, we present practical strategies that can support school leaders in their efforts to genuinely welcome refugee and newcomer students.

CASE NARRATIVE

Preparing to Welcome Afghan Evacuee Students at Grange Road

Four weeks into the new school year, Ms. Baker received email notification from the Local Authority that her London secondary school, Grange Road, would be receiving twelve recent evacuee students from Afghanistan on a temporary basis.[1] As the headteacher, she believed it was important to create a welcoming environment for the children and families, but she wanted more information about the new students: What are their ages? Do they speak any English? She was also concerned about resources and funding. What will the government provide in terms of support for these children's transition to our school? The Local Authority provided minimal information—twelve students, aged between eleven and sixteen, all living with their families temporarily in the same hotel in the adjacent neighborhood, not easily accessible to Grange Road. She also did not know what "temporarily" really meant or how long the students would be at her school. She assumed she would receive more information about the incoming students prior to their arrival and information about how to access translators and other social services. However, getting this information and any funding or support from the government ended up being like pulling teeth. A few days before the students were due to arrive, Ms. Baker received a list with their names, dates of birth for some, the names of their fathers, and contact numbers. She realized that she and her team were going to have to create a transition plan for these students on their own.

Ms. Baker was focused on making sure the students would be able to integrate into the school smoothly. She assembled a transition team including the English as a Second Language (ESL) teacher, assistant headteacher, the inclusion leader, and the school counselor to work together to put in place supports for the new students. They created a welcome pack with a school uniform and translations of the schedule and school rules in Pashto and Dari, and arranged for translators to be at school. During the first team meeting, Ms. Baker explained, "I want to raise the empathy of the teachers; I want them to be friendly and supportive to the new students, not put them on the spot or exclude them if their English is limited." Although Grange Road was rated a "Good" school and had stated values of inclusion, the school had a predominantly white, British middle-class staff and student population. Ms. Baker was concerned that the incoming students would stand out and may face discrimination from their peers and teachers. Her priorities were to preempt resistance from teachers and current students and make sure that the new students knew what to expect when they arrived. She anticipated some culture shock not only for the Afghan evacuee students but also for the teachers and current students at Grange Road.

The First Three Weeks: Culture Shocks and Learning Curves

Ms. Baker had many worries running through her mind: Would her teachers welcome the Afghan students? Would the current students be friendly? How long would they be at our school? What if they are suffering from trauma after fleeing a conflict zone? Was Grange Road ready to welcome these students? The transition team decided it would be best to ease the students into the school routine by setting up a two-week "immersion" program. The new students would spend half the school day with the ESL teacher, Ms. Burns, working on English-language skills and they would have lunch with all students and attend electives, such as music, drama, and physical education, in the afternoons. Ms. Baker was adamant about not segregating the new students. She wanted them included in the regular classes as soon as possible, but she also worried that jumping right into a "typical" school day might be jarring for the students.

The first three weeks were a roller-coaster ride. There were many unanticipated interactions that surprised the headteacher, and she was not sure how to balance respecting the needs and values of the new students with adhering to the ethos and rules at Grange Road.

One of the first surprises was that only the fathers attended the welcome meeting. Ms. Baker wondered why their mothers didn't come too. The translators explained that it was "normal" for mothers to stay home. Ms. Baker did not know what to make of the translator's response—was this a cultural thing? Should she push back and ask to meet the mothers at school? She was not quite sure how to broach this with the fathers without offending them.

She had not anticipated the fathers' specific concerns about their children's education. She was caught off guard by Mr. Aziz, for example, the father of Karim, age thirteen, who wanted to know where the children would pray during the school day. She had not realized this would be important to the families and children. Grange Road had some other Muslim students, but she had never been expected to accommodate prayer in the school day before.

Another big surprise was the school uniforms. On their first day of attending Grange Road, the four girls, Fahra, Hafiza, Zayna, and Amina, did not arrive in their school uniforms. A charity that worked with the school had given every student a uniform (skirt, several white shirts and a blazer, black tights, and flat, black dress shoes). Ms. Baker was confused and brought them into her office with Ms. Najiba the translator and Ms. Evans, the inclusion leader, to find out why. With help from Ms. Najiba, they explained that their fathers would not let them wear the uniforms as this was not considered "appropriate" dress for young women. Ms. Baker was irritated. She wondered whether their fathers cared about their daughters' education. Did they not understand the expectations and rules that their children must comply with at the school? She had made it very clear to the fathers that uniforms are required. She was also frustrated that they did not seem to understand how this would make the girls feel out of place and different from their peers in class, at a time when it is most important for them to feel that they fit in! With the help of Ms. Najiba and Ms. Burns, and agreement from the girls, they compromised. The girls would come to and from school in their "home" clothes and wear uniforms during the school day.

At lunch break, Ms. Baker found Mr. Roberts, the history teacher, waiting for her. Perspiring a bit and red-faced, Mr. Roberts asked if they could have a word. "I can't see how I can teach these children if they don't speak English. What do I do?" he said. Ms. Baker was frustrated and annoyed with his lack of empathy, but she tried to mask it. She hoped his resistance was based on wanting to be a good teacher to these students, not because they were evacuees. She tried to reassure him that the students being included was important for learning English and to feel a sense of belonging. She also offered to support him with assistants and a translator. "Don't ignore them, include them in the activities, and the assistant can modify the work and sit with them," she advised. Ms. Baker and the transition team had also enlisted student "buddies" for each new student. Later that day, she went to Mr. Roberts's classroom with John and Amanda, two students who had volunteered to be buddies, and they discussed how they could all work together to help the new students be part of the class.

Settling In

After the first three weeks, things seemed to be settling down. The transition team had worked with Ms. Najiba, communicating with the fathers by phone, and negotiated some accommodations at the school for the Afghan students. She hoped the changes would be more culturally appropriate for the students and their parents. Ms. Baker still wanted to meet their mothers. She was confused that neither the fathers nor the mothers came to the school to pick up their children. The Local Authority provided the students with taxis or transit cards to get to school, which meant the parents rarely entered the school, met any teachers, or spoke with Ms. Baker face to face. She wondered why they did not seem interested in coming into the school and being more involved.

At 8 a.m. on Monday, there was a knock at Ms. Baker's door and Fahra, Zayna, Hafiza, and Amina entered her office. They said good morning, and the girls went to a corner with a screen and began changing out of their "home" clothes and into their school uniforms. This had become the routine. The "changing room" was Ms. Baker's office. It was a bit awkward for her to have students changing their clothes in front of her, so she left her office for ten minutes when they arrived, so they could have some privacy. This was a new experience for her, but she wanted to make it work for the students and their parents, and this seemed, so far, to be a workable solution.

The transition team set up a prayer schedule and found a quiet room for the students to use during the school day. As the students would be praying during some class periods, they created special hall passes for them to use in case they were questioned for being out of class. The whole staff was briefed on the new process, and there was some grumbling and complaining that this was not "fair" to all other students. Ms. Baker responded to their concerns: "We all need to compromise and ensure that the new students feel welcomed and respected. We need to be culturally sensitive and we can provide the same accommodations for other students if needed. Let's just try this out and see how it goes."

At dismissal, Fahra came to Ms. Baker's office. "Miss, my father needs to talk to you," she said, with Mr. Yusufzai, her father, trailing behind her along with Ms. Najiba. Ms. Baker had met Mr. Yusufzai only once before, at the welcome meeting, but she smiled and gestured to the chairs for them to take a seat. "How can I help?" she asked. Mr. Yusufzai tried to explain, with the help of Ms. Najiba, that Fahra was quite unhappy. She was being seated in her classes with another Afghan student, Hafiza, and she didn't like it. In fact, according to Fahra and her father, neither girl wanted to sit with the other, as they were not friends. Ms. Baker was a bit stunned, as she realized that it had never occurred to her, and probably not any of the members of the transition team, that not all the Afghan students were friends.

At the end of the day, Ms. Baker met with the transition team to evaluate progress with the new students. The team members reported that the students seemed happy and were making astonishing progress in their English speaking. She was happy to hear this, but she told them about the meeting with Fahra. She reflected, "I assumed they all know each other and like each other, because they are all from Afghanistan and they all live in the same hotel. But why would that be true? Why didn't we ask them what they wanted, instead of assuming that the students are one homogenous group? What else are we assuming about them and their experiences at school, instead of asking them what they feel and need? We need to do better."

TEACHING NOTES

For the past ten years, Afghanistan has been one of the top ten asylum applicant–producing countries in the UK. After the fall of Afghanistan in August 2021, 15,000 people were evacuated between August 13 and 28, 2021, to the UK, of whom 2,000 were children.[2] The Home Office launched "Operation Warm Welcome," a cross-sectional government support program to assist with the resettlement of Afghan refugees.[3] The UK Department for Education allocated £12 million for schools to recruit translators and provide transportation and other support. Local authorities were mandated to enroll all Afghan children in public schools with at least a rating of "Good" by Ofsted.[4]

Access to school and education undoubtedly assists Afghan refugee children in quickly settling and integrating into their new environment.[5] Schools play a critical role in supporting and nurturing the social, academic, and physical needs of all children, particularly refugees. These needs may be related to trauma experienced by losing everything when fleeing their country, undergoing family separation, or being victims of abuse.[6] The situations refugee children have experienced can influence their adjustment to school, their educational outcomes, and their language learning.[7] Access to education and school are recognized as crucial factors for refugee children's resettlement, in part because they connect children to the wider community and contribute to their psychological well-being.[8] The quality of the school experience determines how successfully refugee children adjust to their new environment.[9] Schools are frequently the sole statutory organizations that work with and formally support refugee children in England. Apart from providing educational opportunities for the refugees, schools are the key place where newcomers are integrated into mainstream society. Therefore, school administrators and teachers should consider the experiences of refugees and devise strategies to assist the refugee students in adjusting to, restoring a feeling of security in, and forming new aspirations in their new environments.[10]

Previous studies indicate that policy reforms regarding immigration and asylum seeking in England are influenced by international discourses and educational reforms. School headteachers bridge how these discourses should be put into practice while attempting to respond morally and "compassionately" to the refugees' needs.[11] Indeed, school leaders fill the educational gap created by the government by improvising and innovating to support these children who are experiencing a state of uncertainty about their future.[12] As a result, school leaders may be required to strike a delicate balance between internal and external forces such as governmental policies, schools' financial situation, concerns of the established parental-school community, and preparation of skilled practitioners to teach "home" and "refugee" children.[13] Conceptualized as "boundary spanners," school leaders who are focused on building trust, brokering relationships, and "networking across disciplinary and organizational boundaries," are positioned as advocates and are better able to enact equitable educational experiences for refugee students.[14] School leaders must constantly rethink their work in reshaping educational processes that serve all students and promote the best outcomes, while also ensuring that they are guided by their values and ideas about the purposes of what they do.[15]

Research focused on the experiences of English school leaders when welcoming refugee students into their schools has identified several areas of challenge that are reflected in the case narrative: communication, navigation of competing demands, and cultural competence. These challenges are interconnected and intersect in ways that may inhibit the authentic inclusion of refugee students. For example, communication is related to issues of cultural competence on the part of the school staff, which may indicate that staff need to develop further their skills and understanding of their students, learn about their students as individuals, and deepen their knowledge of their students' cultural, religious and ethnic backgrounds. Relatedly, communication issues have tangible resource implications that may require the school to allocate funds to support translators. These challenges are conceptualized as not only interconnected but also, in some instances, interdependent, highlighting the need for a holistic approach to addressing them and encouraging a more "welcoming" school community for these students.

Communication issues arising from limited English proficiency on the part of refugee students and their families and the limited availability or skills of school staff to speak students' first language present a myriad of barriers. Not only do these language barriers create challenges for communication for a variety of purposes, but limited ability to communicate in a common language presents a challenge for headteachers and their staff to determine students' academic skills and performance levels. The communication issues extend to school-family interactions, meaning that interactions with the parents of refugee children may be poor or ineffective.[16] Communication issues also extend to the limited information shared with leaders prior to refugee students attending their schools and limited knowledge sharing of expectations about what the school should be providing to these students. This lack of information sharing with or from government organizations inhibits the leaders' ability to prepare for the arrival of refugee students, putting them in a reactive rather than a proactive position.[17] Research with English secondary-school leaders found that they do not want to label or stereotype refugee students and they recognize the need to deepen their understanding of the cultural and ethnic backgrounds of their students to provide better supports.[18]

The communication challenges illuminate the underlying and interconnected issues of cultural competence and cultural relevance and responsiveness on the part of school leaders and staff. School leaders' and teachers' limited cultural awareness, unexamined xenophobia, racism, and ethnocentrism may add to the marginalization of refugee students and contribute to poor school transitions.[19] Drawing on social justice–oriented and inclusive leadership approaches, such as community-based leadership (CBL) and culturally responsive school leadership (CRSL), may provide the guidance and transformation of leaders' values and practices necessary to being more genuinely welcoming to refugee students.

CBL principles are informed by a social justice orientation of valuing all members of the community and a "social vision" that prioritizes building authentic partnerships with all relevant stakeholders. Key aspects of CBL include critical thinking, creativity, and a development of community knowledge and empathy for all community members. In this narrative, Ms. Baker formed teams to enhance collaboration within the school and with evacuee families, providing a way to solve problems and resolve conflicts. Another strategy would be to engage and involve the wider school community through more structured and interactive "communication channels." This approach could build more shared understandings and deepen awareness of the perspectives and needs of stakeholders. Explicitly developing more power-sharing with community members, especially the evacuee students and other students, through participation in school decision-making could support more cross-cultural understanding and awareness of marginalizing practices in the school.[20]

CRSL principles resonate with CBL and emphasize the "cultural needs of students, parents and teachers."[21] CRSL focuses on the development of an inclusive and "continuously responsive" climate for marginalized students through actively and explicitly working to counter oppression. Much as with CBL, CRSL leaders engage in critical self-reflection and actively encourage teacher development to institute culturally relevant and responsive pedagogy in their classrooms. This activist orientation cultivates awareness and examination of social injustices and works to dismantle them. Furthermore, CRSL leaders seek to promote achievement for students from historically marginalized backgrounds by building on their cultural values and creating "anti-oppressive school contexts."[22] Key strategies include engaging in authentic collaboration with stakeholders, partnering with students and families in decision making, actively adopting a school-wide approach to instituting culturally responsive and relevant curriculum, and engaging in regular audits, evaluations, and reflection so as to improve equity across the school. Ms. Baker exhibits some critical self-reflection and attempts respond to cultural values, however such practices are not embedded throughout the school community. The case narrative highlights cultural misunderstandings and assumptions on the part of the school staff and a lack of meaningful engagement with the parents as partners. Furthermore, building on the funds of knowledge and cultural values of the Afghan students in their teaching and learning would enrich the entire school community and advance student agency.

Discussion Questions

Imagine being in Ms. Baker's position and facing communication challenges and cultural misunderstandings. Consider the following questions:

1. What strategies could be enacted to enhance communication with the evacuee students and parents prior to the first day of school?
2. What resources are available in your community or neighborhood to support newcomers? How could relationships with these services be built?
3. What practices are in place to involve students in decision making in the school? How does your school engage or elicit student voices?
4. What practices or systems are in place for supporting students who may be experiencing trauma or mental health issues?
5. How does your school engage with students' parents and families? How do parents and families respond to these practices? Are there other strategies that could be piloted that could bring parents and families into the school building? What strategies could the school pilot to go out into the community and students' homes and build relationships with families?
6. How does your school community assess or evaluate the interventions put in place to support students? How do you determine if these interventions have the intended impacts?
7. What principles, values, or philosophical positions inform your decision making in terms of student supports?

Teacher Activities

Activity: Think-Pair-Share

Use the literature on community-based leadership and culturally responsive school leadership to consider the following scenarios.

1. Consider the tenets of CBL. Valuing all members of the school community is a key principle. In what ways does the narrative reflect this

principle? What would you do differently than Ms. Baker to enact this principle?

2. Consider the tenets of CRSL. In what ways could culturally relevant practices enhance the experience of the evacuee students at Grange Road? Their families? What specific steps would you take to enact a more CRSL-aligned approach?
3. CBL and CRSL are complementary approaches. How could CBL and CRSL principles be integrated or woven together to develop an authentically responsive, welcoming, and positive school setting for refugee and evacuee students and their families?

CHAPTER 9

Equity Beyond Inclusion for Newcomer Youth in Science Education

MEREDITH BITTEL AND ALEX BITTEL
University of Kansas

ABSTRACT

This chapter presents a case narrative that underscores the complexities and transformative potential of advancing equity for newcomer students beyond mere inclusion in science education. Centered on Grace Etonge, a fourteen-year-old newcomer from western Cameroon, the chapter reveals how the stereotypes and assumptions used by Principal Thompson influenced Grace's early experiences at Greenwood High, a predominantly white, upper-middle-class school. The case narrative exemplifies the broader failure of superficial notions of inclusion to address deeper inequities affecting newcomer students. The chapter delves into two theoretical concepts for fostering equitable and justice-based science education: *community-driven science* and *rightful presence*. These concepts emphasize embracing students' cultural and experiential resources and integrating them in the curriculum so as to enhance engagement and support meaningful learning. It argues for moving beyond tokenistic inclusion to adopt educational practices that genuinely recognize and build on the diverse strengths and experiences of all students, thereby promoting a more equitable and just educational environment. The chapter emphasizes the importance of building deep relationships with newcomer students and families, adapting conventional educational approaches, and creating learning environments that are responsive to students' lived realities. Teaching notes provide actionable strategies for educators to support the integration of students' backgrounds into science education, ensuring a more inclusive and responsive approach. This chapter advocates for a transformative shift in science education that honors and leverages the unique contributions of all students, particularly those from newcomer backgrounds.

CASE NARRATIVE

Greenwood High School, a well-regarded suburban institution known for its academic excellence, primarily serves upper-middle-class students and has a predominantly white student and faculty population. Over the summer and into the fall, substantial infrastructure additions began at the school, and Principal Thompson worked closely with staff to ensure a smooth start to the new school year. During this busy time, Thompson learned that the Etonge family from Cameroon would soon be joining the school community. Fourteen-year-old Grace and her parents, Marie and Samuel, had recently immigrated to the United States, fleeing the political turmoil in the West Region of Cameroon that threatened their safety. The family chose Greenwood because both Marie and Samuel had found jobs in the area, providing the family with stability as they began their new lives. Multilingual and fluent in English, the Etonge family did not require language support, and Grace would not need to enroll in an English-language learner program at her new school. Unlike many families in similar circumstances, the Etonge family had not come to the United States through a resettlement program; instead, they migrated independently and were in the process of seeking asylum.

In a meeting with teachers the week before school began—a meeting dominated by discussion about modified pick-up and drop-off routines and construction timelines—Principal Thompson mentioned the arrival of the Etonge family, which had fled "violence in Africa" (she could not recall the specific country). Assuming Grace was coming from an impoverished, rural background, Principal Thompson urged the teachers to be welcoming and flexible with her and advised that she might need help to "navigate and adapt to a school like ours." Priding herself on a commitment to diversity and inclusion, she advised teachers to help Grace acclimate by pairing her with friendly students during group work and to gently urge her to participate equally in class to signal that she is "a part of our school community like any other student."

Ms. Parker, a biology teacher in her second year at Greenwood, attended the meeting with enthusiasm. Like Principal Thompson, she considered herself to have an inclusive outlook and was eager to welcome Grace into her class. After a successful first year during which her students' impressive test scores earned her praise, Ms. Parker was determined to continue that success. During the meeting, Principal Thompson made a point to mention that "technical content" in subjects like science may be particularly difficult for "a student like Grace." Parker recalled students the previous year who had begun the class behind in their biology knowledge but who had finished the year scoring well on the assessment. She was eager to help Grace overcome any "setbacks" that might carry over from her previous experiences.

Early in the semester, Ms. Parker was happy to see that Grace, though reserved, participated in group work, was attentive in class, and completed her assignments adequately and on time. Ms. Parker, pleased she wouldn't have to worry about Grace, turned her attention to other students. As they approached the middle of the semester, however, Ms. Parker noticed that Grace was becoming increasingly withdrawn and detached in class. First, her participation diminished, then her work was increasingly inadequate, and eventually she stopped turning in work at all. Ms. Parker initially attributed this trend to the challenges of adjusting to a new school and country and expected that Grace would "bounce back" with some support. Following Principal Thompson's advice, Ms. Parker rearranged the seating chart to place Grace next to outgoing students, called on her to answer simple questions, provided flexible deadlines, and used other pedagogical strategies that she found successful with other struggling students. However, Grace's difficulties persisted.

Ms. Parker mentioned Grace's struggles in her class to the principal. After discussion, they concluded that the academic standards in Ms. Parker's course likely outpaced Grace's previous educational experiences. As a result, Grace was moved to a remedial science course with Ms. Gladstone. Grace felt powerless to question the decision.

Outside school, Grace and her family felt increasingly isolated in their new community, in stark contrast to the vibrant life they had enjoyed in Cameroon. There, they had maintained strong connections with extended family, friends, and neighbors who provided unwavering support and a deep sense of belonging. Her walk to school was an important daily social event when she would greet and chat with neighbors and friends. Grace had aspired to become a doctor in Cameroon, driven by a desire to serve her community and make a tangible impact. At Greenwood, though the surrounding community boasted well-funded schools, advanced healthcare facilities, and numerous amenities, Grace struggled to see how the science she was learning connected to her life in her new home. This disconnection was compounded by the difficulty she was having in bridging her past experiences with her current reality. In Cameroon, Grace had thrived in classrooms rich in cultural and linguistic diversity, where students from various backgrounds shared their cultures as an integral part of the learning environment—in contrast to the environment at Greenwood. Despite feeling deeply alienated, Grace resolved to persevere, determined to make the most of her new educational environment and continue pursuing her dreams with a resilience and fortitude beyond her years.

A few weeks after she moved Grace to Ms. Gladstone's class, Principal Thompson received an email from the teacher: Though soft-spoken, Grace demonstrated a strong interest and keen talent in biology; Ms. Gladstone did not believe that Grace belonged in her course and suggested she be moved back to Ms. Parker's biology course.

Perplexed, Principal Thompson finally sat down with Grace, who revealed her passion for science and that she had been a top student at an elite school in Cameroon. Grace also shared that her parents are respected doctors—her mother an ob-gyn and her father a trauma surgeon—both graduates of the highly selective Université de Yaoundé I. Despite the growing conflict in western Cameroon, they chose to stay for as long as they could, deeply committed to serving their community through challenging times, until they decided the threat to their safety was too great. Inspired by their dedication, Grace had always been determined to excel in her studies and continue their legacy. However, she confided to Principal Thompson, she was struggling to connect her studies with her new environment. When asked why she had not spoken up sooner, Grace explained she felt it disrespectful for a student to challenge or question an authority figure. Struck by this, Principal Thompson felt guilty for not recognizing Grace's background and brilliance sooner, realizing she had unfairly stereotyped the Etonge family and unintentionally limited Grace's potential.

TEACHING NOTES

Science Education, Equity, and Newcomer Youth

The science classroom is a distinctive space where the worlds of education and science intersect, carrying both challenges and opportunities for student inclusion. Equity and justice are central concerns in science, and science education plays a dual role, both contributing to and potentially solving these issues.[1] Dynamics of belonging and exclusion can be particularly strong in science classrooms, exacerbated by the demands of keeping pace with curriculum and preparing for assessments. However, science education also has the power to foster genuine inclusion, break down hierarchical barriers, and connect science to students' lives, turning it into a tool for creative problem solving and constructing alternative futures.[2]

Honoring and prioritizing students' existing knowledge and experiences in science education are crucial to enhancing engagement and promoting justice. Community-rich, cross-cultural science experiences help newcomers navigate their resettlement and connect meaningfully with scientific practices.[3] Scholars call for reimagining science education as democratic and reflective of the diverse experiential resources that all students, including newcomer students, bring to the learning space.[4] Science education that is responsive to newcomer students' experiences, values their funds of knowledge, and fosters their full participation not only strengthens their scientific understanding but also empowers them to contribute and engage meaningfully and positively in their community.[5] This approach does not diminish the *rigor* of traditional science curricula; rather, it infuses it with *vigor* by enriching it with the vitality and dynamism that come from connecting science learning to real-life problems in students' personal and community lives.[6]

Two key concepts, *community-driven science* and *rightful presence* in science, are central to developing an equitable and justice-based science education for newcomer youth.

Community-Driven Science

Community-driven science envisions science inquiry as deeply rooted in students' lived experiences and local communities and as a tool for both genuine inclusion and justice.[7] This approach emphasizes that students, such as Grace, should not only be welcomed into the physical space of the science classroom but should also be provided meaningful opportunities to personally connect and engage with the classroom and local community.

Even for students like Grace, whose perspectives and aspirations naturally fit within the frameworks of school science, there remains a critical need for more expansive, imaginative, and socially relevant science curricula. How students construct knowledge in science depends on their unique standpoint, shaped by their goals, contexts, and positionalities. Grace, for example, is not a "disinterested scientist" focused solely on abstract phenomena; she is deeply motivated by the social impact of her future work as a scientist. Her aspirations to serve her community and make meaningful contributions underscore the importance of a science curriculum that has personal and societal relevance. A curriculum that values diverse perspectives and emphasizes science's broader social purposes can foster deeper engagement and equip students to envision and construct better futures for themselves and their communities, whether they aspire to careers in science or not.[8]

This is where community-driven science becomes essential, as it addresses the disconnect by centering learning on community-based phenomena that are not only scientifically rich but also deeply tied to justice and the collective imagining of alternative futures. It validates students' unique experiences, enabling them to see how science can be used to address the issues that matter most to them and their communities by bridging the gap between the science classroom and the world outside. By integrating people, place, and environment into the curriculum, community-driven science fosters belonging, deepens engagement, and empowers agency as students begin to see themselves as active participants in constructing equitable and sustainable futures.[9]

Rightful Presence

The concept of rightful presence complements community-driven science by providing a basis for inherent belonging in science. Thomas M. Philip highlights Tan and Calabrese Barton's notion that "rightful presence is a reminder that every young person, with all their wonder, curiosity, hopes, needs, fears, frustrations, and flaws, fundamentally belongs."[10] Rightful presence challenges conventional notions of hospitality in newcomer-host dynamics, which often provide only a superficial sense of inclusion.

Current practices of equity as inclusion can lead to newcomer youth being welcomed in a way that makes them feel at home but never truly allows them to claim it.[11] Rightful presence goes beyond merely offering a place in the science classroom; it insists that students' lived experiences and cultural backgrounds are central to their educational journey, thereby addressing and dismantling the deeper systemic barriers that perpetuate their marginalization in science education. Science engagement is deeply rooted in students' personal and cultural experiences, including those of their families and communities. By co-generating knowledge within the classroom, educators and students can develop shared experiences that bridge their cultural backgrounds with scientific content and practice, thereby supporting the rightful presence of all students in science.

In Grace's case, while she was welcomed into the science classroom, this inclusion offered no affordances to her perspectives, motivations, or background as an individual. Rightful presence calls for a shift from simply integrating students into existing systems to actively reshaping those systems to respond to the diverse backgrounds and experiences of all students. Rightful presence in science can be thought of as "legitimate membership in a science learning community because of who one already is and not because of who one should be."[12]

NOTES FOR LEADERSHIP IN SCIENCE EDUCATION WITH NEWCOMER STUDENTS

Supporting newcomer youth in science education demands leadership that fosters equitable learning environments. At Greenwood, equity was limited to mere inclusion, focusing on Grace's ability to "navigate," "adapt," and "acclimate" rather than creating a flexible environment. This was evident in her biology course, where Principal Thompson and Ms. Parker emphasized Grace's participation (on their terms) to signal belonging. The focus on assessment outcomes pressured Grace and Ms. Parker to meet rigid criteria, and when she fell short, she was removed from the class.

We acknowledge that the Etonge family does not necessarily represent a "typical" newcomer experience. Grace, for instance, is fluent in English, comes from an affluent science background, and is entering a school with relatively low racial and ethnic diversity—circumstances that differ from those of many newcomer students. However, this narrative was intentionally constructed to prompt readers to reflect on the assumptions often projected onto newcomer students and their families. It underscores the critical point that newcomer students are not monolithic in their characteristics and emphasizes the importance of challenging categorical assumptions while recognizing and valuing the full humanity of newcomer students and their families.

This case demonstrates that equity, when reduced to simple inclusion, fails to address the deeper needs of students, ultimately perpetuating marginalization and limiting their opportunities for success. Freedom is not just about the absence of external restrictions (i.e., access); it is also about the presence of conditions that enable individuals to realize their potential and pursue meaningful goals.[13] Equity beyond inclusion requires an effort to understand and support students' unique experiences and abilities, ensuring that they can fully engage and thrive. Below, we suggest several practical research-based suggestions for school leaders.

(1) Nurture deep relationships with newcomer students and families, relationships that honor and value their knowledge and experiences across multiple dimensions (including, but extending beyond, science-based knowledge and experiences).

Principal Thompson's lack of engagement with the Etonge family and unconscious assumptions highlights the need for building meaningful relationships with newcomer students and their families. Valuing their backgrounds and experiences helps educators support students' transitions and growth. Acknowledging Grace's previous academic excellence and her family's funds of knowledge helps in understanding her brilliance and adapting support to her needs and goals. Such deep relationships go beyond superficial interactions and are crucial for recognizing and valuing the diverse knowledge and experiences that newcomer students bring to the classroom. Students and families who may not have the academic or professional prestige of doctors still possess rich scientific expertise rooted in their lived experiences and problem-solving skills. Science knowledge and acumen extends beyond occupational or socioeconomic categorizations. Recognizing, valuing, and incorporating "nontraditional" forms of scientific brilliance into science education is vital for creating a more inclusive and equitable curriculum. It enriches science education by connecting school science to real-world experiences, affirming students' and families' roles as contributors to science and society.

(2) Disrupt traditional power dynamics at your school and intentionally identify assets that newcomer students and families bring with them, rather than focusing unduly on deficits. Find opportunities for newcomer students and families to be positioned as science experts by teaching and helping others. Deep relationships help in identifying the science-based funds of knowledge of newcomer students and families.

Simply placing a student in a classroom and offering "equal" opportunities to "participate" are insufficient for their full potential to emerge, and frequently results in a focus on how students fall short of expectations. Schools must actively challenge unnoticed power hierarchies, particularly in science education, where deficit framings can fundamentally alter teaching practices in ways that are both harmful and patronizing to students. In Grace's case, her family's rich science expertise was overlooked (and assumed not to exist), missing an important opportunity to position them as leaders and authentically include their contributions. Deficit perspectives not only diminish the value of students' and families' knowledge but also shape teaching practices that fail to recognize or nurture their capabilities. Instead, building deep, respectful relationships with families like the Etonges can reveal and honor their expertise, empowering them to lead, teach, and collaborate in meaningful ways. This shift disrupts traditional power dynamics and fosters a more inclusive and equitable educational experience for all students, creating a space where diverse forms of brilliance are celebrated and elevated.

(3) Support science teachers in leveraging students' cultures and background knowledge in the science classroom. Highlight that these aspects are a central part of doing and learning science, rather than peripheral.

In contrast to Grace's success in a culturally diverse setting in Cameroon, the new environment she encountered at Greenwood was largely indifferent to her culture. This reflects a broader misconception that culturally sustaining pedagogies are possible only in ethnically homogenous or segregated settings. School leaders must guide science teachers to see students' cultures and backgrounds not as obstacles or irrelevant to learning but as resources that enhance and enrich it.[14] Being responsive to who students are is not made difficult by diversity; it is constrained by standardization and assessments that value normativity.[15]

To create an authentically inclusive and meaningful science curriculum, teachers need to learn about and value students' whole selves. This involves inviting students to explore, practice, and even reinvent the ideas and skills valued in science content areas in ways that affirm their identities and lived experiences.[16] Such an approach fosters a classroom environment where diverse experiences drive scientific inquiry, enhancing both understanding and engagement. It transforms science education from a one-size-fits-all model into a dynamic, responsive practice that not only values the diverse knowledge students bring but also positions them as active contributors to the evolution of science.

(4) Identify community-based connections that allow students to use their science knowledge in personally meaningful and hands-on ways. Co-construct a collaborative space and allocate resources for science teachers to adapt existing curricula to support more authentic assessments and activities.

The isolation experienced by Grace and her family in their new community underscores the powerful opportunity afforded in science classrooms to connect students—particularly newcomer students who have experienced forcible displacement—to their local communities through science-based explorations that are personally significant to them. Schools should create collaborative spaces where students can apply their science knowledge in ways that resonate with their lived experiences, fostering a sense of belonging and community connection. By allocating resources to adapt curricula and assessments to reflect students' backgrounds and contexts, educators can ensure that newcomer students see the real-world relevance of their learning, helping them bridge the gap between their past experiences and new educational environments. Even occasional community-focused science lessons can have a significant impact on students.[17]

Grace did not just aspire to a "good job"; she sought to use her science knowledge to benefit her community and create change. However, she found no justice-based connection in the classroom to fuel this motivation. Without these connections, students like Grace may disengage, cutting off critical pathways into science and diminishing their drive to pursue it as a meaningful tool for addressing real-world challenges. Science education must do more than teach content—it must empower students to see themselves as agents of change in their communities and beyond.

Discussion Questions

- How are newcomer students welcomed as legitimate, contributing, and valued members of your school community? What practices or policies contribute to a welcoming environment for newcomer students at your school? What might prevent you from fostering a welcoming environment, and how can you overcome these barriers?
- How are newcomer students' science-related cultural knowledge, practices, and experiences made visible and welcomed at your school?
- How can you support teachers in identifying opportunities for bridging school and community science experiences for students at your school?
- How is students' science learning evaluated at your school? What counts as evidence of students' science learning? How might this evidence be expanded? How can a more expansive view of science learning operate within the bounds of standard curricula and assessment?

Teacher Activities

- *Role-Playing Alternative Endings.* In this activity, participants write and act out alternative endings to the case of Grace in order to explore how assumptions about newcomer students can influence educational decisions. After participants are introduced to the original narrative and its ending, they then work in small groups to imagine a different version of the story, focusing on a newcomer student with a different background (e.g., interrupted education, limited English proficiency) or rethinking how stakeholders like teachers and administrators could respond more equitably. Groups act out their alternative endings, highlighting key decisions and strategies. After each role play, the group reflects on what changed, different strategies that might be effective, and how these strategies avoided deficit-based assumptions.

- *Community Mapping Exercise.* In this activity, participants identify and map local science-related resources, organizations, and cultural institutions that can support newcomer students and help connect classroom learning to the broader community. Using Google Maps or a similar tool, participants collaboratively create a map of their local area, adding pins for relevant sites or organizations such as environmental nonprofits, science museums, libraries, cultural heritage centers, STEM organizations, and community health services. For each pin, they include a brief description of the organization's mission and brainstorm how it could support student learning—such as through field trips, guest speakers, service-learning projects, or mentorship opportunities. After mapping, participants work in groups to brainstorm ways these resources could be integrated into their school's science curriculum to enhance engagement and make science learning more relevant to newcomer students. For example, a local environmental nonprofit focused on urban tree planting could partner with a school to involve students in hands-on projects that connect classroom lessons on ecosystems and climate change with real-world applications. Groups then share their maps and ideas with the larger group, discussing strategies for building relationships with these organizations and tailoring partnerships to meet the needs of newcomer students.

RESOURCES

The teaching notes and suggestions in this chapter are largely drawn from and adapted from the two resources listed below. These books offer further reading with additional examples and practical strategies for advancing equity beyond inclusion in science education.

- Daniel Morales-Doyle, *Transformative Science Teaching: A Catalyst for Justice and Sustainability* (Harvard Education Press, 2024).
- Edna Tan and Angela Calabrese Barton, *Teaching Toward Rightful Presence in Middle School STEM* (Harvard Education Press, 2023).

CHAPTER 10

Unlocking Linguistic Success

Navigating the Benefits of English-Language Learner Summer School Initiatives

RYAN ALVAREZ
Touro University

STACEY TRAN
Washington Unified School District

ABSTRACT

Current world conflicts have caused thousands of children to migrate to the United States and the number of English learners across the country to steadily increase. With this increase, school districts have had to adapt to various challenges in supporting English learners. Various studies focus on summer vacation learning loss that English learners experience. This chapter highlights the current literature on the effects that summer school programs have on English learners' language acquisition, and in particular the special programs and curricula that one district has used to bring about significant improvements in its English learners' outcomes. The district has offered a summer program for English learners for decades, but several new practices have been shown to improve the level of instruction—including strands for newcomers to the United States, long-term English learners, and co-teaching classrooms—for both English learners and students in special education programs. This chapter finishes with practical strategies to help district leadership implement a summer institute tailored specifically to meet student language needs, support staff, and develop curriculum to help the district tackle the challenge of summer vacation regression in their highest-needs students.

CASE NARRATIVE

Located in California's Central Valley, Western Unified School District (WUSD) is home to a variety of English learners (ELs), ranging from students who belong to a long family line of multilingual speakers to newcomers who have recently made the journey to the United States. Summer programming for ELs has been a priority for WUSD for more than a decade; however, Stacey, the director of the ELL Department, recognized an opportunity to enhance support systems to help the district's EL students reach language proficiency more effectively and prevent long-term EL (LTEL) status. Like many districts, Western Unified has seen a large increase in the number of LTEL students due to the COVID-19 pandemic. Without swift intervention, WUSD's EL students could face challenges that could prevent them from accessing future content.

In 2018, Stacey and her team reflected on the current structure of WUSD's English Learner Summer Institute. The format was loose and provided teachers with no specific curriculum or content to guide their instruction, little to no professional development providing support on differentiated instruction for EL students, or any type of coaching support on high-leverage literacy strategies. The lack of structure caused inconsistencies across classrooms, and teachers had little support or opportunity for collaboration, ultimately diminishing the impact that a summer program could have on student learning. With the Board of Education questioning the need of the Summer Institute given the lack of student progress and limited funding, Stacey knew she needed to overhaul the program design. To continue to secure annual district funding, she needed to find a way to show immediate results to Western Unified's Board of Education, as other district initiatives and priorities competed for limited funds. At the time, no one could have imagined the changes and improvements the summer program would undergo and the pivots that the team would have to make in response to the COVID-19 pandemic.

Tasked with reimagining the EL summer program to maximize its impact, Stacey and her team decided to take a two-pronged approach: (1) provide high-quality instruction for the district's EL students, while (2) building teacher capacity and equipping the summer teaching staff with strategies and skills they could employ not only throughout the summer but also during the school year. The overhaul of the WUSD Summer Institute helped improve services to the approximately three hundred students served annually, who composed nearly 30 percent of the district's EL students in kindergarten through grade 8. The Summer Institute's goal is to provide 75 hours of engaging, rigorous language-rich classroom instruction to students, while also supporting teachers with 1.5 hours of daily professional learning and weekly instructional coaching. Preservice professional learning days immerse teachers in high-leverage literacy strategies and acquaint them with the curriculum by focusing on a unique animal (a keystone species), strategies grounded in the California English-Language Development (ELD) standards. This foundation provides teachers from any content area with the ability to successfully teach EL students. Through weekly coaching cycles, teachers have the opportunity to observe demonstration lessons, learn differentiation techniques, and refine their practice in a collaborative, supportive environment.

To measure the Summer Institute's impact each year, pre- and post-Institute assessments are administered to all students, which mirror the task types of the English Learner Proficiency Assessment for California (ELPAC). Stacey and her team created assessments based on the year's keystone species, including a written test to evaluate students' English proficiency and a listening and speaking segment requiring them to summarize an academic presentation. Both oral and written responses were scored using rubrics that mirror those used on the ELPAC exam.

Even with the program model, the curriculum, and pre- and post-assessments in place, the turnover rate of summer school staff each year presented a challenge. Stacey realized that although the assessments were simple to administer, every year her staff needed professional learning sessions to better understand scoring criteria and rubrics and opportunities to work together in scoring students' assessments. This would provide her with consistent data across all grade levels by allowing her staff to calibrate the scoring process. The pre-assessment results allowed Stacey and instructional coaches to tailor professional development to student needs and train teachers to set academic goals specific to each class's needs. On making these programmatic shifts, on average, 98 percent of students grew in both their oral and written skills between the pre- and the post-assessment each summer.

While Stacey predicted that WUSD's Board of Education would be ecstatic with the results of students' growth, she needed more qualitative data proving the efficacy of the Summer Institute in accomplishing its dual purpose—increasing EL success while equipping teachers with best practices. She developed reflection surveys for both teachers and parents that highlighted examples of student growth, such as increased confidence, vocabulary expansion, and improved attitudes about school because of the structure and the skills built during the Summer Institute. Under Stacey's direction, the program thrived for several years, until 2020.

In 2020, the world was forever changed because of the COVID-19 pandemic; classrooms moved to virtual platforms, and coinciding with political unrest, many families immigrated to the United States. This created an influx of newcomer students from across the world, including Mexico, Ukraine, and Afghanistan; the number of students in WUSD from these countries tripled in just eighteen months. With a growing population of newcomer students, many of whom were developing their English proficiency and adjusting to an unfamiliar school setting, Stacey noticed an opportunity to design targeted supports to improve their success. Unfortunately, WUSD did not have much differentiated support for newcomer students that provided targeted instruction for them beyond what other EL students received. Stacey knew she had an obligation to do more for these deserving students, leading to several structural changes in WUSD's Summer Institute.

In contrast to the Newcomer students, a significant population of long-term EL students missed out on key instruction during virtual learning.

This fact prompted Stacey to heavily recruit EL students who were close to reclassifying to participate in the Summer Institute, as these students could communicate effectively in English but needed to boost their academic language skills to reach proficiency.

As the 2019–20 school year ended, district leaders questioned whether a virtual Summer Institute could match the impact of the in-person program. Despite opposition, Stacey recognized its necessity, given the limited access to high-quality English-Language Development for all EL typographies during virtual learning, in which opportunities for authentic student collaboration and structured language development were limited. In preparation for the Summer Institute, teachers distributed student binders, journals, art supplies, and other instructional materials in a socially distanced manner. Although the programs were vastly different from past ones, teachers adapted by creating in-home classrooms while students engaged from home. Teachers facilitated five weeks of live virtual instruction, full of rich literature, singing, in-depth lessons on language features, and countless opportunities for language production. After school hours, teachers participated in virtually delivered professional learning in which best practices were shared and new tech tools were introduced to maximize student engagement. As the teachers supported EL students in all language domains, Stacey observed the same engagement, joy, and progress in virtual classrooms as she had during in-person settings.

Since the pandemic, WUSD has seen a 60 percent increase in the number of newcomer students, leading Stacey to found the year-round Newcomer Center, housed at one of the K–8 schools and designed for students who have been in the United States for less than one year. These three multigrade classes focus on foundational skills, including phonics, orthography, and oral language, in order to accelerate language acquisition at its earliest stages. These newcomer classes also employ trauma-informed practices and embed social-emotional learning strategies in the instruction to meet needs that extend beyond academics. Newcomer classes have become part of the Summer Institute as well, offering instruction and structure similar to what the newcomer students receive during the school year.

With Stacey's eighth year as summer school principal coming to an end, she reflected on the data and reviewed the progress that WUSD's EL Department had made. She realized through teacher surveys and conversations with her coaching staff that both students and teachers had achieved tremendous growth and found their time at the Summer Institute to be extremely valuable. As a result of the daily professional learning sessions and instructional coaching, teachers reported increased familiarity with the English-Language Development standards and felt more prepared to meet their English learner students' needs. Stacey realized how valuable the daily collaboration and planning time was for teachers, as they shared classroom artifacts and had a safe space in which to ask questions and support one another.

One teacher she had a conversation with reflected on her experience: "The Summer Institute is the best way to reinvigorate my passion for teaching. When you match teachers who want to be there with students who are excited about learning and administrator-coaches who are supportive and nonjudgmental, you have magic! I have an environment where I'm free to take risks and try new strategies to see what is most beneficial for my students, and I have time to reflect and refine." In her closing remarks to all staff, Stacey thanked them for committing to 6.5 hours of daily teaching and professional learning for nearly half of their summer break, acknowledging that it was an immense undertaking for any teacher. To hear that it is so enjoyable that it hardly feels like work at all is a testament to the rewarding nature of the program. Stacey closed her remarks by saying, "See you all next summer!"

Stacey's lived experience reflects what research consistently shows: Summer school plays a vital role in fostering students' academic growth and social development. One of the biggest challenges teachers face at the start of each school year is students' limited retention of material from previous academic years. This summer learning loss has been described as a period when students are away from an academic setting and thereby lack opportunities to either gain or retain information.[1] While summer learning loss can affect all subjects, studies have shown significant adverse effects on literacy skills.[2]

Like their peers, EL students experience summer learning loss too, but a structured summer program can afford EL students the opportunity to reinforce their academic skills and continue to develop their multilingual ability. The success of WUSD's summer program demonstrates the impact a well-implemented program can have on summer learning loss. The following section provides multiple teachable moments and key takeaways that Stacey learned through her experience as the summer school principal.

TEACHING NOTES

Multilingual students come to our classrooms with a wealth of background knowledge and experiences. Nevertheless, EL students, including newcomers, are faced with a continuous uphill climb of balancing content standard mastery and English-language mastery simultaneously, demonstrating their resilience and adaptability. Stacey's experience highlights the challenges school districts encounter in supporting their EL students and addressing their diverse language needs. During the school year, many sites have one English-Language Development class for all EL students, regardless of whether they are newly arrived to the country or an LTEL (who already has mastery of conversational English but lacks literacy skills). In addition, many multilingual students come from homes, neighborhoods, and communities where they navigate life almost exclusively in a language other than English, and summer programs are critical in helping to maintain and improve English skills over the summer. Stacey's experiences sheds light on lessons learned and teachable moments for districts that need direction as to best practices for overcoming challenges like summer learning loss for EL students. The best practices include the following:

- Incorporating literacy-rich instructional practices into engaging content lessons
- Developing engaging, language-rich curriculum that aligns with standards and includes multiple opportunities for oral language production
- Creating assessments that mimic standardized tests, with trackable pre—and post–summer program data

- Grouping newcomer students together to provide targeted foundational skills development
- Implementing daily professional development to facilitate teacher collaboration, sharing of best practices, and data analysis
- Providing accessible instructional coaches and weekly coaching sessions

The following sections detail these key takeaways from Stacey's experience that districts can utilize to implement improved summer programs to overcome summer learning loss for EL students and improve language development for all EL students regardless of level.

BEST PRACTICES FOR EL STUDENTS' SUCCESS

Literacy-Rich Instructional Practices

Recognizing the strengths and diverse linguistic abilities of EL students is crucial in implementing an effective, assets-based EL summer program, and centering your state's standards for English-Language Development is key. The curriculum needs to integrate literacy-rich instructional practices. Some suggestions include strategies that rely on repetition and predictable patterns to develop phrases to facilitate language acquisition, allowing students to transition to more conversational activities.[3] Specific strategies include various structured language protocols such as Choral Response, My Turn Your Turn, and Language Pattern Songs.[4]

Curriculum Content

The content used in a summer language development program is flexible and can cover any curricular area if it aligns with the ELD standards for your state. From WUSD's experience, employing content that is engaging, is rich in language, and can be replicated across multiple grade levels helps in developing a successful summer program. Stacey's district uses a different keystone species every year. For example, one year the institute focused on honeybees, the next about polar bears. You can dive heavily into each keystone species by focusing on its role in the food web, its anatomical features, and how it impacts the environment. Each one of these topics has rigorous vocabulary and content that engages newcomers while teaching them academic English.

Assessments

While having high-leverage literacy strategies incorporated into the curriculum is key, it is vital to have strong pre- and post-assessments. To measure exact student growth, the before and after assessments should be similar. For example, one might ask students to write about their knowledge of sharks; while simple, it is an open-ended prompt that provides EL students opportunity to demonstrate their writing ability. Typically, on evaluating student work, the pre-assessment demonstrates limited content knowledge, but after the cycle of learning about sharks, the assessment usually contains more detailed content. Beyond content knowledge, it is pivotal to focus on the student's writing skills in the assessment as well. Teachers need to examine *how* the students wrote their text, not simply what they wrote. In addition to having accurate content, are the EL students using adjectives, prepositional phrases, text connectives, and proper punctuation? Is there mastery of voice, genre, and paragraph structure? These elements are key in assessing growth.

Newcomer Classroom

With massive increases in newcomer populations in the district, Stacey was very intentional about providing added support to newcomers during the summer program. After analyzing achievement data, looking at the students' US entry dates, and identifying specific needs, she decided to implement a few multigrade newcomer classes. These classes put students in three groups: kindergarten to second grade, third to fifth grade, and sixth to eighth. All groups were taught by some of the district's strongest ELD teachers, who were comfortable implementing differentiated strategies and addressing the ELD standards, including those that encompassed foundational literacy skills. By grouping all the newcomers in specific classes, they do not fall through the cracks in other classes with more advanced EL students and they receive specific attention and instruction to facilitate the development of English fundamentals.

Professional Development

Not all teachers are experts in effective EL strategies from the outset, and it is key to include daily professional development focused on high-leverage strategies like structured language protocols. Professional development needs to be centered on student talk and the various strategies we pursue to meet our EL students' needs and promote language development. Centering professional development on EL student strategies has resulted in improved EL performance with English acquisition.[5] One effective way to deepen understanding of EL strategies in professional development is to ask teachers to share sample lessons or discuss what they are doing in their instruction and how it works. Another way is incorporating instructional coaches into your program. Instructional coaches are typically content experts who can provide training on high-leverage literacy strategies through professional development and can then support in-class instruction in a variety of ways.

Instructional Coaches

In addition to delivering professional development, instructional coaches can assist teachers who need support in utilizing specific strategies to meet the needs of EL students. Instructional coaches can play an instrumental role when developing a strong summer program, as they can assist in developing the curriculum and embedding standards-based ELD strategies. Coaches can provide professional development during each meeting. During instructional hours, they can visit classes to observe or to assist with modeling a lesson, co-teaching a strategy, or gathering student data to use for future reflective meetings.[6] Instructional coaches should be available to all teachers, and administrators should encourage weekly coaching throughout the duration of any summer program.

By implementing these key takeaways, district leadership can create an impactful summer learning experience for EL and newcomer students.

With a well-structured summer program that has engaging curriculum and strategies, effective assessments, dedicated newcomer classrooms, structured professional development, and accessible instructional coaches, educational outcomes for EL students and newcomers are likely to improve. Another valuable by-product of professional development and instructional coaching is that teachers learn strategies and techniques that they can integrate into their instructional practice well beyond the summer program.

Discussion Questions

1. *Addressing Newcomers' Needs*: What are the specific challenges faced by newcomer students with limited English skills and prior schooling experience in your district?
   a. What strategies could be employed to support newcomer students in developing their English skills and building on their prior educational experiences?
2. *Teacher Professional Development*: How did daily professional learning and instructional coaching contribute to the effectiveness of the Summer Institute?
   a. What specific benefits did teachers report from these professional development opportunities? What role does collaboration and peer learning play in enhancing teacher effectiveness in the summer program?
   b. How can these elements be implemented within your district? What are current hurdles, and what resources are needed?

Teacher Activities

Activity A: Scenario-Based Role-Play

Create scenarios based on challenges mentioned in the case study; for example, the need to overcome the consistent turnover of summer schoolteachers and teachers' lack of familiarity with the ELD standards. Have participants role-play different educational partners (e.g., teachers, students, administrators) and discuss how they would address these challenges.

Activity B: Action Planning Exercise

Have participants develop an action plan to address a specific challenge highlighted in the case study (e.g., improving support for newcomer students or enhancing professional development). The plan should include the following:

- Specific steps to implement the solution
- Resources needed (staff, materials, funding, training, etc.)
- Potential barriers and strategies for overcoming them
- Timeline for implementation and evaluation
- Success indicators to measure progress

SECTION 3

School Partners and Family Engagement

In Section 3, the chapters focus on how school leaders can build and sustain partnerships both inside and outside school to support efforts to welcome and create a sense of belonging for newcomer students and families in schools. Authors provide case examples for readers on ways that school leaders can better engage newcomer families both ethically and equitably in the work of schools that honor their multifaceted identities and talents. Chapters in this section first familiarize readers with strategies for building equitable partnerships with newcomer families and organizations and then engage them in creative and practical problem solving through reflective discussion questions and activities. Chapter 11, by Liou and Liang, conceptualizes "identity-safe" schooling and how leaders can use a variety of relational practices to counter xenophobia while also building community by prioritizing trust, interpersonal connection, and promoting understanding and voice. Koyama and Kaihan's chapter (chapter 12) takes place in the US Southwest and focuses on how leaders across roles, from administrators to mentors and interpreters for newcomer families, can collaborate and use holistic practices to better engage refugee families and meet their needs. In chapter 13, Hauber-Özer looks at the power and impact of an informal-learning context, in this case an out-of-school program that strengthens the sense of welcome that a young man from Afghanistan experiences. The chapter carries implications for leaders who seek to strengthen refugees' sense of belonging in school and along postsecondary pathways. In chapter 14, Ebied focuses on compassionate leadership. Situated in Canada, where schools interface with "settlement workers"—but with connections to US-based leaders as well—Ebied's work concentrates on helping leaders build their skills to support refugee students with socio-emotional and trauma needs through school-community collaborations.

The vignettes in Rodriguez, Pippin-Kottkamp, and Ramirez's chapter (chapter 15) also underscore how immigrant and newcomer students are racialized and how schools can create cultures of caring to work holistically, across personnel roles and with outside community partners, to amplify student voice and increase their participation and inclusion schooling. Akhi and Lowenhaupt's case (chapter 16) takes place in the Northeast in a district strongly affected by the COVID-19 pandemic. Their chapter stresses the importance of cross-sector coordination and collaboration, including school partnerships with city government, health services, and community-based organizations, cooperation that can enhance immigrant students' socio-emotional well-being in school. Piral Lee and Dorner's case (chapter 17) occurs in a Midwestern rural school district that struggles to integrate and graduate adolescent newcomers. Researchers, educators, and community members come together as a task force to leverage their individual and collective strengths.

CHAPTER 11

Leadership for Identity-Safe Schools

One Southeast Asian American Principal's Antiracist Expectations of Refugee and Newcomer Students

DANIEL D. LIOU
Arizona State University

GRACE JIA LIANG
Kansas State University

ABSTRACT

In this chapter, we present Lawan, a Southeast Asian American school principal, as a case study for fostering identity safety with her refugee students and families. To repudiate the persistent, impoverished outlook on refugee populations, this case describes the role of identity-safe schooling in rejecting xenophobia while advancing social justice through four relational practices carried out with the school community: (1) promoting trust and interpersonal connection; (2) promoting understanding, voice, and responsibility; (3) cultivating diversity as a source of high expectations for teaching and learning; and (4) creating purposeful communities of care and consistency. By telling the story of Lawan, this case highlights the challenges she faced at the intersections of race and gender and the ways she leveraged these experiences in fostering identity-safe schooling. This chapter concludes with recommended practices for supporting school administrators in enacting antiracist expectations vis-à-vis students' lived experiences in school and society.

CONTEXT

Racism and xenophobia are persistent global problems that have been intensifying in recent years. In the United States, these issues fluctuate in a cycle of self-fulfilling prophecy from social policies to hate crimes that scapegoat immigrants and refugees for economic downturns and as people unworthy of being treated as equals. Since schools are not immune to anti-immigrant and anti-refugee sentiment, school leaders and advocates have a legal, moral, and ethical responsibility to ensure a safe, inclusive, and affirming learning environment regardless of students' identities and lived experiences.

In this chapter, a Southeast Asian American school principal by the name of Lawan shares her story about her work with refugee and newcomer students through the concept of "identity-safe schools."[1] We begin this chapter with a description of the local context, followed by the case narrative, and ending with opportunities for leaders and advocates to reflect on the conditions necessary for creating identity-safe schools.[2] This chapter calls on leaders and advocates to ensure that students' access to a high-quality, vibrant, equitable, and just education is not predetermined by who they are or where they come from.

The state where Lawan lives and works has 2,200 public schools, which serve more than 1.7 million students. More than 60 percent of the state's public school students are eligible for free and reduced-price lunch. The largest racial group, white Americans, make up over 40 percent of the total student population, followed by Black students with 30 percent, and Latinx students with 18 percent. In the past decade, Lawan's school system has seen an increase in immigrant and refugee populations, which currently form 10 percent of the state's population. Many of these students in this cohort are Asian, multilingual, and eligible for free and reduced-price lunch.

The town of Hope, which is twenty minutes away from a major metropolitan city, has been a destination for refugee resettlement since the 1980s. Although Hope has historically relied on tourism, a high-tech economy has recently emerged, leading to a demographic transformation with over 60 percent of the population now born outside the country. Lately, tensions have run deep between the newcomers and the "old Hope" residents, who are primarily white, as some of the latter group have become suspicious about the presence of refugees eroding their way of life. Longtime residents lament their inability to maintain a low cost of living and worry about the willingness of the newcomers to assimilate and whether the group will drain its social services and lead to more gang violence, plummeting property values, school budget shortfalls, and other social issues. Without basic infrastructure to support this new population, state and local officials have pled with the federal government to temporarily halt the resettlement program, attributing Hope's social problems to the refugees. Xenophobia has become normalized in Hope, with its residents' sense of safety, including that of refugees, eroded.

CASE NARRATIVE

Bridgewater is a middle school in Hope, tucked away on a street that faces the athletic practice field of a private university. Bridgewater serves a student body over 90 percent of which are people of color, over 80 percent are categorized as English language learners, and 97 percent qualify for free or reduced-price lunch. For the past three years, Bridgewater's overall performance on state tests and other academic and engagement measures (such as attendance, graduation rate, and school environment and safety index) has been higher than over 60 percent of other state public schools. Lawan, the school principal, is proud of what the school has accomplished, but she can still remember what it was like when she first stepped into the role. There was no trust; parents questioned why she, an Asian woman, was there. They did not think she could relate to, understand, or lead them. The staff turnover rate was high, and morale was low. No one thought she would last a semester in the position, yet she is now in her fifth year as the principal.

Treated as an outsider who did not meet the stereotypical expectations of a school principal, who traditionally are white and male in this district, Lawan, who is Thai, female, cisgender, and of refugee status, worked diligently to promote trust and interpersonal connection in and with her school community. Step by step, Lawan earned trust and created a safe and empowering school environment. She also cultivated fundamental shifts in people's mindsets for teaching and learning. Consistent with Hernández and Darling-Hammong, Lawan sees the following four elements are essential for an identity-safe school: (1) promoting trust and interpersonal connection;

(2) promoting understanding, voice, and responsibility; (3) cultivating diversity as a source of high expectations for teaching and learning; and (4) creating purposeful communities of care and consistency.[3]

Promoting Trust and Interpersonal Connection

One aspect of Lawan's work was to foster trust and connections in order to create conditions to support the school community. To foster an identity-safe learning environment, Lawan made sure that the identities of students and staff were not treated as liabilities but as strengths of the school. To reject societal narratives that considered child-rearing a barrier to women's choice and ability to work, Lawan established a nursery room for her pregnant and new-mother teachers. Since a good portion of her students were refugees from the Middle East, she also designated a praying room and called it "The Spiritual Place," so that the students and their families could practice their religious rituals free of Islamophobic ridicule and harassment.

To ensure that students' socioeconomic status did not discourage them from participating in extracurricular activities, Lawan leveraged local resources to create an ecology of support through university-school partnerships. For example, knowing that most of her students' families could not afford to send their children to participate in sports and other extracurricular activities, Lawan reached out to the president of the private university and advocated for a partnership so that her students could have access to its practice field, as well as its athletes and coaches as role models. Since then, the athletes and coaches from the university have been volunteering with the school. They often talk to the students about going to college and even becoming collegiate athletes. Families, many of whom must work long hours, try to attend practices and sports events; even when they cannot, they feel much at ease knowing that their children are with trustworthy people. As Lawan said, "It was so out of my typical character; I rarely just go up to a stranger and ask for something. But I did it for my kids," indicating that she went out of her comfort zone to build trust through this partnership.

Promoting Understanding, Voice, and Responsibility

For her teachers and staff, Lawan expected that they have a genuine understanding of people's lives as the basis for relationship-building. By eliciting the voices of community members, the school was able to shed light on the multiplicity of lived experiences and cultivate cross-racial understanding so as to increase people's sense of responsibility with one another. By rejecting superficial notions of multiculturalism and convening the school community to understand the values, cultures, histories, and strengths of her students and families, Lawan made sure there was equity in how people related with one another.

For example, given the wide range of languages spoken by students and their families, Lawan ensured that all important announcements were translated to remove any hierarchy of languages, appreciatively relying on her students for help with translations. She also leveraged these opportunities to seek input from families about the best ways to affirm all forms of diversity. This affirmation includes connecting families to community-based organizations through celebratory events that also served as learning opportunities for her teachers and staff to critically reflect on their beliefs and expectations of students through the voices of the community. For instance, the school invited a parent who was a highly regarded artist in the Lao community to share his journey to the United States and how art had become his way of re/memorizing the loss and pain, re/defining life and joy, and re/discovering self and home. The event re-created the school into a place that not only recognized one's sense of loss and pain but also cultivated a greater understanding of the community through discussions about collective responsibility for fostering hope and resilience through education.

Cultivating Diversity as a Source of High Expectations for Teaching and Learning

When it comes to supporting teachers' instructional development and overall professional growth, Lawan personally knew the strengths and limitations of each teacher. Any conversation she had with them were never just a critique or fault-finding mission; they were frank discussions, admittedly, but oriented toward solutions and growth. She organized teachers who had complementary skill sets into clusters where they could collaborate and learn from one another. She allocated a generous amount of her annual budget for teacher and staff professional development. Over time, her school has become a preferred destination for teacher candidates as well as teacher applicants.

Given the strong presence of multilingual students in the school, Lawan worked with staff to ensure that teaching was culturally responsive, so that families were part of the key sources that helped build and expand the school's curriculum to reflect the students' lived experiences. To support teachers in creating a heterogeneous knowledge ecosystem, Lawan was deeply invested in the school library. With financial support, the school library has grown its collection to include books written by authors from diverse backgrounds celebrating experiences and perspectives grounded in different cultures. Lawan also worked closely with the district to create a Spanish and English dual-language program and raised money through fundraising and grants to hire tutors while increasing their availability for multilingual students.

By creating a diverse ecology of knowledges and expressions, Lawan was able to leverage local knowledge as a source of high expectations in the classroom. She expected her students to go on to good high schools and continue their educational journey into college. Such high expectations formed a fundamental pillar of the school culture that Lawan had intentionally nurtured to redefine academic success as cultivating "respect, accomplishments, perseverance, and community." Lawan understood that school culture was often strengthened through rituals and common language, and when developed and implemented purposefully, the school becomes a platform for narratives that counter stereotype threats and xenophobia.

Creating Purposeful Communities of Care and Consistency

As a part of school norms, Lawan opened every morning with her students by saying, "I love you dearly the way you are. You are growing stronger and better. And you *are* going to college." As an expression of care, Lawan successfully recruited and retained bilingual faculty over the years to affirm and sustain the rich cultural and linguistic diversity of her teachers and students. These teachers were actively involved in the dual-language program and tutoring sessions and have become an irreplaceable part of the instructional and learning process, serving as linguistic and cultural brokers. Knowing that with her current school enrollment, she was allocated only one full-time and one part-time counselor, Lawan used money generated from other channels to fund two full-time counselors to support students' social and emotional needs at the school. To further contextualize their caring practices, these counselors conducted regular home visits, worked closely with families and social workers to help the families gain access to public resources to which they were entitled, keep the families informed about school and district policies and their students' academic and socioemotional status, and gain an understanding of the families' expectations and hopes for their children.

By creating conditions of trust, high expectations, and inclusivity, Lawan was able to co-construct the school's sense of purpose through the lenses of care and consistency. She envisioned the school having a more cutting-edge facility as another strategy to communicate her sense of care and high expectations of students. To reach this goal, she had been working for several years on a request to her district to relocate Bridgewater to a new location that would provide the necessary space and upgrades to accommodate her growing student population. She finally received a response from the district, approving her request. The new building was much bigger, was well equipped with the latest technologies, and had more space for both instruction and physical activities. The district also laid out the bus routes for transporting current and future students to the new Bridgewater location. This district approval of relocation would have been welcome news except that the proposed location was on the outskirts of the district, outside the close-knit community boundaries.

The Paradox of Identity-Safe School

Despite the progress made, the school still operated in the context of xenophobia. When news of the district's proposed new location broke, Lawan was thrown into a whirlwind of rumors and attacks from her political opponents: "I knew it; she is not with us. . . . See, those rich Asian lawyers and doctors moved in uptown; they and the others have wanted us out for so long!" "This is not a better option! They literally want us to be caught and deported! [The new location] is so far from where we live; how can we know who is who, notice something that is off?!" "How could she let them do this to us? She is too soft! That's why they pick on us, you know—kill one and set an example for the rest!" "Okay, rich side of town . . . gradually they will demand to have different staff and teachers." Suddenly, Lawan's efforts to create identity-safe contingencies started to erode, as people started to attribute her race and gender to her ability to be trusted as a school leader. Within a school that was intended to promote identity safety, Lawan's own sense of identity was no longer safe.

It was easy to see the panic, resentment, distrust, and fear present in student, staff, and family stakeholders in the school. While she felt saddened and hurt by this reaction, Lawan knew it was important for her to remain calm and think things through: This was a community she had worked tirelessly for, and they had experienced so much together.

On a notepad, Lawan wrote:

Unknown—loss of a sense of certainty—fear & distrust.

No trustful connections and safety net / mechanisms outside the community boundaries.

For families, now, older siblings often opt out of the bus service as they need to help with household tasks and look after their younger siblings in the nearby element schools. They can walk from Bridgewater to their siblings' schools and their homes—within walking distance and feel safe, without worrying if someone would report them to border control or something.

Distant to communal supporters / role models (e.g., university coaches & athletes; business owners)

Ongoing tensions fuel such fear & distrust:

- *ongoing border issues (heating up recently)*
- *international tensions in the Mideast regions*
- *the used-to-be un- or less desirable area/neighborhoods have been experiencing significant gentrification as more rich people and private companies moving*

in, buying properties, and building new developments. Complaints and suggestions to relocate the school have been raised several times.

- *some local and state groups petition against the district, claiming misusages or unfair distributions of state/local taxpayers' money for illegal immigrants, hurting the rights and wellbeing of citizens/children*

"Me"—potentially complicating the issue:

- *Asian American sandwiched—neither there nor here in the Black-vs.-white, Black & brown–vs.-white racial binaries*
- *Asian American women—no place in leadership or, even worse, no place in trustworthiness, the stereotypes about us*
- *Southeast Asian refugee—"problem," "a token hire"*

As Lawan put her thoughts down on paper, she started to see viable and concrete steps toward addressing these issues:

Dispel misleading and harmful information, replace with the correct information and facts/data.

Bring experts and reliable sources to campus & community (i.e., civil rights people / advocates, refugee service partners/organizations, university professor).

Cultural insider / broker (parents, staff, . . .)

This was not the first time Lawan had faced misinformation and backlash. Although some might have called her extremely optimistic, Lawan remained hopeful that the school community could overcome these challenges, especially since sustaining identity-safe schools should be a continuous effort, a process that would require a great deal of intentionality, and not a destination or merely an ideal that would be overdependent on a single person.

TEACHING NOTES

According to the United Nations High Commissioner for Refugees, "Refugees are people who have fled war, violence, conflict or persecution and have crossed an international border to find safety in another country."[4] Historically, wars in Southeast Asia, like the Vietnam War, have held a "positive/welcoming" discourse regarding refugees from these regions, portraying the United States as a savior to justify the government's foreign policies, military actions, and occupations in various Asian regions for its geopolitical dominance and control of the Global South.[5] Currently, the general public in the United States considers the welcoming of refugees from Asian regions as a phenomenon of the past, whereas in reality, these regions continue to witness people being forced to seek refuge in the United States for various sociopolitical, economic, and religious reasons.[6] These refugees are rendered invisible, as they are either dismissed because of perceived associations with the model-minority myth—that is, a stereotype portraying Asian Americans as inherently intelligent, hardworking, well adjusted, and successful academically and socioeconomically—or ridiculed and pigeonholed into narratives of dysfunction and vulnerability, stripped of any humanity, and essentialized as a societal "problem."[7]

Lopez and Fernandez note that "the intersectional dimensions of race, assumed 'citizenship' status, language, and notions of illegality are surfaced and yet remain obscured behind a rhetoric of 'protecting Americans.'"[8] While these scholars focus on Latinx immigrants, their critique of the criminalizing and dehumanizing spaces in US policies, politics, and mainstream and social media also speaks to other refugee populations whose statuses are uncertain as they wait for years for their cases to progress slowly through the immigration court system.

This notion is particularly relevant for the case presented in this chapter, as the protagonist, Lawan, comes from a refugee background and leads a school serving refugee students and families from Asian regions. As we situate this case in critical refugee studies, Lawan's experiences underscore the gendered racialization and violence against Asian American women while she worked to repudiate the pathologies of refugee groups through identity-safe schooling.[9] In addition, her racial and gender subjugations also informed her expectations and sense of responsibility as a school principal. Given the ways Lawan was stereotyped as a perpetual outsider, it shows how schools, despite their focus on identity safety, can still operate in contradictory ways. While facing systemic challenges and injustices, the protagonist maintained an orientation and took actions reflective of leadership for identity safety—leadership that is enacted through four relational practices mentioned earlier.[10]

Discussion Questions

1. *Group discussion*: Resources are often tight in schools, particularly for those that serve students of minoritized groups. Furthermore, many schools across the United States are not equipped with the awareness, knowledge, and resources needed to lead and support their administrators, teachers, and staff to advocate and ensure quality and equitable education for their refugee students and families. If you were tasked with crafting a professional development series for staff at a school serving refugees, what topics or recommendations would you have for their leadership team? Consider the following (just to name a few):
   a. Critical literacy on refugee populations
   b. Critical literacy on federal and state policies
   c. Social and emotional well-being for adults and children with refugee experiences and circumstances
   d. Housing and safe spaces outside the students "home" or "lodging place" for sharing experiences and program support
   e. Community partnerships
   f. Partnerships with professional organizations or governmental agencies
2. *Group discussion*: In the case narrative, we present the leadership orientation, actions, and practices that Lawan engages to create a school that provides quality education and empowerment for her refugee students and families. Such orientation and practices closely resemble the dimensions of identity-safe schools, as noted in the "Teaching Notes" section. Given the circumstances of this case, use the four key elements of identity safety and craft a course of leadership actions to address the tensions and issues related to the potential school relocation.
3. *Role play*: Put yourself in Lawan's shoes. Given her personal and professional identities, how would you analyze the relocation situation to find possible solutions? You may consider the following aspects:

a. What frames of reference will you use to define the "issue"?
   i. What is the main issue?
   ii. What are the relevant subissues?
   iii. How will different frames of reference lead to different definitions of the issue?
b. What or whom will you pull in as your resources for problem solving and decision making?
   i. Persons from the school or district
   ii. Persons from the families and their communities
   iii. Persons from organizations or entities beyond the immediate school and district units
c. What criteria will you rely on to weigh potential options?
   i. Interpersonal and communal
   ii. Student centered
   iii. Managerial and operational
   iv. Equity, justice, and humanity

RESOURCES

For greater understanding of Asian American experiences in education and leadership, see the following research-based resources:

- Jia G. Liang and April Peters-Hawkins, "'I Am More Than What I Look Like': Asian American Women in Public School Administration," *Educational Administration Quarterly* 53, no. 1 (2017): 40–69.
- Jia G. Liang, James Sottile, and April Peters, "Understanding Asian American Women's Pathways to School Leadership," *Gender and Education* 30, no. 5 (2018): 623–41.
- Taeyeon Kim, "Becoming Skillful Leaders: American School Principals' Transformative Learning," *Educational Management Administration and Leadership* 48, no. 2 (2020): 353–78.
- Jung Kim and Betina Hsieh, *The Racialized Experiences of Asian American Teachers in the US: Applications of Asian Critical Race Theory to Resist Marginalization* (Routledge, 2021).

CHAPTER 12

"To know us is to be a part of us"

School Leaders Can Collaborate with Refugee Families

JILL KOYAMA AND NASIR KAIHAN

Arizona State University

ABSTRACT

Drawing on data collected in an eighteen-month case study of a southwestern-US school district's response to refugee students and their families, this case study centers on how school leaders engage the families and communities of refugee students. It illuminates the complexities of working with a heterogenous student population and their families, a population that includes among other migrants, recently arrived refugees. The case also brings to the fore the ways school leaders can mistakenly aggregate all migrant students—and, even more broadly, all emergent bilinguals (often referred to as English language learners)—using stereotypes based on deficit thinking.

In the case, the leaders and other school staff initially admit to not knowing much about the refugee students and their families. However, unsatisfied with her lack of knowledge, one principal holds a meeting with staff of the school district's refugee support program to explore what they can do to enact new and meaningful ways to learn alongside refugee families so that they can participate more in the schooling of their children. At the meeting, which is the first of its kind in the six years the principal has been in her position, the participants create a to-do list to better serve refugees in their school.

Drawing on the scholarship on parental and familial involvement and refugee education in the United States, we offer teaching activities based on the case to highlight how interactions with the families and how the families' understandings about, and familiarity with, US schooling can change over time. The scaffolded activities employ the case's to-do list to guide school leaders, leadership teams, and groups of educators in applying what they learn to their own context and to expanding their collective abilities to educate refugee students and engage the students' families.

CASE NARRATIVE

Principal Ana Gómez and Assistant Principal Pam Torrès chat as they walk the short distance from their offices to the middle school's front entrance. Students are lining up outside next to their first-period teachers and parents are saying their goodbyes. The women stop chatting as the front doors open and students stream into the building. They say hello to the students and wave to some of the parents they know. The atmosphere is upbeat and organized. This has been the morning routine at the school for the six years that Principal Gómez has led the school. As she is about to close the front doors, she sees a large family standing on the playground that she does not know. She leans out, says "Good morning," and waves. The family does not respond. "Do you know that family?" she asks Assistant Principal Torrès. Before getting an answer, she says "Oh, I should have said '¡Buenos días!': How stupid of me." Assistant Principal Torrès responds: "Oh, don't blame yourself. They aren't Latinos. They look it, but they're new, somewhere from the Middle East. Their son just started this week. Not your fault. You can't know everyone, and they probably don't speak enough English yet." Principal Gómez agrees that she can't know every family, but also makes a mental note that she should try harder to know the refugee and migrant students who aren't Latinos and whose families don't speak Spanish like hers.

Assistant Principal Torrès's comment about the Middle Eastern family not knowing enough English to engage with the school personnel is repeated later in the day by Patrick, the English Language Development (ELD) teacher to Awad, the son in the family who attends the school. Patrick has come to the main office to get some materials—the attendance policy and the condensed school procedure manual—in Arabic for Awad's family. To the one of the administrative specialists, he says: "I need the basics, you know, for the new refugee family . . . I am guessing I need them in Arabic. The family's from Syria." After receiving the materials, Patrick says hello to Principal Gómez, who, overhearing his request, asks about Awad and his family. Patrick replies that he doesn't know much about them and adds that "they [the family] probably won't get too involved. None of them [refugee families] do. They can't with the language and all." Again, Principal Gómez makes a note to herself to learn more about Awad, his family, and the other refugee students and families attending her school.

Before leaving that evening, Principal Gómez asks for a meeting with the director of the school district's refugee support program, the director of the district's interpreting services, and Mahmoud, a refugee parent who also teaches as a substitute at the school. She wants to know more about the 12 refugee families whose children have started attending her school this fall. Including these new enrollees, 32 refugee students attend the school, and they are part of the larger refugee student population in Desert Unified School District (DUSD), which fluctuated between 771 and 1,104 students during 2013–16, the time frame in which we situate our case study. The middle school led by Principal Gómez, in fact, had the largest number of refugee middle schoolers in DUSD, a large district in southern Arizona with approximately 48,000 students, 62 percent of whom were identified as "Hispanic." The refugee students came from fifty-two different countries, with the majority hailing from either Bhutan, Somalia, or Iraq. Of the 89 schools in the district, all but 10 had at least one refugee student; 2 district high schools had the largest percentage of refugee students—22 percent of the refugee student total attended one, and 10 percent attended the other. The middle school in this case was a feeder school to those two high schools.

DUSD has a department, the Refugee Services Department, that works to integrate refugee youth into schools and helps refugee families transition to living in southern Arizona. The department comprises a director, ten or eleven full-time student-family mentors, and one part-time coordinator. Together, they provide a range of educational and social supports. The educational services, such as school registration assistance, tutoring, and language support, are designed to counteract refugee youth's initial lack of experience with the English language and their histories of intermittent formal schooling. The Refugee Services Department helps secure medical services for the youth and their families, provides ESL tutoring for the adult refugees, and translates school information to parents. The student-family mentors routinely work with refugee support organizations and resettlement agencies, of which there are nearly eighty-five.

THE MEETING: MULTIPLE PERSPECTIVES ABOUT ENGAGING REFUGEE FAMILIES AT THE SCHOOL

Thirteen days after her request, Principal Gómez; Assistant Principal Torrès; Tam, the director of the school district's refugee support program; Jayne, the director of the district's interpreting services; and Mahmoud, a refugee parent who substitute teaches at the middle school, met to talk about what was being done and what should be done to engage refugee families.

Principal

Gómez acknowledged that she and many of the middle school teachers and staff were more familiar with Latino families. Many of them spoke Spanish fluently. Those who didn't could find colleagues who did when they needed to interact with Spanish-speaking families. Principal Gómez, though, felt that she and the entire school could do better in "connecting with, engaging" refugee families. She kept repeating that these families were part of the school community and needed to know that. What, she wondered, was being done and what more could be done? She turned to the other meeting attendees for their expertise and advice.

Assistant Principal

Torrès, who was in her first year of school leadership, said that she felt that she was respecting the refugee families by not requesting anything of them, especially at first:

> I feel like what they need is outside of the school. We will take good care of their kids, but the parents need more than we can, or do, offer . . . I rely

> on the [resettlement] agencies and refugee support and interpreting for connecting with the parents. It's not so much that I don't want to or that I don't see them as part of our school, but they are new, new to the US, new to Arizona, and way new to our school system here, you know. If I were them, I'd be lost about it all . . . Why burden them more by asking them to come to meetings and stuff? Now, at least.

Torrès also stated that her parents, who spoke mostly Spanish, felt very embarrassed when asked to participate in her and her brothers' schooling. She didn't want the refugee parents and families to feel that way.

Director, DUSD Refugee Support Program

Tam, whose staff worked closely with the refugee students and their families, argued that the responsibility to connect was that of the schools for the very same reason given by Assistant Principal Torrès. "The refugees are new here," she said. "They are the ones that need welcoming. It should not be up to the families to connect." Tam continued to explain how the mentors in her program, nearly all of whom were refugees themselves, can be utilized better by the middle school to interact with parents. It would require some advance planning, she warned, so that mentors could be scheduled and so that families could be invited. She gave several examples of mentors meeting with families and teachers at the school within the last month.

Director, DUSD Interpreting Services

Jayne's staff works closely with Tam's, and together, their units are the consistent points of contact for the refugee families. Jayne said, though, that she wished there was more communication between the mentors and interpreters, especially about overall scheduling and concerns and issues that arise for certain families. For instance, she said that she wasn't told about the recent car accident death of a refugee grandparent near a school until she saw it on the news. Jayne's staff had worked closely with the grandparent as he was the primary adult in the family. A refugee mentor had mentioned it in a meeting weeks after the death and the funeral.

Refugee Parent and Substitute Teacher

Mahmoud felt that he had the best of both worlds. He was a refugee but also part of the school staff. He encouraged the others to be more welcoming to refugee families, to see them as part of the school—and to get to know them. "To know us is to be part of us," Mahmoud advised, "and if you want us to become American, like we do, then we need to work together for the good of our children." He reminded everyone that whatever they do needs to be done with the children in mind. Many parents like him, he said, fled their countries to offer better lives to their children. Education was a big part of that. He told the meeting attendees to stop making so many divisions between the refugee families and other families. "We are all families who love our children and want good lives for them, always," he insisted. Mahmoud added that many refugee parents were professionals in their home countries and should not be treated as inferior just because they had not yet learned English fluently. That, he said, was very disrespectful.

Toward the end of the meeting, the attendees created a to-do list to better engage refugee families. It read, in no prioritized order:

- Invite refugee parents to school
- Learn how to pronounce the refugees' names
- Know refugee families' histories and home countries
- Have refugee families come share their stories at the school
- In collaboration with the refugee communities and organizations, conduct resource fairs to introduce refugee families to the US schooling system and other learning opportunities and resources
- Include books from different languages in the library
- Have the mentors and interpreters provide workshops for teachers and staff
- Recruit more refugee families to serve on school committees
- Have meetings with refugee families in community organizations or resettlement agencies
- Learn greetings in different languages, such as Arabic, Kiswahili, and Farsi

TEACHING NOTES: SCHOLARSHIP ON PARENTAL AND FAMILY INVOLVEMENT IN US SCHOOLS

Title I of the federal Elementary and Secondary Education Act (ESEA) requires schools to develop parental involvement policies to increase student achievement. Forty states also have laws encouraging or requiring school districts to formulate and implement policies and programs for parental and family engagement, and many, including DUSD, are evaluated annually on their efforts to engage families. Yet, as Mapp and Kuttner show, state and federal governments assume that school administrators and families are already equipped with the knowledge and skills to develop, implement, and sustain partnerships between schools and homes; however, this is not necessarily the case, especially as student populations change with the influx of migrants, including refugees.[1] Complicating school-home partnerships, even when mandated and measured, is the reality that parental involvement remains vaguely defined and can include a broad range of parenting interventions in the learning and development of their children, from discussion and helping with homework to volunteering at school and attending parent-teacher meetings.[2] It is even difficult to measure narrower definitions of parental involvement, such as the one offered by McKay, which focuses on parenting, communication, learning at home, decision making, volunteering, belonging, and community collaboration.[3] Some scholars have called for parental involvement in school leadership and decision-making boards, councils, and teams.[4]

Overall, parental or family involvement continues to be seen as positively affecting students' schooling experiences and academic achievement.[5] However, Cucchiara and Horvat clearly warn us that some kinds of parental involvement can be detrimental to certain groups of students in schools.[6] Any policies or programs around parental and family involvement that reify static notions of culture and norms, perpetuate gender and ethnic stereotypes, privilege certain knowledges, or deny linguistic diversity can be harmful. This can be particularly true for migrant families. Bolívar and Chrispeels note that opportunities for poor and immigrant parents are limited in both quantity and benefit. They argue that "low-income and non-English-speaking parents seem to benefit little from conventional parent-teacher associations, which seem unable to effectively channel parent power for meaningful participation."[7] Others have demonstrated that linguistically, culturally, and socioeconomically diverse (LCSD) families are persistently positioned as needing "help" and "encouragement" from schools to become involved in their children's schooling.[8] Parental involvement can thus be used as a proxy for socializing and norming LCSD parents to adapt to the mainstream model of family engagement while marginalizing their cultures, languages, and family resources. Such efforts often deauthorize LCSD parents, deny their knowledge, and underestimate their agency.

Refugee families share commonalities with other immigrant families, but have unique experiences and histories that should also inform any strategies to engage them in their children's schooling.[9] Drawing on interviews with a group of Arabic-speaking, recently arrived refugee parents in Canada, Cranston, Labman, and Crook find that schools need to lower the barriers of limited language proficiency for refugee newcomers and develop teachers' cross-cultural and interreligious understandings.[10] As generative AI continues to improve, schools will have more success with free and low-cost translation apps to bridge language differences. Increasingly, as well, portable translation systems and equipment, including booths and multiple headsets, for different languages are becoming more affordable.

When inviting refugee families to engage with schools, leaders must also consider the demands they face to meet basic needs.[11] Efforts to engage refugee families should be undergirded by their cultural strengths, and collaborative school-home-community programs for refugees should be culturally responsive.[12] These efforts should be seen as interconnected, and when possible, there should be an overall strategy, rather than a disjointed piecemeal attempt, to meet the multiple needs and challenges encountered by the refugee families.

Discussion Questions

1. Prioritizing action steps

In groups, take the to-do list generated during the meeting in the case and (1) add action steps and details to each list item. For instance, what events, performances, meetings, and classes could be included under the item "invite refugee parents to school"? (2) Prioritize the items and put them on a realistic timeline, complete with who will be responsible for leading the action on each item and who else will need to be mobilized and involved. And (3) add any other items you think are missing.

FACTORS TO CONSIDER:

- There are 358 total students in the school, nearly 68 percent of whom are Latino.
- There are six ELD teachers; all of them are Spanish-English bilingual.
- The refugee students spend two-thirds of the school day in extended ELD classes.
- The parent-teacher advisory board of eight members currently has no refugee members.
- Interpreters must be scheduled one week in advance of any interpreting assignment; exceptions can be made in emergencies.
- There are ten refugee mentors for the entire district, which includes eighty-nine schools.
- There are minimal amounts of discretionary funds for new programs in the budget; however, some funds are available for translation equipment and software.

2. Exploring knowledge gaps and biases about refugee families

Individually, create a list of things you would like to know about refugees and their experiences with formal schooling. What do you believe refugee families want for their children's education?

Use the lists to have a facilitated small-group discussion. Be aware of patterns of bias and stereotypes during this activity. Be prepared to talk about them critically and with civility.

HERE ARE SOME POSSIBLE ISSUES TO DISCUSS MORE DEEPLY IN THE GROUP AFTER YOU'VE CONTRIBUTED WHAT YOU WANT TO SHARE FROM YOUR LISTS:

- Some refugee families choose their preferred resettlement countries based on the schooling for their children.
- Refugee students and parents are unfamiliar with US school policies, pedagogies, and practices.
- Many refugee families include members who have college degrees and who were professionals in their home countries.
- Many, if not most, refugee families are multilingual.

As a group, make a list of resources where you can find more information about refugee education. This list should be made available to everyone working in the school.

CHAPTER 13

Out-of-School Programs for Refugee Youth

Community Partnerships to Extend School Capacity

MELISSA HAUBER-ÖZER
University of Missouri

ABSTRACT

This chapter examines the role of a community-based organization providing post-resettlement services for refugees in a small Midwestern city, focusing on an out-of-school program. Led by a former instructional aide for newcomer middle school English learners, the program is designed to support refugee youth in high school and postsecondary transitions in partnership with the school district. The weekly time is loosely structured, comprising about an hour of homework help from volunteer tutors (mostly undergraduate students from the nearby university), a guest presentation or activity, and dinner. Through the eyes of a young man from Afghanistan, the chapter offers a window on the welcoming environment created in this informal learning context, insight into challenges and successes, and implications for school leaders seeking to foster belonging and strengthen postsecondary pathways for refugee students.

The case highlights the many responsibilities that refugee-background youth juggle, including learning English, catching up on high school credits, serving as language brokers, and working to contribute to family expenses. It also demonstrates how informal learning in community-based organizations can complement school services and how meaningful connections with both those from a similar background and local community members can support positive integration experiences and educational progress. Educational leaders benefit from an understanding of the range of experiences and knowledges that refugee-background youth bring to meet their linguistic, academic, and socioemotional needs and support them in reaching their potential. Insights from the case and the accompanying discussion questions and activities can aid school administrators and leaders of out-of-school programs in developing effective partnerships to foster integration and school success for newcomer and refugee youth.

CASE NARRATIVE

Amanullah, a reserved, sixteen-year-old sophomore from Afghanistan, parks at the Welcome House community center of the Youth Impact Program at around 5 p.m. on Thursday evening. Amanullah recently got his driver's license after Ali, a professor from Turkey at the local university, helped him study the manual and practice driving. Amanullah's father, who works second shift at a factory like many of the other Afghan men in the area, has not yet passed the driver's test due to his limited English. Now the entire family depends on Amanullah for transportation from their modest, sparsely furnished home on the outskirts of town. Amanullah also works at Walmart after school and on the weekends to contribute to family expenses, sometimes skipping classes to pick up an extra shift. He comes to the Youth Impact Program on the rare Thursdays that he isn't scheduled to work and hopes to study computer science after graduating.

First, however, Amanullah needs to master English and earn enough credits for his high school diploma. Since he's enrolled for a third year in the newcomer program housed in the alternative high school, he has to make up for lost time before aging out of public schooling at twenty-one. Amanullah would be the first in his family to graduate, since neither of his parents had the opportunity to go to school in Afghanistan. As the oldest of five children, the most proficient in English, and the most literate member of the family, he regularly serves as a language broker for his parents, translating during parent-teacher conferences and doctor's appointments and trying to make sense of bills and humanitarian parole notices. In short, Amanullah faces significant challenges in school and juggles multiple additional responsibilities.

Welcome House is a nonprofit organization located in downtown Truman (a pseudonym), a college town of about 130,000 in the US Midwest. It was founded in 2010 to supplement the initial support provided by Catholic Charities, the federally contracted resettlement agency in the region. Resettlement in Truman and the surrounding area corresponds to national trends and has risen after several years of record lows during the COVID-19 pandemic and the previous presidential administration. Recent arrivals originate primarily from the Democratic Republic of Congo, Syria, Myanmar, and Sudan, along with more than three hundred Afghans evacuated from Kabul after the Taliban takeover in 2021. These newcomers represent diverse cultural, linguistic, religious, and socioeconomic backgrounds. The majority of local residents are white, monolingual-English speakers, but the Truman community is generally open-minded and welcoming. This marks a stark contrast with the politically conservative, mostly rural state, which has become notorious for legislative attempts to curb immigration and ban diversity, equity, and inclusion efforts.

Welcome House distributes food bank boxes, clothing, and hygiene products and assists clients in applying for jobs, medical aid, social benefits, and citizenship. The organization's education services consist of English, driver education, and artisan classes for adults; afterschool programs for K–12 students; and a newly opened multicultural preschool that fosters school readiness and intercultural understanding between refugee and nonrefugee children. A staff of eighteen runs these programs and raises funds through a combination of private donations, grants, and thrift store sales to serve more than fifteen hundred clients. More than two hundred weekly volunteers provide vital supports for refugee families gaining independence in their new community, including English practice, transportation, and childcare while parents attend classes or meetings.

Furthermore, Welcome House functions as a crucial intermediary between refugee families and school administrators. Since staff work with clients individually and the organization operates outside the funding restrictions and bureaucracies governing both public schools and resettlement agencies, Welcome House can identify and respond to gaps with relative dexterity. The Youth Impact Program was launched in January 2023, following requests from the local refugee population for more educational support for youth. The program aims to help refugee-background high school students build relationships with others who have similar experiences and prepare for postsecondary education and career pathways. This type of support is crucial for youth like Amanullah.

Truman Public Schools (TPS) enroll around 19,000 students living within the city limits and the semirural surrounding county in twenty-three elementary schools, seven middle schools, four high schools, and a career center offering occupational training, continuing education, and adult English-language classes. TPS teachers are highly qualified—nearly three-quarters have a master's degree or higher—but are mostly white, monolingual English speakers, like the broader community. Although the district boasts high rates of graduation and postsecondary education, almost half of students qualify for free or reduced-price lunch. During the 2023–24 academic year, student demographics were recorded as 54 percent white, 21 percent Black, 8 percent Hispanic, 6 percent Asian, and 10 percent multiracial. The percentage classified as English learners (ELs) has risen sharply in recent years, from 3.4 percent in 2009 to 8.5 percent in 2024, or about 1,500 students. Although EL services are now offered across the district, one middle and one high school house Newcomer Centers—sheltered English programs for about 450 students who test at the beginner level on the WIDA (World-Class Instructional Design and Assessment) exam. A large proportion of ELs in Truman have refugee backgrounds, including dozens of Afghan students like Amanullah who arrived suddenly during the 2021–22 school year.

The TPS director of EL services has worked tirelessly to increase the district's capacity to serve refugee students' academic, cultural, and socio-emotional needs, including by requiring professional development in trauma-informed instruction and allotting funds from the federal Office of Refugee Resettlement to get more teachers certified to teach ELs. She has also emphasized family communication, in part through strengthening the district's relationship with Welcome House as a trusted intermediary, and honored Muslim newcomers' religious practices by designating rooms for prayer. In fact, she was chosen for the district's 2024 "Outstanding Administrator" award in recognition of her efforts. Despite these significant improvements, however, teachers can effectively address only a portion of newcomers' needs, making Welcome House a crucial partner.

Amanullah enters the community center hesitantly, breaking into a grin when he sees his favorite tutor, Asif, a Pakistani American medical student. A group of sophomore girls from South Sudan, Eritrea, and Afghanistan take selfies and chat animatedly about an upcoming honors chemistry test and basketball tryouts at their mainstream high school. Ms. Michelle, the Welcome House school liaison, arrives from a van run to pick up the Kenyan and Congolese youth who live north of town and greets Amanullah warmly. Ms. Michelle was previously an instructional aide with the middle school newcomer program but now helps parents navigate the school system, from initial enrollment and vaccination records to school portals, parent-teacher conferences, and report cards. In the evenings, she runs a weekly Homework Helpers program for elementary and middle school students and the Youth Impact Program for high schoolers. She also oversees a Homework Helpers program run by an intern at a Burmese-speaking church on the western outskirts of town where most of the families from Myanmar have settled.

More volunteer tutors, mostly students from the nearby university, trickle in and join the clusters of youth tackling homework assignments and playing lively games of UNO and chess. A young man from Nigeria who is working on a PhD in math education chats with Congolese boys about their experiences learning math during their years in refugee camps. A professor who used to teach ELs waves Amanullah over to join a few other Afghan newcomers in reading a graphic novel about immigrant journeys.[1] Although the images and relatable story help him follow along, he soon becomes frustrated by unfamiliar words. Later, Amanullah's EL teacher, Ms. Jessica, and instructional aide, Ms. Vanessa, stop by, accepting hugs from their current students and former newcomers who had transferred to the mainstream high school and checking in about their academic progress and family life.

Each week at the Youth Impact Program, a presentation or activity by a community member follows about an hour of unstructured time to work on homework, play games, or read. Recent presentation topics, based on student requests or staff-identified challenges, have included finding a summer job, opening a bank account and budgeting, and applying to college. Activities have ranged from art therapy and photography to visiting a radiology lab at the university teaching hospital and attending the county fair. Shortly before 6:30, the guest speaker from the county historical society arrives. Amanullah tries to follow the presentation as the man talks about local history and shows artifacts. After a short explanation about the state's role in the Civil War, he unsheathes an ornate sword with a flourish. Amanullah instinctively recoils, later explaining to Asif that the Taliban used similar swords. Dinner arrives around 7:00, eliciting groans from some youth when they see that it's pizza again. Afghan families tend to be devout Muslims and there's only one halal restaurant in Truman, so Ms. Michelle tries to include a vegetarian option each week. Amanullah double-checks with her that the veggie pizza is halal before taking a couple of slices. Since he avoids eating at the school cafeteria due to the lack of halal options, he's famished by dinnertime.

Amanullah feels more at home at Welcome House than at school. He likes hanging out with refugee teens who have successfully transitioned to the mainstream high school, which often feels unattainable given his slow progress learning English and his numerous responsibilities outside school. The tutors, especially the men from similar cultural and religious backgrounds, have helped him gain confidence and attain specific goals, like getting his driver's license. Although Ms. Michelle and most tutors have limited knowledge about his culture and no experience of forced displacement, they're kind, caring, and willing to learn. Their support helps him believe that he's capable of finishing high school and pursuing his dream of a college education.

TEACHING NOTES

By the end of 2023, an unprecedented 117 million people were forcibly displaced by conflict, persecution, or other forms of violence.[2] This includes more than 43 million refugees who were unable to return to their countries of origin due to "a well-founded fear of being persecuted for reasons of race, religion, nationality, membership of a particular social group or political opinion."[3] Those deemed particularly vulnerable are referred to potential resettlement nations, such as Canada, the United States, and Australia, which implement additional rounds of security checks and interviews.[4] In the case of the US Refugee Admissions Program, this process takes eighteen to twenty-four months and includes a few other categories of international protection, such as the Special Immigrant Visa (SIV) for Afghan and Iraqi nationals who worked in some capacity for the US military or government.[5] Resettlement and SIV status include work eligibility and a pathway to permanent residency. Asylum status, temporary protected status, and humanitarian parole (the category used for many Afghan evacuees) are more precarious, with restricted rights and benefits, increased surveillance, and limited-term residency.

Refugee youth have varied premigration experiences and face unique and multifaceted challenges. Some have spent their entire lives in refugee camps or conflict zones with limited or interrupted access to formal education, while others have faced sudden disruption of stable lives with consistent, high-quality schooling. Like Amanullah, many are overcoming trauma and shouldering significant financial and caretaking responsibilities while adapting to a new culture, learning a new language, and catching up in school. They may encounter isolation or discrimination in their new communities and schools. Regardless, these youth possess diverse cultural, linguistic, and religious knowledge and have high aspirations for the future.[6]

Belonging is an important component of positive adaptation to a new community and a supportive factor in education.[7] Along with familiar cultural and linguistic practices and group affiliations, the degree to which a refugee feels accepted as part of the host community influences this sense of belonging.[8] Supportive relationships with teachers, other adults, and peers are also vital for fostering personal resilience, which in turn contributes to positive coping and academic success.[9] In other words, establishing meaningful connections with both those from a similar background and local community members supports positive integration experiences and educational progress. Role models from similar cultural backgrounds can have a powerful impact on refugee youth's sense of belonging and success inside and outside school, as Ali and Asif do for Amanullah.

Amid divisive political rhetoric and changing demographics, school administrators play an important role in establishing community partnerships, shaping organizational cultures, and creating welcoming environments. Furthermore, in meeting the linguistic, academic, and socio-emotional needs of refugee-background youth and supporting them in reaching their potential, educational leaders benefit from an understanding of the range of experiences and knowledges these youth bring. They must also understand the additional responsibilities these youth bear—acting as language brokers, caring for siblings or elderly family members, contributing to the household income—while adapting to a new culture and language. As administrators build capacity to meet newcomers' needs at the school and systems levels, partnerships with community-based organizations can help fill in remaining gaps. Similarly, leaders of out-of-school programs designed for newcomer and refugee youth must consider both the challenges they face and the importance of supportive factors—including family ties, friendships, and cultural and religious practices—in overcoming them. Liaisons like Ms. Michelle with deep knowledge of school systems, local resources, and refugee students' lives play a crucial role in facilitating effective school-community partnerships.

Discussion Questions

1. How does the refugee population at Welcome House compare to that of your area and your school?
   a. What are newcomers' linguistic, academic, and socioemotional needs?
   b. Which and whose needs are not sufficiently met in school, and why?
2. What community resources exist for meeting these needs (e.g., EL programs, a school liaison, nonprofit organizations, after-school

programs, houses of worship)? How could your school establish or expand partnerships to address newcomers' specific needs?

3. What pathways exist in your community for completing high school and transitioning to postsecondary education or careers?
   a. Do newcomers earn high school credits while receiving EL services? Are there options for making up credits, such as summer school?
   b. What are state and district policies on "aging out" of PK–12 education? Are there alternative or accelerated options for earning a high school diploma?
   c. What financial and practical supports (e.g., dual-credit programs, scholarships, in-state tuition, SAT or ACT prep courses) are there for facilitating access to career and technical education, community college, or four-year university programs?

Teacher Activities

1. Map resources in your community that could fill newcomers' unmet needs, including nonprofit organizations, cultural centers, houses of worship, and individuals. Which community leaders, role models, and groups could help foster a sense of belonging and resilience? What partnerships are in place to connect newcomers to these resources? Consider gaps or obstacles to access and the roles of policy, procedure, and transportation in facilitating access to these resources.
2. Design an activity for refugee youth in your school. Which organizations, businesses, educational opportunities, and arts, sporting, and entertainment opportunities might be of interest? Consider costs and logistical aspects (e.g., transportation, interpretation, permission slips, chaperones) as well as students' practical needs and socio-emotional well-being.
3. Draft a job description for a refugee school liaison—what skills, experience, qualifications, and dispositions would this person need to effectively serve newcomers and more established refugee children and youth? Alternatively, find a posting for a similar position online and critique it. Based on the case study, what would you add or change?

4. Outline a training session for volunteer tutors working with refugee youth. What topics would you cover? What kinds of background information do they need to know? What skills or dispositions would be useful for them to develop?

CHAPTER 14

Compassionate Leadership for Newcomer Refugee Students

A Holistic and Resilience-Based Approach

RAGHAD EBIED

Wilfrid Laurier University

ABSTRACT

The number of refugees worldwide reached approximately 36.8 million at end-2024, of whom 40 percent are children and youth under age eighteen. There is an emphasis on the important role of school leaders to create inclusive and welcoming school cultures that support refugee students' integration. My doctoral study investigated school-community collaborations with settlement or community organizations that hire settlement workers in schools, also known as "cultural support workers, community liaison personnel, and cultural brokers," to support newcomer refugee students' resettlement in Canadian schools. This chapter informs school leaders about support for refugee students with socio-emotional or trauma needs. The Settlement Workers in Schools (SWIS) program collaborates with school leaders and staff to shape a safe and caring school culture, provide professional development for educators, and support the social and emotional well-being of refugee students through cultivating strong relationships with newcomer students and their families and offering information and referrals to relevant services. Thus, I found settlement workers offered support for newcomer students through a holistic, compassionate, and resilience-based approach, at the individual, family, school, community, and societal levels. This chapter discusses the importance of school leaders' strengthening such school-community collaborations, which enable settlement workers to play a key role in enhancing intercultural competence of school staff in order to aid in promoting integration and a sense of belonging and well-being for newcomer refugee students.

CASE NARRATIVE

Mrs. Nicholson is the principal at a suburban secondary school in a mid-size city. She has met Ahmad, who is sixteen years old and came to Canada as a refugee originally from Syria, after being displaced to a nearby country in the Middle East for more than five years. Ahmad came with his parents and three younger siblings: Saja, who is fourteen; Hassan, who is eight; and Noor, three. Due to their displacement, Ahmad, Saja, and Hassan all experienced interrupted education since there was a lack of access to consistent formal education. Principal Nicholson also learned that, with Ahmad being the oldest in the family, he needed to prioritize work to support his family financially while they were living in a refugee camp. Even when education was possible, Ahmad preferred to work, which further impacted his educational progress.

In addition to the challenges of learning a new language, Principal Nicholson became aware that Ahmad and his sister Saja experienced social challenges related to making friends and experiencing a sense of belonging—more so than their younger brother, Hassan, an elementary school student, who was able to adapt more quickly by learning English more readily. Ahmad and Saja experienced a type of identity crisis; they felt connected to their original roots in Syria and were uncertain how they would fit into a new environment and culture, especially since Saja wore the hijab, the headscarf worn by some Muslim women. They experienced teasing and bullying from their peers at school, and many times thoughts of going back to their homeland surfaced for them. They also struggled with being pulled in two different directions between their new context and their country of origin. This struggle led Ahmad and Saja to question their culture and decisions, such as how they dress and to feel greater pressure to "fit in."

Principal Nicholson was familiar with the way Ahmad and his family, like many other refugees, had experienced multiple stressful and traumatic situations, including separation from loved ones, witnessing violence, and lack of access to basic needs in refugee camps. These challenges led to some concerns related to trauma and mental health, which manifested in behavioral challenges for Ahmad. He found it very difficult to sit through seventy-five minutes of class without feeling frustrated or agitated, especially if he was teased about his culture or his inability to readily understand or complete a task. His sister, Saja, sometimes felt withdrawn and anxious, exhibiting symptoms of posttraumatic stress. It was difficult for them to express these feelings, which sometimes made it increasingly challenging to adapt to a new school environment.

Fortunately, Ahmad and Saja were introduced to the school's settlement worker, Hanan, who works with newcomer families to support their transition to schools by providing information, orientation, and referrals to school and community resources. Hanan is employed by a community settlement agency to support newcomer students and their families in schools by advocating for their needs, facilitating interculturally sensitive communication between school staff and newcomer families, and providing staff with information helpful in understanding the needs of newcomer families. Hanan was a newcomer herself over ten years ago and speaks Arabic. Principal Nicholson was not fully aware of all the tasks Hanan could be involved in, as the role of the settlement worker was usually reduced to that of a translator. However, Hanan had connected with Ahmad's family at the beginning of their transition to Canada and supported his parents by finding English-language classes for adults and helping the children transition into the public school system.

Hanan supported Ahmad and Saja by assisting the school with their placement in the appropriate English-language learning level, according to their English competency. Once Ahmad and Saja completed their English-language learning classes, Hanan advocated for them, at their request, to be placed in an academic stream that would enable them to attend university, despite having faced some discouragement from school staff that they may not be able to meet the demands of academic-stream courses. There are typically two streams of courses in Canadian secondary schools, one for colleges that offer shorter, "diploma and certificate programs . . . with emphasis on . . . practical hands-on training for specific careers or industries." The other, an academic stream is intended for "universities which offer undergraduate and graduate degrees with a focus on academic and professional education . . . and research."[1] Two years into academic stream courses, Ahmad and Saja were doing their best and were able to meet expected requirements in most cases. Ahmad hoped to be an engineer, and Saja hoped to be a doctor.

One of the other important roles Hanan played as a settlement worker was to be a trusted adult to whom Ahmad and Saja could express their concerns and frustrations. While Hanan is not trained as a social worker or mental health counselor, as a newcomer herself several years ago, she is familiar with the challenges faced by newcomers, and she supported Ahmad and Saja with their struggles related to "identity crisis." She supported them with the understanding that as individuals, they can make their own decisions aligned with their values, without feeling that their culture and identity are at stake due to being in a new environment. She also encouraged them to volunteer to become more familiar with the Canadian context and to develop confidence and leadership skills. Furthermore, she planned events for all students in the school, including newcomer students and established Canadians, to support integration rather than separation, such as a Mother's Day celebration. She also organized support groups to assist newcomer refugee youth in navigating the public school system. On identifying the likely impact of trauma and potential mental health concerns that Ahmad and Saja might be experiencing, Hanan provided referrals to resources, though culturally sensitive mental health services were scarce.

While Ahmad and Saja missed their country of origin, with the type of support offered by Hanan, they became more comfortable with their new environment and looked forward to succeeding in their studies. The challenge was that there were only a handful of settlement workers, while there were hundreds, if not thousands, of newcomer refugee families who needed support. In addition, the role of settlement workers is not sufficiently understood in schools. This left Principal Nicholson with many demands to support newcomer families that were difficult to meet and a lack of clarity around the role of settlement workers in schools.

TEACHING NOTES

The number of refugees worldwide has reached approximately 36.8 million, 40 percent of whom are children and youth under eighteen years of age, with more than 24 million refugees coming from Syria, Ukraine, Venezuela, and Afghanistan.[2] More recently, the number of Palestinian refugees has reached 5.9 million globally as a result of a long-standing conflict spanning more than seventy-five years. School leaders play an important role in cultivating inclusive and welcoming school cultures that support refugee students' integration. Several scholars state that cultivating environments that encourage refugee students to succeed is instrumental in fostering their academic success, social cohesion, economic prosperity, sense of belonging, and transition to citizenship.[3] This chapter explores school-community collaborations in Ontario, Canada, with settlement or community organizations who hire settlement workers in schools, also known as cultural support workers, community liaison personnel, and cultural brokers, to help newcomer refugee students resettle in schools.

The SWIS initiative is an important partnership between schools and community agencies, which entails settlement workers supporting school leaders, teachers, and staff, such as guidance counselors and English as a second language teachers, to cultivate a safe and caring school culture and encourage effective teaching and learning. Creating a strong relationship with schools can encounter challenges such as understanding the roles of settlement workers and school staff in the partnership. As I have written elsewhere, "The primary role of SWIS is that of a liaison, in which they act as the link to connect newcomer students, families, school staff and community involvement; therefore, their role as compassionate connectors is key in cultivating support at multiple levels on the individual, family, school, community and society level."[4]

My doctoral research explored settlement workers collaborating with school leaders and staff, including classroom teachers and English as a second language teachers to create and maintain a safe and caring school culture, provide professional development for educators, and support the social and emotional well-being of refugee students through cultivating strong relationships with newcomer students and their families, and offering information and referrals to relevant services. I found that settlement workers offered support for newcomer students through a holistic, compassionate, and resilience-based approach. In examining different approaches that acknowledge the impact of trauma on newcomer refugee students, I found Lavelle and colleagues' and Pieloch and colleagues' review of programs active from 2006 to 2016 in Australia, Canada, Europe, and the United States to be most relevant.[5] To reflect holistic support for newcomer refugee students that reaches beyond meeting second-language-learning needs, I merged both the compassionate and resilience-based approaches in my framework.[6] The compassion-based framework considers the following six elements, which guided an initial exploration of SWIS support for refugee students: "i) school leadership, ii) a safe and caring school culture, iii) effective teaching and learning, iv) parental and community involvement, v) compassion training programs, and vi) professional development for educators."[7]

I define compassionate leadership as the ability to acknowledge our common humanity in order to alleviate individual and collective adversity in our schools and organizations. By building trust, practicing emotional intelligence, and demonstrating moral courage, we can engage in ethical decision making that contributes to well-being and equity. Through cultivating cultural proficiency and collaboration, we can build a thriving spirit of community, which leads to resilience and belonging in our diverse learning environments. Leading with compassion at schools for newcomer refugee students is embodied through prioritizing cultural, spiritual, ethical, psychological, and emotional safety and well-being at school infused into a safe and caring school culture that values students' unique strengths and cultural heritage.

Also compassionate teaching and learning emphasizes the need for teachers to understand students' previous experiences, as well as their current needs and goals for the future. This process requires the support of school leaders and other staff, including settlement workers and school counselors, as well as building parental and community engagement with settlement and culturally relevant agencies to draw on the expertise, strength, and networks that constitute social capital for newcomers.

Compassionate leadership also recognizes that newcomer refugee students may have experienced "triple trauma"—in their war-torn countries of origin, during their transition to other countries or refugee camps, and on their arrival in Canada. Research shows that up to 40 percent of racialized youth reported experiencing discrimination from peers in Canada.[8] Far greater numbers of racialized and refugee youth likely experience implicit bias and prejudice or do not report their experiences of discrimination. Discriminatory attitudes from some teachers can adversely impact refugee students' self-esteem, academic achievement, and social integration. Overall, discrimination can contribute to a lack of belonging among newcomer youth, isolation, and behavioral concerns, all of which can lower academic performance, leading to lower rates of employability. These experiences can be considered a type of racial trauma that adversely impacts newcomer refugee students' well-being and therefore demands the special attention of school leaders to address through the compassion-based framework described above, which includes professional development. One particular area of professional development identified by research on SWIS, as well as the literature for school leaders and educators, is intercultural competence. A pan-Canadian research report that examined literature and policy between 2007 and 2017 on support for refugee students indicated that schools and policy makers continue to require additional learning in intercultural competence and social justice.[9] Intercultural competence is "a set of knowledge, feelings, and skills that enable a person to communicate, work and function effectively in pluralistic contexts. It involves increasing one's own sensitivity about differences in values, beliefs, and behaviours, and developing skills to determine the most appropriate practices and behaviour to communicate and work effectively and respectfully across cultures."[10] Ongoing professional development of intercultural competence is required in order to support the work of school leaders and staff working with newcomer refugee students.

It is also important for school leaders to strengthen school-community collaborations that enable SWISs to play a key role in "enhancing intercultural competence of school staff in order to aid in promoting integration, a sense of belonging, and well-being for newcomer refugee students."[11]

With the wide variety of challenges encountered by newcomer refugee students, school leaders need to work with settlement workers to offer support for students beyond schools on a more comprehensive level at the individual, family, community, and society level, as described in the resilience-based approach. As Pieloch and colleagues outline, "Resilience reaches beyond an individual's capacity (e.g., grit) and interacts with family (e.g., resources, employment, extended family support), school (sense of belonging, positive school experiences), community (community engagement and support networks), and society (e.g., maintaining family, cultural and religious values and practices)." Thus, resilience is not solely the responsibility of an individual refugee student to develop: "Meeting basic needs is the first step to cultivating resilience which includes the need for refugee students to be viewed as children first, and refugees second; to have stable housing; to be able to attend school and learn English; and to have access to health care services such as immunizations."[12] Resilience is further cultivated through strong connections to family and drawing on community resources. Promoting resilience at multiple levels can contribute to enhancing the positive adaptation of newcomer refugee students and acknowledges the importance of supporting refugee students "through a lens of recovery and resilience because focusing on risk alone paints an incomplete picture of refugee youth's lives."[13] Thus, both the compassion-based and the resilience-based approach draw on an asset-based perspective, highlighting strength and empowerment, versus a deficit-based perspective.

SWIS Collaboration with Schools

First, collaboration between settlement workers and school leaders builds an important foundation for the partnership between settlement workers and the school. For example, in the case of conflict related to newcomer refugee students, school leaders usually ask the settlement worker to communicate with parents and invite them to meet with the school. Settlement workers also fulfill the role of mediators and advocates for newcomer students and their families. They may assist school staff with understanding the underlying reasons of behavioral challenges for newcomer refugee students, such as aggression. Instead of reaffirming "aggressiveness" or "lacking in social skills," labels sometimes attached to newcomer refugee students with behavioral challenges, settlement workers draw on an asset-based approach to offer ongoing education and professional development to support school leaders and staff by reframing the deficit-based view of newcomer refugee students. For example, settlement workers strive to share the perspective that newcomer refugee students have developed great resilience, and instead of lacking skills, they have developed a different set of "survival skills" that enabled them to live under the difficult circumstances of conflict and refugee camps. Therefore, settlement workers encourage school staff to support newcomer refugee students with developing a new set of skills to help them adapt to their new environment, and staff who acquire this new perspective are more helpful to the students.

While many teachers may be largely from middle class, homogenous backgrounds and may have limited intercultural training due to competing demands and heavy workloads, settlement workers can communicate to teachers the underlying sociocultural background and experiences of diverse students who may be having challenges, academically or behaviorally. This can contribute to less stereotyping and marginalization of students and aid with promoting integration, a sense of belonging, and well-being for newcomer refugee students.

Supporting the Role of Settlement Workers in Schools

Since settlement workers play such a pivotal role in supporting newcomer refugee students, strengthening the partnership between schools and community agencies that hire settlement workers is important in that it provides school staff information on the SWIS role and offers opportunities for regular communications between school leaders and SWIS management at settlement agencies. Since settlement workers in Ontario, Canada, are currently externally hired staff, they do not always have access to space in schools, school email accounts, or student records. Alternatively, the school board could, as in districts in British Columbia, hire settlement workers so they are considered internal school staff. This direct employment could prevent settlement workers from being viewed as outsiders by school staff and could provide them the tools and resources they need to support their work with students. Furthermore, hiring a greater number of settlement workers with different languages and competencies in order to be able to respond to the needs of a growing and diverse population of refugee students in schools is helpful. Also, offering settlement workers additional professional development, particularly on how to promote intercultural competence at schools, is helpful for settlement workers, students, families, and school staff. Settlement workers have also explained that navigating limited resources was another common challenge; therefore, reviewing the financial and human resources available to support the school-SWIS partnership is necessary. Canada's Immigration, Refugees, and Citizenship Canada (IRCC) federal department, recommended developing a clear definition of the role of settlement workers, articulating a strategy to capture their work with schools and their community agencies, and developing an agreement between schools and SWIS to ensure clarity as to settlement worker roles.[14] Therefore, in order for there to be more proactive measures to support the increasing number of refugee students in schools, there needs to be greater involvement at a systems level when it comes to policies, funding, and organizational structures to allow for more school-community collaborations such as the SWIS program to grow and succeed.

Teacher Activities

Below are suggested activities that settlement workers in schools can work on in collaboration with school leaders and staff to support newcomer refugee students. If SWIS is currently not available in certain areas, school leaders can request support from their school district or engage with ESL teachers, school counselors, social workers, or parent or community volunteers with a diversity of backgrounds who demonstrate intercultural competence through having the knowledge, skills, and experience to support newcomer refugee students.

- *Planning events for all students to support integration versus separation and to encourage newcomer refugee students to volunteer*

Some settlement workers I spoke with shared that newcomer refugee youth may experience separation or "segregation" when they begin attending a new school, especially if they are in a separate stream for English-language learners. Thus, planning events that encourage all students to participate and engaging both newcomer and established students to volunteer can support integration. For example, planning a Mother's Day celebration or another type of charity event may be helpful. Organizing such events promotes social integration of newcomer children and youth, which can contribute to their success in schools as well as transition to citizenship and leadership roles in the future. Also, encouraging newcomer refugee students to volunteer at such opportunities provides them with experiences to develop leadership skills and a sense of agency and empowerment, which can support their integration and positive adaptation.

- *Organizing support groups for newcomer refugee youth*

Organizing support groups for newcomer refugee youth, such as "Let's Get Talking" (shared by SWIS), supports their integration by offering them opportunities to connect with other newcomer refugee students and ask questions of settlement workers and other guests. During this program, newcomer refugee students have an opportunity to acquire information related to the school system, exam preparation, requirements to complete their high school diploma, postsecondary pathways, and the like. The support group is a safe space for refugee students to bring their questions and concerns. It may be similar to a life skills group, which can provide students with an opportunity to increase their connectedness to others and their confidence and strengthen decision-making skills.

- *Engaging in a multidisciplinary team approach*

Due to the complex needs of newcomer refugee students, which may involve trauma, resettlement, and behavioral challenges, a multidisciplinary team approach is required that engages multiple staff in supporting students. Settlement workers I spoke with describe this multidisciplinary team as typically including "the school principal and/or vice-principal, learning support teacher (LST), classroom teacher, ESL teacher, SWIS worker, parents, and if necessary other specialists such as an educational assistant, social worker, or school psychologist."[15] Settlement workers play an important role in mediating the relationship between school staff and parents.

- *Using forum theater*

To support newcomer refugee students with behavioral challenges, one creative strategy that draws on the arts is forum theater. If a teacher has a specific concern, they can connect with a settlement worker, school counselor, or social worker to engage newcomer refugee students in forum theater where students participate in role play and an audience is available to provide their own solutions to a particular challenge instead of giving them direct instructions. This strategy can complement the work of teachers, and programming can change based on the need. Further exploration of the impact of these types of creative, arts-based programs to support newcomer refugee students who have experienced trauma is an important consideration.

- *Podcast*

While settlement workers operate in schools during the school year, since they are usually hired by a community agency, they also fulfill an important role during the summer as "community connectors or integrators." One innovative idea is a weekly podcast called "Cup of Coffee with SWIS," to which the host would invite different guest speakers, such as a dietician or librarian, to discuss important topics and resources in both Arabic and English, since many newcomer refugee families in the area of my research were Arabic-speaking. Such a creative activity can foster connection and a sense of belonging for newcomer refugee families as they learn about resources and services in their community.

Discussion Questions

- How can school leaders facilitate further understanding and support for the role of settlement workers in schools, through encouraging collaboration with school staff and providing resources and other types of support for settlement workers?
- Which processes can school leaders engage in to strengthen school-community partnerships more broadly on a systems level including policy, funding, and organizational structures? How can strengthening these partnerships aid in promoting resilience among newcomer refugee students at the individual, family, school, community, and societal levels?
- In which ways can school leaders further promote positive integration, well-being, and belonging for newcomer refugee students?
- Given multiple training demands on school leaders and educators, how can they advocate for compassion training programs that can support both newcomer refugee students as well as school staff with increased resilience and well-being?
- Intercultural competence, equity, diversity, and inclusion training for school staff may have varying levels of priority and effectiveness. In what ways can engaging in this type of personal and professional development shift from performance to transformation in more sustainably promoting social justice and equity for students?
- How can school leaders practice compassionate school leadership, particularly when it comes to shaping a school culture that prioritizes cultural, spiritual, ethical, psychological, and emotional safety; as well as supporting effective teaching and learning and cultivating parental and community engagement?

CHAPTER 15

"Our Students Matter"

District Leaders' and Educators' Efforts to Center Immigrant Youth and Families in Building Caring School Systems

SOPHIA RODRIGUEZ
New York University

STACI PIPPIN-KOTTKAMP
University of Maryland

GISELL RAMÍREZ
University of Maryland

ABSTRACT

In this book chapter, we draw on data from a larger, mixed-methods study about how public school districts manage the welcome and inclusion of immigrant youth in the context of racial justice. The embedded case study design and multiple-case analysis here draw from interviews with school leaders in the US mid-Atlantic and Midwest regions who discussed their efforts in meeting the needs of immigrant youth in a responsive and inclusive manner. Previous scholars have argued that urban schools do not meet or respond to the needs of immigrant youth. Within the context of many district efforts to implement racial equity plans, this chapter includes vignettes in which district leaders share localized and system-wide efforts to meet the needs of immigrant youth. They identify three ways they strive to provide inclusive and responsive services to immigrant students, including (1) having in-school personnel to focus on the holistic services for newcomers; (2) including student voices in school-wide decision making; and (3) collaboration with outside agencies. Based on these narratives, we conceptualize *community-based partnerships of care* so that district leaders can reflect on their ongoing efforts and work toward a system of care that supports the whole well-being of immigrant youth and their families.

CASE NARRATIVE

Sitting in class with Ms. Ava, a bilingual educator in a racially diverse public school, I [Sophia Rodriguez] was struck by the warmth of her attentiveness to the newcomers arriving weekly to her language-learning classroom.[1] I remember talking with Juan in Ms. Ava's class, a newcomer from El Salvador, who described for me his migration trauma as he had to "cross multiple times" with several failed attempts. He would often sit quietly staring out the window of Ms. Ava's room. Some educators might think he was inattentive to the lesson, but Ms. Ava gave him space because she knew the reasons his family came for a "better life" and sent Juan by himself with all of the money they had saved. She told me, as did he in later interviews, that he wasn't sure he would be able to see or talk to his mother again. Ms. Ava explained that we have to "hear and understand their stories" as they impact youths' educational experiences. Listening to Juan recall migration stories when he stayed in filthy abandoned homes and was at the bottom of a pile of human males in a pickup truck traversing often dangerous routes from El Salvador to Mexico, I thought about the need to listen, to develop the type of empathy that comes from listening to their stories.

This theme of listening arose also during a conversation with an educator, Mr. Raul. He shared that educators need to help "reshape their [immigrant youth' and families'] relationship to school. Many of the young people coming to his schools, he explained, face significant barriers to meeting basic needs. "Some come through the door after living in jungles, getting evicted, experiencing forms of violence . . . where's the resources for that?" He explained that many families are going through things and need help navigating systems, so the school tries to think about where they can "story-listen," as they develop programs and practices for families. He described how many immigrant mothers felt that they could not provide for their families through simple things like cooking—since many were living in hotels or other temporary housing and felt "powerless"—so the school was able to offer a community kitchen and families could use it and take food home. While perhaps a small gesture, it was another practice that was rooted in *listening* to families.

The perspective of a leader and district equity director can be critical in shaping systemic responses from school districts. For instance, one district equity director, Ms. Alejandra, talked about listening and understanding immigrants' experiences. She explained:

> For our larger [group of] Hispanic students, we are learning that they are in need of mental health services. As a school leader, I keep saying are we aware? I mean, are we mindful of this specific trauma that different cultures bring? We can talk about trauma generally, or you can delve deeper and realize that it looks different if you migrate here. We can't know the depths of trauma that they've experienced just getting here. There's a level of humanity that I just feel like we as people need to exude, and I guess a lot of it is getting blocked by our own selves.

This leader encourages a deeper understanding of migration experiences and potential trauma that youth experience that could be ongoing if their families face deportation threats or have insecurities in relation to their immigration status.

TEACHING NOTES

In recent decades, more than 1 million Central Americans, like Juan, have been uprooted from their home countries and forced to migrate due to, among other things, violence, persecution, and poverty.[2] Specifically, migrants from El Salvador, Guatemala, and Honduras, known as the Northern Triangle, constitute the largest Central American–born population in the United States today. Forced to emigrate due to extreme conditions in their home countries, these individuals come to the United States in search of a better life. However, many are challenged by constraints imposed by their undocumented status. The path to citizenship is difficult and unpredictable. The process can take decades and is costly, and many applications are denied due to variability in immigration adjudication. In 2021, this population has grown to more than 3.8 million people, with the majority having come from the Northern Triangle.[3] In 2017, the US president terminated the Central American Minors Program, which was designed specifically to aid children and their families from the Northern Triangle who met certain requirements.[4] Children in the Northern Triangle experience difficulties similar to older family members in their home countries including extreme poverty, gang violence, and persecution.[5] These factors force children and youth to uproot their lives and undertake a traumatic journey to the United States, a journey that affects their experience as students.

Immigrant students in the United States hold various status labels.[6] Some qualify as refugees, allowing them a pathway to citizenship. Others hold temporary status, allowing them to work for a limited period of time.[7] Unaccompanied minors are children who arrive in the country with no parent or legal guardian.[8] One challenge faced by newcomer students is dehumanization due to anti-immigrant discourse and policies.[9] Immigrant youth are usually designated as English learners or English language learners, labels created from a deficit perspective. Efforts to achieve inclusivity have seen schools now use the terms *multilingual learner* or *emergent bi- or multilingual learner*, in recognition of newcomer linguistic assets. As exemplified in Ms. Alejandra's statement, it is important for schools to recognize that newcomer children and youth have experienced trauma in their home countries and during migration, making mental health resources a necessity.[10] Many immigrant children have experienced limited or interrupted formal education and may have gaps in academic knowledge and skills.[11] In addition, not all school districts require families to report their immigration status. As a result, true data on newcomer youth is difficult to achieve. Thus, schools and districts need to have resources in place to best serve the needs of this student population.

School leaders can create *community-based partnerships of care* (CBPCs) to build systems that support the well-being of newcomer youth and their families. CBPCs organize noninstructional in-school personnel to provide inclusive, responsive holistic services to newcomers.[12] While other staff can engage in collaborative efforts to support newcomers, they often juggle multiple roles and responsibilities.[13] By contrast, teams focused on newcomer needs have the capacity to deeply understand the unique needs of newcomers and provide *comprehensive and collaborative intake processes.* Team members often include mental health and social workers with expertise in serving students dealing with sensitive topics of legal status and poverty.[14] Effective teams (a) conduct an intake assessment for each newcomer, (b) provide on-site mental health support, and (c) utilize deep relationships to discover and meet invisible needs.[15] One principal whose school serves newcomers told us, "My intake team meets one-to-one with each newcomer," collecting data on social emotional concerns so that students can be immediately referred for support in coping with migration or other trauma. This principal provides an advisory hour at the end of each day so newcomers can meet with a trusted adult to receive support and discuss their personal challenges. Using Google Tools (i.e., shared Sheets, Forms, and Docs), advisers alert the intake team when newcomers need academic, social, emotional, or material support throughout the year.[16]

Schools that are responsive to the holistic needs of newcomers realize that *collaboration with outside organizations* is necessary to meet newcomers' diverse needs.[17] One school counselor collaborates regularly with four external organizations. She cited one organization in particular as crucial in providing afterschool and virtual academic support for students with limited or interrupted formal education.[18] According to the counselor, this immigrant-serving organization provides a myriad of services in addition to academic support, including legal services "when families are struggling" or "face legal issues with immigration."[19] Working together, school counselors and community partners can support persistence and decrease the burden of legal precarity for students striving to complete their education.[20] An assistant principal of a newcomer school collaborates with local healthcare providers to increase access to medical services by "providing dental services and vaccination clinics" onsite. He schedules services over several days and on weekends to accommodate the schedules of students and families.[21] Partnering with community based organizations for various services connects newcomers to beneficial community spaces while fostering and increasing a sense of belonging in schools.[22]

Finally, schools developing a CBPC create mechanisms for students to express their wants and needs and use this data to inform programs and initiatives.[23] Educators we spoke with in our research shared that they have different groups at their schools "to get them involved and give us their voice." In addition to affinity groups, this newcomer school conducts an annual school climate survey in students' native languages to understand how students feel about the classroom and school environment, instructional practices, and peer relationships. These data help staff understand the mental health of newcomers and how it is impacted by the school environment and outside factors including immigration enforcement.[24] At this school, student feedback is used in the creation of timely professional development, culturally appropriate restorative justice practices, and the development of accessible, timely programs for family engagement and support.[25]

Discussion Questions

Martin and Suárez-Orozco have identified characteristics of schools that effectively include and serve newcomer students. This chapter addresses two of these characteristics: *comprehensive and collaborative intake procedures* and *collaboration with outside organizations*.[26] This chapter also discusses the importance of including newcomer student input. Drawing from the Case Narrative and Teaching Notes, reflect on the following questions.

1. How are mental health and social support services provided in your school or district? How do school systems and processes support or constrain collective efforts to include and respond to the needs of newcomer students?
2. How can school personnel be responsive to the needs of newcomers? How might they communicate and validate these responsive actions to multiple stakeholders (e.g., the principal, superintendent, district leaders, community members)?

3. Many schools lack resources to hire additional newcomer-focused staff. How might tasks and responsibilities be reorganized to create an in-school team focused on newcomer needs?
4. In what ways can partnerships with community-based organizations enhance the educational experiences of and outcomes for students in your school or district? Reflect on specific examples in which these partnerships might provide additional resources, support, or opportunities that complement your teaching and address students' diverse needs.
5. Consider how your school or district gathers student input and feedback.
   a. What type of input and feedback are requested?
   b. To what extent are these data used to inform schooling practices?
   c. What specific practices are impacted by this data?
   d. What's missing from this process?
6. How can building strong, supportive relationships with immigrant students and their families help educators better understand and address their unique needs and challenges?
   a. How might your school or district build capacity for developing leaders within immigrant families and immigrant communities?
   b. Reflect on specific ways these relationships can reveal insights into cultural, emotional, and academic needs that might not be apparent through formal assessments alone.
7. The concept of community-based partnerships of care is based on efforts to create a system of care that will support the whole well-being of immigrant youth and their families. What other facets of a "system of care" would you include that are not mentioned in this article?

Teacher Activities

Activity A. Building Relationships

One challenge facing schools is meeting the unique holistic needs of newcomer students. These needs may include academic support, legal services, and food or clothing assistance. Consider the benefits of partnering with outside organizations that have expertise and resources needed by newcomers and their families.[27] These partnerships provide holistic support to immigrants and also connect them to the wider community outside school.[28] For this activity, brainstorm a list of outside agencies and organizations that could be beneficial partners in supporting newcomer students and families.

1. List the resources and types of support available through each agency or organization.
2. Consider drawing a web describing how the organizations and agencies are connected to one another.
3. On the web, list which school personnel might be responsible for leading the partnership. Add names of other school personnel who should be informed about and involved in the collaboration.
4. Identify any immigrant community leaders or school parents who demonstrate leadership or potential leadership.
5. What systems are already in place that would be useful for supporting collaboration with outside agencies? What systems need to be created so that the community partnership includes school staff and students for whom it is most beneficial?

Activity B. Inclusion of Student Voice

When schools ask newcomers about their experiences and perceptions, they gain valuable insights that can make systems and programs more effective and accessible to immigrant families. In addition to district-wide climate surveys, schools may conduct their own school survey specific to their student demographics and language needs. Schools can also intentionally create the space and time needed for newcomers to develop deep relationships with at least one trusted adult.[29] Insights gleaned from newcomers can inform school practices, including parent-teacher conferences, onsite family activities and information sessions, homework, instructional practice, sports, and discipline procedures. As a group, brainstorm ways use of student voice can be increased and included in school decision making.

1. In what ways does your school or district already obtain student input?
2. What barriers exist to gaining student input (e.g., language, technology)?
3. What resources are in place to support this effort (e.g., language line, bilingual assistants)?
4. What resources are needed?
5. What tools (e.g., Google Forms, Google Classroom) does your district or school already have or could it easily obtain to support this effort? Are these tools anonymous and secure when necessary?
6. In what ways does your school or district support deep relationship development between newcomers and staff? How can it build capacity and modify school practices to support deeper relationships?
7. What barriers exist for newcomers in building relationships? How can these be overcome?
8. Are newcomers and other immigrant students represented in student advisory groups? How might we build their capacity for leadership (e.g., mentoring)?

EDUCATOR RESOURCE FOR FURTHER LEARNING

- M. Martin and C. Suárez-Orozco, "What It Takes: Promising Practices for Immigrant Origin Adolescent Newcomers," *Theory into Practice* 57, no. 2 (2018): 82–90, https://doi-org.10.1080/00405841.2018.1425816.

CHAPTER 16

Collaborating to Support Immigrant-Origin Youth and Their Families

A Case Study of Cross-Sector Leadership to Address Well-Being

NISHAT TASNIM AKHI AND REBECCA LOWENHAUPT

Boston College

ABSTRACT

In this chapter, we share the case of a cross-sector initiative established in an immigrant-serving city in the US Northeast that was hard-hit by the COVID-19 pandemic. We describe how local educational, government, and community leaders came together to establish a new collaborative partnership in the form of a Children's Cabinet to coordinate responses to the crisis and address youth well-being. The case examines the superintendent's leadership of the cross-sector initiative focused on emergent issues and structural gaps in services and her efforts to strengthen collaboration among leaders in the local school district, city government, health services, and various community-based organizations (CBOs) serving immigrant families. Prior research in low-income communities has demonstrated that the lack of coordination between schools, social services, and families can adversely affect immigrant youth outcomes including their socio-emotional well-being. Our case illustrates how a coalition of institutional and community leaders sought to amplify care and support for immigrant-origin youth via coordinated efforts to respond to crisis and meaningful connections for supporting their well-being.

CASE NARRATIVE

In a small, immigrant-serving city in the northeastern United States, youth were struggling. It was spring 2021, a little over a year after the COVID-19 pandemic had shut down in-person schooling and led to major health and financial challenges in the dense, tight-knit community of Gaudet.[1] In particular, the large number of recently arrived immigrant families were having a hard time accessing employment opportunities and healthcare and engaging in school, which had shifted to online modes of learning for over a year, longer than neighboring communities that were not as hard-hit by the pandemic. Youth in the community were shouldering additional burdens in caring for family members, coping with physical and mental health challenges, earning an income, and trying to navigate their education at the same time.

The school superintendent was troubled that these challenges, impacting the city as a whole, were being addressed in disconnected ways by different members of the community. While everyone seemed to be trying to solve these issues, there was little consensus or coordination about just what needed to happen to respond to growing concerns about the well-being of Gaudet's youth in the aftermath of the pandemic. Given a growing awareness of just how acute the situation was, the superintendent recognized the need for a cross-sector approach that could provide some coherence and momentum for the city to work together to support youth during this difficult time. She envisioned that at the very least, a cross-sector initiative had the potential to help everyone learn from one another about how they were impacted by and responding to the emerging crisis in youth well-being. As she invited her associate superintendent and other district and city leaders to support the initiative, they all viewed it as an opportunity to work toward coordinating care for youth by building a cross-sector network to address their well-being.

A dense, bustling city with a population of roughly forty thousand people, Gaudet served a majority of individuals identifying as Hispanic or

Latinx (70 percent), of whom approximately 45 percent were recent immigrants. In the low-income community, a significant portion of families in the city already faced financial challenges prior to the pandemic with nearly a quarter of children living in poverty.[2] Over the past decade, the city has become a key destination for recently arrived families with school-age children, as well as unaccompanied minors settling with extended family members in the city. Despite concerns arising from increased immigration law enforcement nationally, local institutions such as city government and local law enforcement agencies, as well as community organizations, remained committed to providing support for the immigrant community, including those without documentation. For example, the police department prided itself on proactively building relationships and embracing culturally responsive approaches to policing and community engagement. The public library incorporated multilingual resources and support for immigrant families. In many ways, this vibrant community has had a history of supporting immigrant families with a robust set of resources distributed via formal institutions, social service agencies, and a wide range of deeply embedded community-based organizations, all striving to address the needs of its residents. While all of these resources were in place, they were not coordinated enough across sectors to facilitate comprehensive, systemwide support for the community.

Heavily impacted by the pandemic, the city relied heavily on these institutions and organizations to address myriad issues of health, poverty, and access to resources exacerbated by disruption. A year into the pandemic and recognizing the needs of youth in particular, the superintendent consulted the associate superintendent, whose office was directly next to hers and who was responsible for overseeing student services. Exasperated, she exclaimed, "This is terrible! We have to do something, and we can't do it alone!" The associate superintendent quickly agreed and suggested that they explore the idea of bringing all the important leaders in the community together at one table. They had both heard about a few other communities implementing something called a Children's Cabinet and had worked as part of one in their previous roles at another school district. After some discussion about how the initiative might look different in Gaudet, in spring 2021 they reached out to the city director to elicit his support for the collaborative effort to address the well-being of youth. As the superintendent said multiple times, and all the partners echoed, "It truly takes a whole village to support the kids in this community!"

Drawing on existing relationships and a connection with a local university, the superintendent and her associate established a university-district partnership with the authors of this chapter. The research team from the local university was on board, having prior experience in partnership with the district, and together they came up with a plan for bringing leaders together to focus on supporting the well-being of youth in the community. Together, they founded the Children's Cabinet, building on a model of cross-sector collaboration used in several cities around the country and with support from a network of similar initiatives nationwide.[3] The Cabinet brought together institutional and community leaders from across sectors to identify collaborative approaches for addressing immigrant youth well-being and construct more purposeful networks of care for these youth. Members included school district administrators, directors of social services and health agencies, government leaders across departments, and directors of local nonprofit organizations, along with the university partners, who both helped facilitate meetings and served as embedded researchers documenting the process (see figure 16.1).

As the conveners of the Cabinet, the superintendent and her associate compiled a comprehensive list of organizations and individuals representing diverse facets of the local youth support network to launch the initiative. While the exact makeup of the group evolved over the years as leaders came in and out of their roles and new members of the community were identified, throughout the collaboration, the superintendent ensured that key sectors were always represented, including the school district; city officials, including the recreation department, police, housing, and public library), healthcare providers, and community-based organizations, including the city's business leaders.

FIGURE 16.1 Children's Cabinet partnership

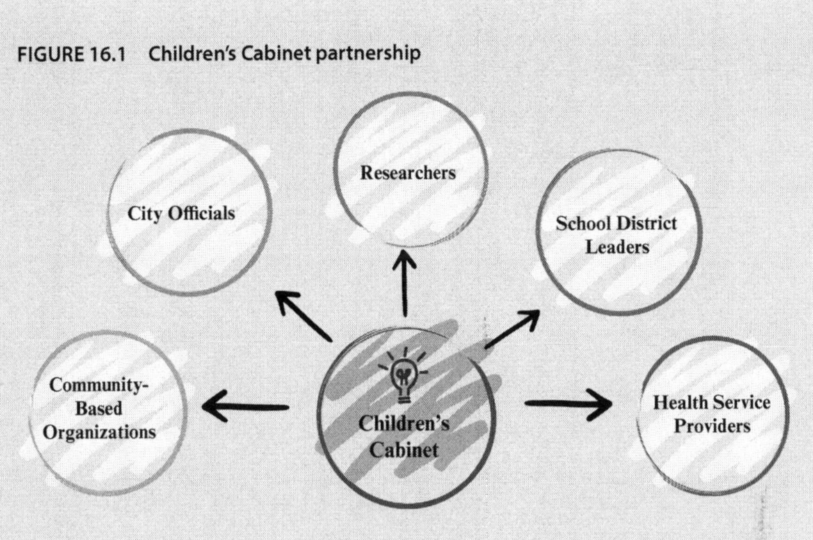

From the outset, the superintendent relied on support from the research team to co-plan and facilitate meetings. The research team helped design various methods to support cross-sector collaboration via in-person meetings, monthly online sessions, and half-day in-person retreats for Cabinet members. The superintendent and other leaders said they found these meetings helpful for sharing ideas, developing collaborations, and building awareness of one another's efforts to support youth well-being. For example, during one cabinet meeting, the district connected with a CBO that offered after-school activities in order to work together to provide tutoring offsite.

As far as the nuts and bolts of the initiative, the primary mode for coordination and collaboration has been the monthly cabinet meetings on Zoom, typically attended by approximately thirty members. District leaders and researchers iteratively designed meeting agendas to develop an engaging format that has included setting goals and objectives with the district, focusing on actions needed to achieve those goals, utilizing breakout groups for focused discussions, and ending with reflection and takeaways. As the initiative evolved and as the research team gathered feedback, the agenda for the meetings has evolved. In the second year of the initiative, a new mode of active engagement was employed, with one cabinet member presenting a problem of practice and soliciting insight from other cabinet members who engaged in conversations, gave advice, and co-constructed strategies to address the problem.

Although the Cabinet continued to meet regularly with consistent support from the superintendent, some community leaders wondered how to bring conversations from the Cabinet outside the meeting space and turn them into actionable tasks. At the same time, they felt that having people in leadership positions such as the superintendent and city director helped move the conversation forward and gave access to different community members to directly engage with district and city leaders, which otherwise they might not have done. For example, a few years into the initiative, the city director solicited advice about how to address issues of youth violence that had arisen in the city. District and community leaders, along with the police, offered to join efforts to host a citywide peace vigil in response.

Throughout this process, the Cabinet hoped to foster more intentional collaboration among leaders from various youth-serving sectors, all of whom were committed to improving youth well-being in the city. The overarching goal of these initiatives was to foster holistic well-being among the city's youth, not only encouraging their educational achievements but also nurturing their social and psychological development.[4] Moreover, the goal the superintendent set at the start of the initiative and that guided her work with the school district was "to know every student by name, strength, and story," focusing on a motto aimed to foster an environment where every child feels seen and supported while addressing systemic challenges at every stage of a child's development. This philosophy shaped and guided initiatives with the cabinet members and was spread community-wide to address youth's individual needs. Within this broad goal, three key areas emerged as crucial to this effort: (1) building out-of-school opportunities, (2) ensuring college and career readiness, and (3) supporting mental health. More recently, housing and safety emerged as key issues impacting youth well-being in the city, particularly as large numbers of immigrant families arrived who were unhoused or were doubling up with other families.

FIGURE 16.2 Map of Cabinet initiatives

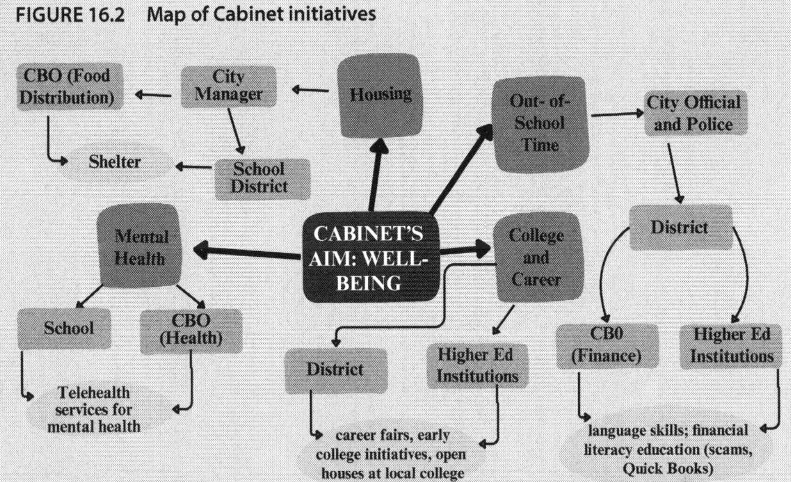

As illustrated in figure 16.2, the Cabinet sought to bring leaders together from different sectors to address issues related to these topics with implications for the various youth-serving institutions and organizations in the city. For example, identifying additional ways to support youth mental health was one of the Cabinet's top priorities from the beginning. Given barriers that can keep immigrant families from accessing mental health support, such as linguistic differences and stigma surrounding mental health, school-based approaches have been embraced by many immigrant-serving communities.[5] And that's what Gaudet's school district set out to implement. Further, community-wide initiatives also offer opportunities to combat these barriers. To address these barriers, the superintendent and her team collaborated with health sector CBOs to apply for city funds, made available via Cabinet discussions, to support embedding additional mental health support within the school through adopting innovative technologies, including a mobile app to provide early prevention and intervention for students. In addition, the district with support from Cabinet members built out a now annual community-wide "Well-Being Day" to showcase the myriad resources available to address mental health in the city.

Figure 16.2 illustrates the interconnected organizations and services contributing to the Children's Cabinet's strategic goal of improving youth well-being. The central node, labeled "Cabinet's Aim: Well-being," represents this goal. The various elements, differentially shaded for clarity, demonstrate the numerous services involved and the many stakeholders committed to promoting well-being in the community. The medium-gray boxes denote regions of support associated with direct services provided, encompassing housing, mental health, and college and career preparedness. Light-gray boxes represent key partners (institutions and organizations), such as the school district, the city director, and higher education institutions, through which these services are made possible. Dark-gray ellipses highlight specific initiatives or resources, like telehealth services, career fairs, and financial literacy education, that support overall goals of well-being within the community. Arrows indicate the direction of relationships or processes between entities and demonstrate how these organizations interact and support one another in order to provide an integrated response to well-being.

For instance, the school district is involved in collaborative partnerships with mental health service providers, shelter organizations, and higher education institutions, partnerships that basically reflect a multisector approach with the aim of meeting the various needs of students both within and outside the school. The map further underscores partnerships involving food distribution and extracurricular activities, thus highlighting broad-ranging efforts aimed at supporting overall youth well-being in the community. This framework effectively encapsulates the intricacies of providing support for youth well-being, all the while ensuring transparent communication regarding the function of each participating entity.

As the Cabinet started its third year, the superintendent prided herself on different successful initiatives that had been achieved through its formation. Bringing all the leaders into one space inspired them to work collaboratively across sectors to ensure the well-being of immigrant youth in the community. One example occurred when the city leader shared in a Cabinet meeting that housing posed a significant challenge in the city especially given the continuous influx of new immigrants joining the population.

Working with the housing department, the city was in the process of establishing new shelters, and city leaders shared this news with the Cabinet. In the conversation, leaders from both the school district and community-based organizations came forward to support the initiative. Research has shown that ensuring housing to youth from vulnerable groups adds to their college and career readiness and requires cross-sector support.[6] Through efforts proposed by the city director along with support from the superintendent and other community members, this collaboration aimed to bring in such results.

While leaders from particular sectors continued to work hard to address ongoing challenges in the community through their own initiatives, the Cabinet meetings served as important sites to share concerns and coordinate efforts, and at times, they led to concrete collaborations to support immigrant youth and families that wouldn't have been possible otherwise due to lack of communication and coordination. Even though at times, power structures and tensions between individual and collective aims arose, the Cabinet provided timely opportunities to work together rather than compete. While the full impacts of these efforts have yet to be completely documented, the continued engagement and collaborations are promising.

TEACHING NOTES

Given the global increase in the numbers of refugees and immigrants who are displaced from their home country due to various disruptions such as war and climate change events, the global population of school-aged immigrant and refugee children doubled by the end of 2022 from the past few years.[7] In the United States, the impact of global migration has been felt across the field of education with emerging responsibilities for the educational leaders in immigrant-serving communities.[8] Challenges outside education, including stringent federal immigration policy and limited access to opportunity, have profound impacts on immigrant and refugee youth and their experiences of schooling.[9] For example, policies that concern the livable wages for refugees lead to barriers to adequate health care, safe housing, and community integration that affect the well-being of people belonging to the immigrant status.[10] Consequently, educational leaders at different levels directly observe the consequences for immigrant and refugee students.[11]

Cross-Sector Collaboration

Recent research about the integration of immigrant-origin and refugee youth has explored how their experiences of belonging are interwoven with layers of social policies and community support and among youth-serving institutions.[12] Therefore, collaborative actions across sectors in a community are needed to ensure youth well-being in the community.[13] Research in poorer communities has revealed that when schools, social services, and families don't work together well, it affects how well young people do in school and how they experience it.[14] Misalignment of efforts and policies for offering provisions to immigrant-origin youth can negatively impact access to these supports.[15] For example, efforts to develop sanctuary communities can fall short when local policies do not align across government, law enforcement, and other sectors.[16] When cross-sector services are not coordinated, immigrant youth and their families can more easily fall through the cracks.

Supporting students from immigrant and refugee backgrounds extends beyond educational institutions and requires whole systemic change to address fragmentation among different institutions.[17] As an approach to addressing social problems, collective impact initiatives that foster cross-sector collaboration by bringing together various systems to coordinate different policy interventions have been found to lead to greater accessibility of resources.[18] The Children's Cabinet model has been identified as one promising approach to coordinating collaboration and supporting collective impact since it works to organize and facilitate the conversations across institutions in a structured way.[19]

At the same time, cross-sector initiatives can encounter challenges such as tensions between collective and individual objectives, competition for limited resources, and the need to overcome institutional barriers that can strain efforts to collaborate.[20] Hence, having a coordinated structure for cross-sectoral partnership and collaborations can enhance the flow of resources through a coordinated medium.[21]

Building Social Capital

Considering the possibilities for the Children's Cabinet to support immigrant and refugee youth, one might frame the initiative in terms of social capital theory. As a humanizing space to proactively address community-wide issues impacting youth well-being, the Children's Cabinet provides opportunities for leaders across institutions, organizations, and communities to build social capital.[22] Social capital is a useful way to theorize the benefits of creating collaborative efforts and coordinated services because it emphasizes how social interactions function as a resource that can buffer individuals from disruptive conditions and foster positive outcomes.[23]

Two components of social capital that are particularly relevant for serving immigrant and refugee communities are trust and care. Trust is a vital ingredient of social capital that is crucial for effective collaboration among partners dealing in immigrant-origin communities.[24] For many newcomers who have left contexts of disarray and upheaval, distrust in formal institutions and government is understandable, particularly given federal anti-immigrant policies in the United States.[25] At the same time, purposefully building relational trust within and across sectors by leaders has the potential to help immigrant families feel safe and valued in the school community. Also relevant, care and caring, conceptualized as both a resource and a relational practice that exists through interactions, are crucial to supporting immigrant families.[26] By emphasizing care in relations with immigrant communities, leaders can highlight the value of connection despite complexity.[27]

Given the rich variety of different cultural and linguistic backgrounds that immigrant students bring with them, the city needed to develop social capital for understanding the unique cultural context of these students. This social capital is indispensable for leaders in schools to ensure that support systems are found to be effective and inclusive. It would also mean the availability of resources in multiple languages, recognition of needs as diverse within immigrant families, and attention to how local policies and practices may inadvertently create barriers to access. Engaging in cross-sector collaboration to support immigrant and refugee communities has the potential to amplify social capital among leaders serving youth, thereby supporting the flow of care resources and relational practices as leaders collaborate to identify and address gaps in care, bridge institutions, and leverage existing resources.

Discussion Questions

1. *Mapping cross-sector supports in your community.* Given the importance of contexts of reception for immigrant communities, identifying the various institutions, organizations, and agencies that support newcomers is essential for ensuring that immigrant-origin students are nurtured across institutions.[28] The Children's Cabinet in Gaudet sought to include leaders from all of these key entities in order to coordinate care more effectively. In your context, which entities would you want to invite to participate in such an initiative? Which sectors are most relevant to serving newcomers there? Are there informal leaders or community members who are also crucial to caring for newcomers?
2. *Overcoming systemic barriers.* Immigrant-origin students commonly experience various barriers to engaging in education, due to poor proficiency in the dominant language, cultural disparities, and legal issues. Education leaders need to champion policies and practices that minimize these several barriers and promote equity, from specialized support services, such as language assistance programs and legal aid, to the advocacy of a welcoming school environment for all students. How can leaders assess whether or not cross-sector initiatives are supporting efforts to overcome systemic barriers for immigrant-origin youth? What do you think are the most salient outcomes to look for?
3. *Sustaining the initiative.* One of the challenges facing educational leaders is how to sustain cross-sector initiatives given rapid turnover in leaders across sectors. Long-term support of immigrant-origin students

requires sustained collaboration across sectors. One way that the Cabinet in this chapter's case was sustained was through the ongoing participation of research partners who facilitated routine meetings and evaluation of progress. What advice would you give leaders of such an initiative that might help sustain the work? What structures or supports are important to put in place to keep the initiative going?

CHAPTER 17

El Pueblo Unido

Relationship Building, Collaborative Advocacy, and Transnational Family Leadership for Newcomer Education

SOPHIA PIRAL LEE AND LISA M. DORNER

University of Missouri

ABSTRACT

School and district leaders who serve newcomers with different migratory backgrounds, statuses, languages, and needs may wonder: How do we advocate for equity in policies and practices to genuinely care for newcomers while navigating the policies and expectations of powerful stakeholders at state, district, and community levels? This chapter describes how a Midwestern rural school district struggled to integrate and graduate adolescent newcomers and asylum seekers from Guatemala. The chapter starts with the story of one bilingual English teacher who faced these challenges, and how a task force of educators, community members, and researchers collaborated to brainstorm new and flexible practices for newcomer education. After presenting the case narrative, the chapter reviews theoretical and practical tools for educators and leaders facing similar situations, with a focus on the importance of relationship building, collaborative advocacy, and transnational family leadership. The chapter concludes with discussion questions and activities, including how to map one's political contexts and develop advocacy plans for stronger and more equitable partnerships for newcomer education.

CASE NARRATIVE

Context

It's 2023. Wars, violence, and poverty—especially in the Global South but also in Europe—have led to one of the highest rates of migration and displaced people in recent history: 1 in 69 individuals had to move within their own country or to a new one in 2023, double the proportion of people forced from their homes just ten years before.[1] Youth from Central America are an important part of these numbers, as more and more have traveled unaccompanied to the United States since 2011, applying for asylum as soon as they reach the US border.[2]

The case narrative that follows is based on a real situation facing a rural town in the US Midwest. (This is a fictionalized narrative based on fact, with demographic data and identities adapted for anonymity.) Here, Spanish-speaking immigrants have settled in increasing numbers, from 10 percent of the population in 2000 to over 30 percent in 2020. In the schools, 40 percent of students come from Central America, with the majority qualifying for English-language development classes. In 2022, the enrollment of adolescents from Guatemala reached record numbers, with new high school students arriving every month. We start this narrative by telling the story of a high school "Beginner English" teacher who works closely with newcomers who bring their dreams and overcome many challenges to enter her classroom.

Ms. Juárez and High School English Education—Plus More!

Ms. Juárez loves her job, and students love her. Originally from California, with family roots in Mexico, she grew up speaking Spanish and English. She has worked as a teacher for more than ten years at various grade levels, but her favorite spot is right here at the high school. Her goal in teaching newcomers is twofold: She aims to help them develop initial academic skills in reading, writing, comprehending, and speaking English, and she also helps them integrate into US society and schooling. Toward this end, each day, Ms. Juárez teaches four English-language development classes along with environmental science. She also tutors and advises students on a volunteer basis; communicates regularly with students' family members about their progress in their home language of Spanish; adapts and creates students' course schedules; and supports homeschooling as necessary, such as for new moms who are caring for their infants. Students also consider her a friend and confidant and often ask her for advice or share their personal situations with her.

The long list of Ms. Juárez's daily work is extraordinary, but she does it because she knows time is short. One of her gravest concerns, and that of the district's, is how to support youth who arrive at the high school with only a few years to learn English, pass the state-required "end of course" exams, and obtain enough credits to graduate. She knows many have arrived unaccompanied, after leaving their closest family members behind, traveling long distances, suffering trauma, and, for some, experiencing violence along the way. Nonetheless, the students are eager to learn and want to be in school; as one teacher shared, "They have dreams; they want to become professionals, pursue college, have their own businesses, and be successful adults."

The Newcomer Experience in the Midwest

Today, Fausto, who is sixteen years old and in his first few months in the United States, stays after class to figure out his path to graduation. He chats in Spanish with Ms. Juárez:

FAUSTO: Ms. Juárez, I'm wondering how to get my high school diploma. I don't know who to talk to. It seems like I have a lot to do, but I'm not sure. When I try to ask questions, it's hard to say what I mean in English and then people just ignore me. I don't know what to do.

MS. J: Oh, I hate to hear that—teachers or office staff just ignoring you? I remember when my mom first came to the states, people would do the same thing to her. She's told me how she cried—every single night—out of frustration and loneliness. Could you tell me more about what you want to do, and what you did for school in Guatemala?

FAUSTO: Well, right now, I live with my uncle and sister. In Guate, I finished la primaria y básicos (through ninth grade), and I was just starting my first year of carrera (tenth grade).

MS. J: Ah, what subject were you studying in carrera?

FAUSTO: Industrial electricity.

MS. J: So, you want to be an electrician?

FAUSTO: Well, honestly, I'm not sure. I had to stop studying to travel here. I came all by myself. It's hard to be on my own without my mom anymore. But I know I don't want to sit in front of a computer all day, and back in Guatemala, I needed a job to make money. So, I thought being an electrician, I could do that. My real goal now is to graduate high school, so I can pay my bills here and help my mom, who has always worked so hard for me. Maybe build a house for her. She separated from my dad when I was six years old because he was so violent to her. So my goals have always been for her, you know, to give her the best, whatever I can do. Eventually, I want to go to college. So, do you know what I need to do now?

MS. J: Here, let's take a look at your schedule and see what options you have. Did you know you have until twenty-one years old to finish high school? Even though that makes you older than most students here, that's okay. There's also something called the HiSET exam. It's a test you can take, rather than taking classes to graduate, and you can take it in Spanish. It's called an "equivalency" diploma. Also, maybe you can have a flexible school schedule if you want to get a job.

FAUSTO: I never heard of that! Can you help me figure this out?

For the next ten minutes, Ms. Juárez and Fausto lean over the computer, Fausto skipping lunch and Ms. Juárez eating bits of her sandwich as she can. They are still digging through paperwork and files from previous students to find helpful information when the bell rings.

Addressing Challenges: The High School Newcomer Task Force

As Fausto leaves for his next class, Ms. Juárez writes down all of their questions, which she promises to bring up at the High School Newcomer Task

Force meeting today. This is a new committee designed by the district's language education director.

Later that afternoon in the district office, Ms. Juárez sits next to her friends, two high school Spanish teachers, who are from California just like her. The meeting is well attended and includes a number of stakeholders: four district leaders (the assistant superintendent of curriculum, the language education director, and two instructional coaches who help teachers work with designated English learners); two bilingual community members who used to work for the district (a family-school liaison-teacher and a translator); and two university partners, one from Guatemala.

During the meeting, Ms. Juárez brings up Fausto's questions and shares how she spends many hours creating and fixing newcomer students' schedules for their second year in high school. Someone asks, shouldn't that be the role of the school counselor? Ms. Juárez says that the counselors annually visit "English Language Arts" classes, but they often forget or skip the English classes for newcomers. Many of them also really don't know how to create the best schedule for very recent arrivals; they think that they all should just follow the same path, despite the range of options actually available. The assistant superintendent explains to the group that each counselor takes a group of students split alphabetically by their last name. They switched to this approach a few years ago, partly to make sure everyone at the school feels responsible for all their students, including newcomers, but the group questions whether this is working.

The former family-school liaison, who speaks Spanish as her second language, explains that she used to act as the main counselor and teacher for newcomers when she worked in the district about fifteen years ago. She made home visits, helping students and their families understand their choices, from their first day at school until graduation. Loving the idea of home visits and working with families, the Guatemalan university researcher then wonders aloud: Do the teachers ever connect virtually with parents still in Guatemala? The language education director makes notes of all these questions.

Then, another major issue comes up: the number of credit hours required by the district for high school graduation, 27, rather than the state average and coordinating board's recommendation, which is 24. To alleviate this high bar, the high school's instructional coach says she's working on a new process that would give high school credit to students for their jobs; she wants to make sure newcomers get course credit for work just like US-born students can do. She has had to be creative in designing this, however, because some students and businesses are worried about signing the necessary paperwork due to students' migratory status.

In this conversation, one teacher proposes, "Why can't we just reduce the number of credit hours for graduation somehow?" The assistant superintendent responds that, even though the district could create specialized plans for newcomers based on the state's policies, this may be unfeasible, as the school board and community pride themselves on having "high standards" with their higher number of required credits. The university researchers say that they'll look into this matter. They also promise to explore opportunities to design more classes in Spanish using resources from the Guatemalan Ministry of Education. The meeting ends with the language education director thanking everyone for their time and setting up the next meeting.

TEACHING NOTES

Research consistently documents a gap in four-year graduation rates between US-born students and those designated as English learners (84% versus 69%, respectively, in 2019).[3] The reasons for the gap are as varied as students' home countries: Most high schools lack the necessary multilingual resources, curricula, teachers, and understanding of newcomers' needs and desires; in addition, adolescent immigrant students need time to learn English, work, or catch up with classes after interrupted schooling.[4] Anti-immigrant discourses and policy making matter too; powerful stakeholders may defend the status quo, claiming to uphold community values and preferences, rather than attending flexibly and caringly to newcomers' circumstances.[5]

In this narrative, the district assembled diverse stakeholders in a task force designed to assess the challenges the district faced, as recommended by research.[6] Together, they unearthed practices that historically have made it difficult for newcomers to graduate before they aged out of the system. That is, even though the district followed state policy and allowed students to attend school until age twenty-one, it still had (1) a requirement for a higher-than-average number of required credits for graduation, which leaders said they could not change per the Board of Education's and long-term (white, US-born) residents' beliefs and desires; (2) a difficult process for designing flexible course schedules and obtaining credit for work outside school, particularly for immigrant students; and (3) a standard approach to counseling—splitting up all students alphabetically—rather than providing one immigrant-knowledgeable counselor to all adolescent newcomers. Although the task force documented these issues, change proved difficult, at least in part because of organizations' tendency to stick to the (racialized) status quo.[7] The following sections briefly highlight the necessity of broad relationship building, advocacy coalitions, and transnational family leadership to move beyond the norm and create caring newcomer education.

Relationship Building

This Midwestern district built on existing relationships to create its High School Newcomer Task Force. Importantly, the task force invited educators from various programs across the district (career and technical; English learner; counseling; special education), school and district leaders (assistant superintendent, director of language education, instructional coaches), community leaders (parents, advocates, and translators who used to work in the district), and university partners. Such relationships are essential not only to assessing challenges but also to building on a wide knowledge base and expertise, and to most thoroughly understanding and connecting with existing resources.[8] For instance, through the task force, the district leaders realized that the community member (former family-school liaison) used to make home visits and take care of course scheduling for all newcomers; perhaps they could return to this practice. In addition, the university research partners learned that the district did not have enough multilingual resources, knowledge about Guatemala, or regular connections with

Guatemalan family members; they promised to look into bringing such expertise and available educational resources into the high school.

Advocacy Coalitions

The district's task force may be viewed as an advocacy coalition, a group with shared beliefs and values that aims to strategically influence policies and practices.[9] Advocacy coalitions consist of various actors with different levels of power, resources, and tools.[10] Coalitions are often demarcated by social status and shaped by their historical and sociopolitical contexts. For instance, this chapter's narrative suggests that there are at least two advocacy coalitions in the district: (a) the new task force advocating for newcomers and (b) dominant stakeholders advocating for white or "all" students. To agitate for change, it's important to understand advocacy coalitions' perceptions and beliefs, and which coalitions might be in conflict.

Transnational Family Leadership

For a coalition advocating for newcomers to be most strategic, resourceful, and relevant, it must include those most impacted by newly proposed policies or practices. In educational spaces, family members and students are the central policy agents, and schools must design collaborative spaces where families have agency to codesign students' education and opportunities.[11] Family and student agency means that newcomers, their families, and other community members who represent their interests should have been invited to the task force. Moreover, families, even if they are living in Guatemala and other countries, must be included in decision making and conversations about their children's future. While this may seem challenging, there is precedence: Teachers have started to use various social media tools to include parents in conversations when they are unable to meet face-to-face.[12]

Conclusion

This Midwestern school district and others like it are working hard to create equitable education for newcomers. As one educator shared with immigrant families: "We want you to know that we want your children to be safe. We want your children to be healthy. We want you here in our community." Continued relationship building, advocacy coalitions, and transnational family leadership should ensure ever more equitable and greater opportunities for adolescent newcomers to reach their own goals—both in high school and beyond.

Discussion Questions

1. What challenges existed for newcomer education in this case narrative? Discuss the extent to which these challenges were impacted by school-, district-, and state-level practices. Then, consider your own context and brainstorm your challenges, and at which level(s) you need the most advocacy. You could create and fill out a table like this one:

	Practice or policy impact?			
Challenges in the narrative	*State level*	*District level*	*School level*	*My context's challenges*

2. What creative opportunities did the task force identify to address their challenges? How could they improve their process and outcomes by considering the context of their district within the framework of advocacy coalitions?
3. Discuss or reflect: Who joined and who was missing from the task force? Then, create a political map of stakeholders in your community. Note where and with whom they have power. Use your map to design a task force for your context. You may use this tool as a resource: https://tinyurl.com/yvs9ak4a.[13]
4. Consider the proposal to reduce the number of high school credits needed for graduation; then, answer these questions:[14]
   a. What are the intentions of having 27 required credits for graduation versus 24? What does this policy aim to accomplish?

b. How might this graduation requirement align with what happens inside the high school; for instance, with course scheduling for newcomers?
c. Who benefits from this policy, and who is negatively affected? Consider how this policy is affecting immigrant high schoolers in particular.
d. Who has a voice in the policy process and whose voice is currently silenced? How could the voices of newcomers, other designated English learners, and immigrant families be elevated in the policy process?
e. What policies exist at other levels that could help influence change? For instance, in Missouri, it is possible for districts to create alternative pathways to graduation for particular circumstances.[15]

Conclusion

This book provides school leaders with tools to navigate the complexities of supporting refugee and newcomer students. These chapters speak to only a fraction of the challenges leaders may encounter and thus serve as a starting point for developing strategies and critically engaging with these issues. It would not be possible to include every issue in this book, and, honestly, we conceptualized and planned this book before the second Trump administration's takeover of the federal government and recommitment to strict immigration policies. The work has changed, and we recognize this fact. However, we believe essential lessons can be learned from the experts in this book, and we view it as a reminder that there are faculty, leaders, and teachers worldwide committed to supporting newcomers using meaningful and thoughtful strategies.

There are a few enduring themes across the book's sections that apply regardless of any given administration's policies and support. The first section, "Policy and Administration," reminds us of the challenges policy environments create as we support newcomer students. At times, leaders must navigate policies ethically to mitigate harm, and at other moments, shifting political and policy environments offer more support. School leaders must think critically about policy interpretation and implementation, constantly interrogating how their actions and responses to policy shape the well-being and success of newcomer students. In the second section, "Within-School and Classroom Considerations," we learn strategies for creating inclusive, just, and academically effective school environments that consider newcomer students' unique challenges and experiences. A commitment to the goals of inclusivity, justice, and rigor remains paramount to creating the best schooling experience for newcomer students. The third section, "School

Partners and Family Engagement," shows that school leaders do not act in isolation. Despite the current political hostility toward work supporting newcomer students, leaders must never forget that they are part of a broader network of educators, families, and community partners committed to this work.

There are countless other themes and topics beyond the sections of the book. All of them coalesce around a fundamental principle: School leaders must remember that newcomer students are children like any other children—each with their own dreams, hopes, and desires. These young people did not choose the difficult circumstances they face, and educators are responsible for providing the supportive environments necessary to fulfill these children's right to a healthy and happy life. Education is a human right, and ensuring that right for newcomer students is a moral obligation. Denying them access to meaningful educational opportunities is an injustice. School leaders, often the final safeguard in upholding this right, must use every available tool to ensure that newcomer students receive the education and support they deserve.

Leaders will face myriad challenges in pursuing strategies to educate newcomer students. These challenges range from intercultural differences to a lack of policy support or resources at various levels of the educational system. While these obstacles are significant, they are not insurmountable. This book presents strategies to navigate some of these difficulties, emphasizing the importance of collaboration, patience, resilience, and adaptability. There is no doubt that political movements shape conversations and opportunities, but the work must continue regardless of the climate. At times, we may find ourselves to be the only source of support for these students; at other times, broader support systems will be in place. Either way, newcomers will be here seeking our support because global migration will continue and will likely increase as political strife and the climate crises accelerate. It is not unimaginable to think that any one of us and our children could be displaced and become newcomers in a distant land. The compassion, dignity, and commitment to justice we extend to newcomers should reflect the support we hope to receive if our families were ever forced to seek refuge elsewhere.

Appendix

Chapter Context and Key Topics

Section	*Chapter*	*Geographic Context*	*Key Topics*	*Grade Level(s)*
1. Policy and Administration	1. Testing for "Success"?: Considerations for Assessing Student Growth in Content and Language	Missouri	English-language and school testing, reading, state policy, leadership	Elementary
	2. Working with Socioculturally Diverse Immigrant and Refugee Families to Meet the Needs of Students with Disabilities	Minnesota	Students with disabilities, federal policy, sociocultur-ally responsive communication	Elementary and pre-K
	3. It's Not About Silos! School Leadership to Address the Learning Needs of All and Include Immigrant and Refugee Students		Professional learning, instruction, data and evidence use for English-language development	Elementary
	4. Changing Times: Exploring the Role of Culturally Responsive Leaders in New Immigrant Destinations	Texas	New immigrant destinations, leadership; local- and state-level agencies, policy design	District-wide K–12
2. Within-School and Classroom Considerations	5. What's Your Birthday? The Birthday Mystery and the Enrollment Conundrum	Southern US	Enrollment and registration, documentation, cultural views of birthdays	Elementary and middle school
	6. School Leadership Democratic Practices: Welcoming and Integrating Newcomers		Democracy, integration, working through student behaviors and conflicts	

(*continued*)

Section	*Chapter*	*Geographic Context*	*Key Topics*	*Grade Level(s)*
	7. Creating Schools That Are Inclusive Places for Newcomer and Refugee Students	Suburban public school	Radical hospitality, mitigating bias against newcomers, religious practices, theories of place	High school
	8. Welcome? A Headteacher's Approach to Integrating Afghan Evacuee Children in a London Secondary School	London, England	Cultural differences, community-based leadership, unexpected arrivals	Secondary school (UK)
	9. Equity Beyond Inclusion for Newcomer Youth in Science Education	Suburban public school	Science education, student cultural and experiential resources, student acclimation and relationship building	High school
	10. Unlocking Linguistic Success: Navigating the Benefits of English-Language Learner Summer School Initiatives	California	Long-term English learners, professional development, instruction, summer programming	Elementary and middle school (K–8)
3. School Partners and Family Engagement	11. Leadership for Identity-Safe Schools: One Southeast Asian American Principal's Antiracist Expectations of Refugee and Newcomer Students	Public school in a metropolitan city	School-university partnerships, community-based organizations, promoting recognition of students' lived experiences, cross-cultural understanding	Middle school
	12. "To know us is to be a part of us": School Leaders Can Collaborate with Refugee Families	Southeastern US	Refugee support programming, collective leadership, refugee parent engagement	District-wide K–12
	13. Out-of-School Programs for Refugee Youth: Community Partnerships to Extend School Capacity	Midwestern US	Community-based organizations, youth programming, school partnerships	District-wide K–12
	14. Compassionate Leadership for Newcomer Refugee Students: A Holistic and Resilience-Based Approach	Canada	Settlement workers in schools, community organizations, student sense of belonging	Secondary school

Section	*Chapter*	*Geographic Context*	*Key Topics*	*Grade Level(s)*
	15. "Our Students Matter": District Leaders' and Educators' Efforts to Center Immigrant Youth and Families in Building Caring School Systems	Mid-Atlantic and Midwestern US	System-wide collaboration, student voice in decision making, urban schooling systems, caring partnerships	District-wide
	16. Collaborating to Support Immigrant-Origin Youth and Their Families: A Case Study of Cross-Sector Leadership to Address Well-Being	Northeastern US	Post-pandemic effects, crisis responses, social services, youth well-being, district and city collaboration	District-wide
	17. El Pueblo Unido: Relationship Building, Collaborative Advocacy, and Transnational Family Leadership for Newcomer Education	Midwestern US	Rural schools, changing community demographics, coalition building, student acclimation and aspirations	High school

Notes

Foreword

1. United Nations Department of Economic and Social Affairs (UNDESA), *International Migration Report 2025* (2025), United Nations, https://www.un.org/development/desa.
2. United Nations High Commissioner for Refugees (UNHCR), *Global Trends: Forced Displacement in 2025 (*2025), https://www.unhcr.org.
3. Khalid Arar, Emily R. Crawford, Deniz Örücü, and Ira Bogotch, *Educational Leadership for Refugee Inclusion: Policy, Practice, and Perspectives* (Emerald, 2025).
4. Emily R. Crawford and Lisa M. Dorner, eds., *Educational Leadership of Immigrants: Case Studies in Times of Change* (Routledge, 2019).
5. Khalid Arar, Deniz Örücü, and Sedat Gümüş, "Educational Leadership and Policy Studies in Refugee Education: A Systematic Review of Existing Research," *Educational Review* 76, no. 4 (2024): 1032–56.
6. Alba A. Ortiz, María E. Fránquiz, and Gilberto P. Lara, "Educational Equity for Emergent Bilinguals: What's Wrong with This Picture?," *Bilingual Research Journal* 45, no. 1 (2022): 1–7.
7. Laurie Porter, Maria Vazquez Cano, and Ilana Umansky, *Bilingual Education and America's Future: Evidence and Pathways (*Civil Rights Project / Proyecto Derechos Civiles, 2023).
8. Emily R. Crawford, "Community-Building for Educational Equity: Fostering Relationships Between Schools and Refugee Families," *International Journal of Leadership in Education* (December 2023): 1–23.
9. Monisha Bajaj, Daniel Walsh, Lesley Bartlett, and Gabriela Martínez, *Humanizing Education for Immigrant and Refugee Youth: 20 Strategies for the Classroom and Beyond* (Teachers College Press, 2022).
10. USA for UNHCR, *Refugee Facts: Refugees in America* (2025), accessed September 15, 2025, https://www.unrefugees.org/refugee-facts/usa/.
11. Crawford, "Community-Building for Educational Equity"; Sarah Dryden-Peterson, "Refuge Education: The Crossroads of Globalization," *Educational Researcher* 45, no. 9 (2016): 473–82.

Introduction

1. "Refugee Statistics," USA for UNHCR, accessed August 20, 2025, https://www.unrefugees.org/refugee-facts/statistics/.
2. "Refugees in America," USA for UNHCR, accessed August 20, 2025, https://www.unrefugees.org/refugee-facts/usa/.
3. Global Refuge Staff, "U.S. Resettles Most Refugees in Three Decades, Maintains FY 2025 Refugee Cap at 125,000," press release, Global Refuge, September 20, 2024, https://www.globalrefuge.org/news/refugees-resettlement-three-decades/.
4. "Ukraine Situation: Flash Update #82," UNHCR, July 28, 2025, https://www.unhcr.org/media/ukraine-situation-flash-update-82.

5. Camilo Montoya-Galvez, "In 2 Years Since Russia's Invasion, a U.S. Program Has Resettled 187,000 Ukrainians with Little Controversy," *CBS News*, April 24, 2024, https://www.cbsnews.com/news/ukrainian-refugees-us-uniting-for-ukraine-russia-invasion/.
6. "Where Do Refugees Resettle in the U.S.?," USAFacts, September 27, 2021, https://usafacts.org/articles/where-do-refugees-resettle-in-the-us/.
7. "Realigning the United States Refugee Admissions Program," White House, January 20, 2025, https://www.whitehouse.gov/presidential-actions/2025/01/realigning-the-united-states-refugee-admissions-program/; "After Day One: A High-Level Analysis of Trump's First Executive Actions," American Immigration Council, January 22, 2025, https://www.americanimmigrationcouncil.org/research/after-day-one-high-level-analysis-trumps-first-executive-actions.
8. Kara Arundel, "Schools No Longer Protected from Immigration Raids," *K–12 Dive*, January 21, 2025, https://www.k12dive.com/news/schools-protected-areas-immigration-enforcement-Trump/737926/.
9. Emily R. Crawford and Rebecca Lowenhaupt, "The Cost of ICE Raids," *The 74*, February 4, 2025, https://www.the74million.org/article/the-real-costs-of-ice-raids-at-schools-and-what-educators-should-do/; Patricia Gándara and Jongyeon Ee, *Schools Under Siege: The Impact of Immigration Enforcement on Educational Equity* (Harvard Education Press, 2021).
10. Tim Stanley and Peter Smith, "Refugee Resettlement Agencies Scramble After Trump Orders Them to Halt Their Federally Funded Work," Associated Press, January 29, 2025, https://apnews.com/article/trump-refugees-resettlement-funding-pause-afghan-allies-3f35577f504246132ede00dddff46f27.
11. Crawford and Lowenhaupt, "The Cost of ICE Raids"; J. J. Kirksey and Carolyn Sattin-Bajaj, "Immigration and Customs Enforcement Raids the Pillar of a Community: Student Achievement, Absenteeism, and Mobility Following a Large Worksite Enforcement Operation in North Texas," *American Behavioral Scientist*, November 28, 2023, https://doi.org/10.1177/00027642231215992.
12. Universal Declaration of Human Rights (1948), Article 26, accessed December 15, 2023, https://www.un.org/en/about-us/universal-declaration-of-human-rights.
13. Sarah G. Naylor, "Lawmakers Introduce Bill to Keep Undocumented Students Out of Public Schools," *Chalkbeat Tennessee*, February 5, 2025, https://www.chalkbeat.org/tennessee/2025/02/05/republican-lawmakers-introduce-bill-keep-undocumented-students-out-of-school/; Lau v. Nichols, 414 U.S. 563 (1974); Plyler v. Doe, 457 U.S. 202 (1982); Refugee Act of 1980, Pub L. 96-212.
14. Khalid Arar, *School Leadership for Refugees' Education: Social Justice Leadership for Immigrants, Migrants, and Refugees* (Routledge, 2021); Sarah Dryden-Peterson, "Refugee Education: The Crossroads of Globalization," *Educational Researcher* 45, no. 9 (2016): 473–82; Rabia Hos, "The Lives, Aspirations, and Needs of Refugee and Immigrant Students with Interrupted Formal Education (SIFE) in a Secondary Newcomer Program," *Urban Education* 55, no. 7 (2020): 1021–44.
15. Kristen Brezicha and Chandler P. Miranda, "Actions Speak Louder Than Words: Examining School Practices That Support Immigrant Students' Feelings of Belonging," *Equity and Excellence in Education* 55, nos. 1–2 (2022): 133–47; Kristina F. Brezicha, "Legislating What Matters: How Policy Designs Shape Two New Immigrant Destinations Schools' Responses to Immigrant Students," *Education Policy Analysis Archives*, January 25, 2022, https://epaa.asu.edu/index.php/epaa/article/view/5089/2896;Jill Koyama and Julie Kasper, "Pushing the Boundaries: Education Leaders, Mentors, and Refugee Students," *Educational*

Administration Quarterly 57, no. 1 (2021): 49–81; Rebecca Lowenhaupt and Todd Reeves, "Toward a Theory of School Capacity in New Immigrant Destinations: Instructional and Organizational Considerations," *Leadership and Policy in Schools* 14, no. 3 (2015): 308–40.

16. Emily R. Crawford, "The Ethic of the Community and Incorporating Undocumented Immigrant Concerns into Ethical School Leadership," *Educational Administration Quarterly* 53, no. 2 (2017): 147–79; Sophia Rodriguez and William McCorkle, "On the Educational Rights of Undocumented Students: A Call to Expand Teachers' Awareness of Policies Impacting Undocumented Students and Strategic Empathy," *Teachers College Record* 122 no. 12 (2020): 1–34; Julie Kim Yammine and Rebecca Lowenhaupt, "Educators' Perceptions of Immigration Policy Implications on Their Schools: A Mixed-Methods Exploration," *Teachers College Record* 123, no. 12 (2021): 97–124; Rebecca Lowenhaupt and Megan Hopkins, "Considerations for School Leaders Serving US Immigrant Communities in the Global Pandemic," *Journal of Professional Capital and Community* 5, nos. 3–4 (2020): 375–80, https://doi.org/10.1108/JPCC-05-2020-0023.
17. Emily R. Crawford and Noelle Witherspoon Arnold, "'We Don't Talk About Status; We Talk About Helping Children': How School Leaders Shape School Climate for Undocumented Students," *International Journal of Educational Leadership and Management* 5, no. 2 (2017): 116–47; E. N. Bonney, V. N. A. Bonney, and H. Sweeney, "Schools Alone Cannot Educate Refugees: It Takes a Community," in *Refugee Education Across the Lifespan: Mapping Experiences of Language Learning and Use*, ed. D. S. Warner (Springer, 2021), 17–34.
18. Marjorie F. Orellana, María Meza, and Kate Pietsch, "Mexican Immigrant Networks and Home-School Connections," *Practicing Anthropology* 24, no. 3 (2002): 4–8.
19. Margie McHugh and Caitlin Doxsee, "English Plus Integration: Shifting the Instructional Paradigm for Immigrant Adult Learners to Support Integration Success," Migration Policy Institute, 2018, https://www.migrationpolicy.org/sites/default/files/publications/AdultEd_EnglishPlusIntegration_Final.pdf.
20. Carola Suárez-Orozco, Hirokazu Yoshikawa, and Vivian Tseng, "Intersecting Inequalities: Research to Reduce Inequality for Immigrant-Origin Children and Youth" (William T. Grant Foundation, 2015); Yammine and Lowenhaupt, "Educators' Perceptions of Immigration Policy Implications on Their Schools"; Vanessa Wight, Kalyani Thampi, and Michelle Chau, *Poor Children by Parents' Nativity: What Do We Know?* (National Center for Children in Poverty, 2011), http://www.nccp.org/wp-content/uploads/2020/05/text_1006.pdf.

Chapter 1

1. Mo. Rev. Stat. § 167.645 (2021).
2. Julian Vasquez Heilig, Thomas J. Brewer, and Jose Ojeda Pedraza, "Examining the Myth of Accountability, High-Stakes Testing, and the Achievement Gap," *Journal of Family Strengths* 18, no. 1 (2018): article 9, https://doi.org/10.58464/2168-670X.1389.
3. Wayne Wright, *Foundations for Teaching English Language Learners: Research, Theory, Policy, and Practice*, 3rd ed. (Calson, 2019).
4. Michael Hopkins and Julie Sugarman, *State Accountability for English Learners* (Migration Policy Institute, 2024), https://www.migrationpolicy.org/sites/default/files/publications/mpi-nciip_state-accountability-english-learners-2024_final.pdf.
5. Kenji Hakuta, Yuko Goto Butler, and Daria Witt, *How Long Does It Take English Learners to Attain Proficiency?* (University of California Linguistic Minority Research Institute Policy Report 2000-1, September 2000).

6. Ilana M. Umansky, Rebecca M. Callahan, and Jennifer C. Lee, "Making the Invisible Visible: Identifying and Interrogating Ethnic Differences in English Learner Classification," *American Journal of Education* 126, no. 3 (2020): 335–88.
7. Margarita Huerta, Tanya Garza, and Fuhui Tong, "Examining Validity and Accommodations for English Learners in High-Stakes Content Area Standardized Tests," in *Teaching on Assessments*, ed. Sharon Nichols and Divya Varier (Information Age, 2021), 173–94.
8. J. L. Moore, T. Li, and Y. Lu, "Reliability of English Learners' Test Scores," *ACT Research and Policy* (2020): 1–10, https://files.eric.ed.gov/fulltext/ED606154.pdf.
9. "Digital Technology and Literacy," CORE (Cultural Orientation Resource Exchange), accessed August 21, 2025, https://www.coresourceexchange.org/activity-bank/digital-technology-and-literacy/.
10. Jonah A. Heissel, Elijah K. Adan, Jennifer L. Doleac, David N. Figlio, and Jonathan Meer, "Testing, Stress, and Performance: How Students Respond Physiologically to High-Stakes Testing," *Education Finance and Policy* 16, no. 2 (2021): 183–208.

Chapter 2

1. Muna Sunni, Mohamed Farah, Christine Hardie, Abdirahman M. Dhunkal, M. Jennifer Abuzzahab, Jennifer H. Kyllo, et al., "Understanding Cultural Beliefs in Families of Somali Children with Diabetes in the Twin Cities, Minnesota," *Journal of Community Health* 40 (2015): 827–33.
2. Ahmed Ismail Yusuf, *Somalis in Minnesota* (Minnesota Historical Society Press, 2012).
3. Bernard Guerin, Pauline Guerin, Roda Omar Diiriye, and Susan Yates, "Somali Conceptions and Expectations Concerning Mental Health: Some Guidelines for Mental Health Professionals," *New Zealand Journal of Psychology* 33, no. 2 (2004): 59–67.
4. Mildred Boveda, "Beyond Special and General Education as Identity Markers: The Development and Validation of an Instrument to Measure Preservice Teachers' Understanding of the Effects of Intersecting Sociocultural Identities" (EdD dissertation, Florida International University, 2016).
5. Kimberlé Williams Crenshaw, "Mapping the Margins: Intersectionality, Identity Politics, and Violence Against Women of Color," in *The Public Nature of Private Violence: The Discovery of Domestic Abuse*, ed. Martha Fineman and Roxanne Mykitiuk (Routledge, 2013), 93–118; Martina Barnevik-Olsson, Christopher Gillberg, and Elisabeth Fernell, "Prevalence of Autism in Children Born to Somali Parents Living in Sweden: A Brief Report," *Developmental Medicine and Child Neurology* 50, no. 8 (2008): 598–601; Jennifer Hall-Lande et al., "Age of Initial Identification of Autism Spectrum Disorder in a Diverse Urban Sample," *Journal of Autism and Developmental Disorders* 51 (2021): 798–803.
6. Hassan A. Hassan, "Qualitative Analysis of the Experience of Minnesota Somali Parents with Students with Disabilities in Distance Learning During the COVID-19 Pandemic" (EdD dissertation, University of St. Thomas, Minnesota, 2023); Deeqaifrah A. Hussein, "Somali Parents' Experiences with Autism and the Special Education System" (EdD dissertation, University of St. Thomas, Minnesota, 2022).
7. Grace L. Francis et al., "Hispanic Caregiver Experiences Supporting Positive Postschool Outcomes for Young Adults with Disabilities," *Intellectual and Developmental Disabilities* 56, no. 5 (2018): 337–53.
8. Sarah Geenen, Laurie Powers, Alfonso Lopez Vasquez, and Hank Bersani, "Understanding and Promoting the Transition of Minority Adolescents," *Career Development for Exceptional Individuals* 26, no. 1 (2003): 27–46.

9. Hussein, "Somali Parents' Experiences with Autism."
10. Su-Je Cho, Betsy Brenner, and George H. S. Singer, "A Comparison of Adaptation to Childhood Disability in Korean Immigrants and Korean Mothers," *Research and Practice for Persons with Severe Disabilities* 18, no. 1 (2003): 9–19.
11. Guerin et al., "Somali Conceptions and Expectations Concerning Mental Health"; Amy N. Esler, Jennifer Hall-Lande, and Amy Hewitt, "Phenotypic Characteristics of Autism Spectrum Disorder in a Diverse Sample of Somali and Other Children," *Journal of Autism and Developmental Disorders* 47 (2017): 3150–65.
12. Jessica Kuenzli, "The Somali Community's Experiences with Autism: An Exploratory Study" (MSW thesis, University of St. Thomas, Minnesota, 2012).
13. Amy Hewitt, Jennifer Hall-Lande, Kristin Hamre, Amy N. Esler, Judy Punyko, Joe Reichle, et al., "Autism Spectrum Disorder (ASD) Prevalence in Somali and Non-Somali Children," *Journal of Autism and Developmental Disorders* 46 (2016): 2599–608.
14. Hussein, "Somali Parents' Experiences with Autism."
15. Chun Zhang and Tess Bennett, "Facilitating the Meaningful Participation of Culturally and Linguistically Diverse Families in the IFSP and IEP Process," *Focus on Autism and Other Developmental Disabilities* 18, no. 1 (2003): 51–59.
16. Maria Arboleda, Kathleen Call, Xai Gao Sheng Chang, Mariam Egal, Donna McAlpine, Walter Novillo, et al., *A Qualitative Study of Families of Children with Autism in the Somali Community: Comparing the Experiences of Immigrant Groups*, Report to the Minnesota Legislature, Minnesota Department of Health, 2014.
17. Amal M. Hussein, Elizabeth Pellicano, and Laura Crane, "Understanding and Awareness of Autism Among Somali Parents Living in the United Kingdom," *Autism* 23, no. 6 (2019): 1408–18.
18. Muideen O. Bakare and Kerim M. Munir, "Autism Spectrum Disorders (ASD) in Africa: A Perspective," *African Journal of Psychiatry* 14, no. 3 (2011): 208–10.
19. Z. Rossetti, M. M. Burke, O. Hughes, K. Schraml-Block, J. I. Rivera, K. Rios, et al., "Parent Perceptions of the Advocacy Expectation in Special Education," *Exceptional Children* 87, no. 4 (2021): 438–57.
20. Hewitt et al., "Autism Spectrum Disorder (ASD) Prevalence in Somali and Non-Somali Children."
21. Hassan, "Qualitative Analysis of the Experience of Minnesota Somali Parents."
22. Hussein, "Somali Parents' Experiences with Autism."
23. Lucy Ellen Selman, Fiona Fox, Nura Aabe, Katrina Turner, Dheeraj Rai, and Sabi Redwood, "'You Are Labelled by Your Children's Disability': A Community-Based, Participatory Study of Stigma Among Somali Parents of Children with Autism Living in the United Kingdom," *Ethnicity and Health* 23, no. 7 (2018): 781–96.
24. Joseph K. Gona, Charles R. Newton, Kenneth Rimba, Rachel Mapenzi, Michael Kihara, Fons J. R. Van de Vijver, et al., "Parents' and Professionals' Perceptions on Causes and Treatment Options for Autism Spectrum Disorders (ASD) in a Multicultural Context on the Kenyan Coast," *PloS ONE* 10, no. 8 (2015): e0132729; Kathryn Munroe, Linda Hammond, and Susanna Cole, "The Experiences of African Immigrant Mothers Living in the United Kingdom with a Child Diagnosed with an Autism Spectrum Disorder: An Interpretive Phenomenological Analysis," *Disability and Society* 31, no. 6 (2016): 798–819.
25. Hassan, "Qualitative Analysis of the Experience of Minnesota Somali Parents."
26. Joanna E. Bettmann, Deb Penney, Pamela Clarkson Freeman, and Natalie Lecy, "Somali Refugees' Perceptions of Mental Illness," *Social Work in Health Care* 54, no. 8 (2015):

738–57; Shanna Miller-Gairy and Saul Mofya, "Elements of Culture and Tradition That Shape the Perceptions and Expectations of Somali Refugee Mothers About Autism Spectrum Disorder," *International Journal of Child and Adolescent Health* 8, no. 4 (2015); Claire Decoteau, *The Western Disease: Autism and Somali Parents in the Twin Cities* (University of Chicago Press, 2017).
27. Hussein, "Somali Parents' Experiences with Autism."
28. Abdullahi S. Elmi, *A Study on the Mental Health Needs of the Somali Community in Toronto* (Toronto: York Community Services; Rexdale Community Health Centre, 1999); Fiona Fox, Nura Aabe, Katrina Turner, Sabi Redwood, and Dheeraj Rai, "'It Was like Walking Without Knowing Where I Was Going': A Qualitative Study of Autism in a UK Somali Migrant Community," *Journal of Autism and Developmental Disorders* 47 (2017): 305–15.
29. Erving Goffman, *Stigma: Notes on the Management of Spoiled Identity* (Simon and Schuster, 2009).
30. Laura Sweeney, "Somali Parental Participation in School-Based Autism Treatments: A Cultural Perspective" (EdD dissertation, Northcentral University, 2018), https://www.proquest.com/openview/19a5937351be4552a5f514d304f52dbe/1?pq-origsite=gscholar&cbl=18750.
31. Karen Burkett, Edith Morris, Patricia Manning-Courtney, Jean Anthony, and Donna Shambley-Ebron, "African American Families on Autism Diagnosis and Treatment: The Influence of Culture," *Journal of Autism and Developmental Disorders* 45, no. 10 (2015): 3244–54; Victoria Mutiso, Abdulkadir Hussein Warsame, Edna Bosire, Christine Musyimi, Abednego Musau, Maimuna Mohamud Isse, et al., "Intrigues of Accessing Mental Health Services Among Urban Refugees Living in Kenya: The Case of Somali Refugees Living in Eastleigh, Nairobi," *Journal of Immigrant and Refugee Studies* 17, no. 2 (2019): 204–21.
32. Miller-Gairy and Mofya, "Elements of Culture and Tradition That Shape the Perceptions and Expectations of Somali Refugee Mothers."
33. Harker et al., "Challenges for Healthcare Providers and Educators with Somali Refugee Families."
34. Hussein, "Somali Parents' Experiences with Autism."
35. Hassan, "Qualitative Analysis of the Experience of Minnesota Somali Parents."

Chapter 3

1. "Global Trends Report 2023," UNHRC (United Nations Human Rights Commission): The UN Refugee Agency, 2023, https://www.unhcr.org/global-trends-report-2023.
2. Emily R. Crawford, and Sarah L. Hairston, "He Could Be Undocumented: Striving to Be Sensitive to Student Documentation Status in a Rural Community," *Journal of Cases in Educational Leadership* 21, no. 1 (2018): 3–15, https://doi.org/10.1177/1555458917718008.
3. "Designing, Delivering, and Evaluating Instruction and Services for Multilingual Learners Guidebook," Colorado Department of Education, 2023, https://www.cde.state.co.us/cde_english/eldguidebook.
4. "Designing, Delivering, and Evaluating Instruction."
5. "Designing, Delivering, and Evaluating Instruction."
6. "Designing, Delivering, and Evaluating Instruction."
7. "Designing, Delivering, and Evaluating Instruction."
8. "Global Trends Report 2023."

9. George Theoharis, "Social Justice Educational Leaders and Resistance: Toward a Theory of Social Justice Leadership," *Educational Administration Quarterly* 43, no. 2 (2007): 221–58, https://doi.org/10.1177/0013161X06293717.
10. James McLeskey, Larry Maheady, Bonnie S. Billingsley, Mary T. Brownell, and Timothy J. Lewis, eds., *High Leverage Practices for Inclusive Classrooms* (Taylor and Francis, 2019).
11. Laura Stelitano, Jennifer Lin Russell, and Laura E. Bray, "Organizing for Meaningful Inclusion: Exploring the Routines That Shape Student Supports in Secondary Schools," *American Educational Research Journal* 57, no. 2 (2020): 535–75, https://doi.org/10.3102/0002831219859307.
12. Silvia Molina Roldán, Jesús Marauri, Adriana Aubert, and Ramon Flecha, "How Inclusive Interactive Learning Environments Benefit Students Without Special Needs," *Frontiers in Psychology* 12 (April 2021), https://doi.org/10.3389/fpsyg.2021.661427.
13. Richard Villa and Jaqueline Thousand, *Leading and Inclusive School* ASCD (Association for Supervision and Curriculum Development, 2017).
14. Wendy Murawski, and Lisa Dieker, "Leading the Co-Teaching Dance: Leadership Strategies to Enhance Team Outcomes," Council for Exceptional Children, 2013.
15. Laura Hedin and Greg Conderman, "Shared Promises and Challenges of Coteaching: General-Special Education and Mentor Preservice Partnerships," *Action in Teacher Education* 37, no. 4 (2015): 397–417, https://doi.org/10.1080/01626620.2015.1078756.
16. Regional Education Laboratory Southwest, "Collaborative Framework to Support English Learner Students Instruction: Collaboration Guide," IES: Institute of Education Sciences, 2022, https://ies.ed.gov/ncee/rel/regions/southwest/publications/pdf/sw_main_031522.pdf.
17. "English Language Toolkit," National Clearinghouse for English Language Acquisition, 2017, https://ncela.ed.gov/educator-support/toolkits/english-learner-toolkit

Chapter 4

1. Different authors offer different definitions of new immigrant destinations. Winders suggests five characteristics of a new immigrant destination: a rapid change in population, little institutional infrastructure, few formal and informal networks to support immigrant arrivals, a missing link between immigrants and the area's past, and rapid changes in demographics and settlement patterns in the area. Jamie Winders, "New Immigrant Destinations in Global Context," *International Migration Review* 48 (2014): S158–61, https://doi.org/10.1111/imre.12140.
2. "Texas Immigrant Population Now Rivals New York's in Size," Pew Research Center, April 21, 2016, https://www.pewresearch.org/short-reads/2016/04/21/texas-immigrant-population-now-rivals-new-yorks-in-size/.
3. Alejandro Portes and Rubén G. Rumbaut, *Immigrant America: A Portrait* (University of California Press, 2006), 37–66; Alex Stepick and Carol D. Stepick, "Diverse Contexts of Reception and Feelings of Belonging," *Forum Qualitative Sozialforschung* 10, no. 3 (2009), https://doi.org/10.17169/fqs-10.3.1366.
4. Kristina Brezicha and Megan Hopkins "Shifting the Zone of Mediation in a Suburban New Immigrant Destination: Community Boundary Spanners and School District Policymaking," *Peabody Journal of Education* 91, no. 3 (2016): 366–82, https://doi.org/10.1080/0161956X.2016.1184945; Anne L. Schneider and Helen M. Ingram, *Policy Design for Democracy* (University Press of Kansas, 1997); Kristina F. Brezicha, "Legislating What Matters: How Policy Designs Shape Two New Immigrant Destinations Schools' Responses to Immigrant Students," *Education Policy Analysis Archives* 30, no. 4 (2022): 1–35,

https://doi.org/10.14507/epaa.30.5089; Tanya Golash-Boza and Zulema Valdez, "Nested Contexts of Reception: Undocumented Students at the University of California, Central," *Sociological Perspectives* 61, no. 4 (2018): 535–52, https://doi.org/10.1177/0731121417743728; Megan Hopkins, Hayley Weddle, Peter Bjorklund Jr., Ilana M. Umansky, and Dafney Blanca Dabach, "'It's Created by a Community': Local Context Mediating Districts' Approaches to Serving Immigrant and Refugee Newcomers," *AERA Open* 7, no. 1 (2021): 1–13, https://doi.org/10.1177/23328584211032234.

5. Muhammad A. Khalifa, Mark A. Gooden, and James E. Davis, "Culturally Responsive School Leadership: A Synthesis of the Literature," *Review of Educational Research* 86, no. 4 (2016): 1–40, https://doi.org/10.3102/0034654316630383.
6. Gloria Ladson-Billings, "Toward a Theory of Culturally Relevant Pedagogy," *American Educational Research Journal* 32, no. 3 (1995): 465–91, https://doi.org/10.3102/00028312032003465; Django Paris, "Culturally Sustaining Pedagogy: A Needed Change in Stance, Terminology, and Practice," *Educational Researcher* 41, no. 3 (2012): 93–97, https://doi.org/10.3102/0013189X12441244.
7. Muhammad A. Khalifa, *Culturally Responsive School Leadership* (Harvard Education Press, 2018), 13–21.
8. David E. DeMatthews and Elena Izquierdo, "Supporting Mexican American Immigrant Students on the Border: A Case Study of Culturally Responsive Leadership in a Dual Language Elementary School," *Urban Education* 55, no. 3 (2020): 362–93, https://doi.org/10.1177/0042085918756715.
9. Khalifa, *Culturally Responsive School Leadership*, 9.
10. Kristina F. Brezicha and Chandler P. Miranda, "Actions Speak Louder Than Words: Examining School Practices That Support Immigrant Students' Feelings of Belonging," *Equity and Excellence in Education* 55, no. 1–2 (2022): 133–47, https://doi.org/10.1080/10665684.2021.2021633; Kristin A. Sinclair, Sophia Rodriguez, and Timothy P. Monreal, "'We Can Be Leaders': Minoritized Youths' Subjugated (Civic) Knowledges and Social Futures in Two Urban Contexts," *International Journal of Qualitative Studies in Education* 36, no. 3 (2023): 392–410, https://doi.org/10.1080/09518398.2022.2025488.
11. Nathern S. Okilwa, Amanda J. Cordova, and Kerry Haupert, "Learning in a New Land: School Leadership in Support of Refugee Students," *Leadership and Policy in Schools* 21, no. 3 (2022): 710, https://doi.org/10.1080/15700763.2020.1843061.
12. Khalifa, *Culturally Responsive School Leadership*, 11–12.
13. Terrance L. Green, "From Positivism to Critical Theory: School-Community Relations Toward Community Equity Literacy," *International Journal of Qualitative Studies in Education* 30, no. 4 (2017): 370–87, https://doi.org/10.1080/09518398.2016.1253892.
14. Ann M. Ishimaru, "When New Relationships Meet Old Narratives: The Journey Towards Improving Parent-School Relations in a District-Community Organizing Collaboration," *Teachers College Record* 116, no. 2 (2014): 1–56, https://doi.org/10.1177/016146811411600206; Christine M. McWayne, Gigliana Melzi, and Jayanthi Mistry, "A Home-to-School Approach for Promoting Culturally Inclusive Family-School Partnership Research and Practice," *Educational Psychologist* 57, no. 4 (2022): 238–51, https://doi.org/10.1080/00461520.2022.2070752.
15. Khalifa, *Culturally Responsive School Leadership*, 64–65.
16. Deborah K. Palmer, "Middle-Class English Speakers in a Two-Way Immersion Bilingual Classroom: 'Everybody Should Be Listening to Jonathan Right Now . . . ,'" *Tesol Quarterly* 43, no. 2 (2009): 177–202.

17. H. Samy Alim, "'The Whig Party Don't Exist in My Hood': Knowledge, Reality, and Education in the Hip Hop Nation," in *Talkin Black Talk: Language, Education, and Social Change*, ed. H. Samy Alim and John Baugh (Teachers College Press, 2007), 15–29.
18. Khalifa, *Culturally Responsive School Leadership*, 21.
19. Ramona Fruja Amthor and Kevin Roxas, "Multicultural Education and Newcomer Youth: Re-Imagining a More Inclusive Vision for Immigrant and Refugee Students," *Educational Studies* 52, no. 2 (2016): 155–76, https://doi.org/10.1080/00131946.2016.1142992.
20. Brezicha and Miranda, "Actions Speak Louder Than Words," 133–47.
21. Reva Jaffe-Walter and Stacey J. Lee, "Engaging the Transnational Lives of Immigrant Youth in Public Schooling: Toward a Culturally Sustaining Pedagogy for Newcomer Immigrant Youth," *American Journal of Education* 124, no. 3 (2018): 257–83.
22. Khalifa, *Culturally Responsive School Leadership*, 21.
23. Luis Moll, Cathy Amanti, Deborah Neff, and Norma Gonzalez, "Funds of Knowledge for Teaching: Using a Qualitative Approach to Connect Homes and Classrooms," *Theory into Practice* 31, no. 2 (1992): 132–41.
24. Barbara Czarniawska, *Social Science Research: From Field to Desk* (Sage, 2014), 43.

Chapter 5

1. "Apprehensions and Expulsions Registered by the United States Border Patrol from the 1990 Fiscal Year to the 2023 Fiscal Year," Statista, 2024, https://www.statista.com/statistics/329256/alien-apprehensions-registered-by-the-us-border-patrol/.
2. "Data and Statistics: Global Trends" United Nations High Commissioner for Refugees, accessed September 5, 2024, from https://www.unhcr.org/global-trends.
3. "4 Ways to Facilitate Migrants' Access to Identity Documents," International Organization for Migration, accessed September 17, 2024, from https://www.iom.int.
4. "4 Ways to Facilitate Migrants' Access to Identity Documents."
5. J. Tim Goddard, "A Tangled Path: Negotiating Leadership for, in, of, and with Diverse Communities," *Leadership and Policy in Schools* 14, no. 1 (2015): 1–11.
6. Cathyrn Magno and Margo Schiff, "Culturally Responsive Leadership: Best Practice in Integrating Immigrant Students," *Intercultural Education* 21, no. 1 (2010): 87–91; James Ryan, "Inclusive Leadership and Social Justice for Schools," *Leadership and Policy in Schools* 5 (2006): 3–17; Marcelo M. Suárez-Orozco, "The Challenge of a Changing Nation," in *21st Century Principal: Current Issues in Leadership and Policy*, ed. M. Pierce and D. L. Stapleton (Harvard Education Press, 2003); George Theoharis and Julie Causton-Theoharis, "Include, Belong, Learn," *Educational Leadership* 68, no. 2 (2010): 1–6.
7. John Boli, Francisco O. Ramirez, and John W. Meyer, "Explaining the Origins and Expansion of Mass Education," *Comparative Education Review* 29, no. 2 (1985): 145–70; Shunah Chung and Daniel J. Walsh, "Unpacking Child-Centredness: A History of Meanings," *Journal of Curriculum Studies* 32, no. 2 (2000): 215–34.
8. Gary R. Howard, "As Diversity Grows, So Must We," *Educational Leadership* 64, no. 6 (2007): 16–22; Muhammad Khalifa, Mark Gooden, and James Davis, "Culturally Responsive School Leadership: A Synthesis of the Literature," *Review of Educational Research* 86, no. 4 (2016): 1272–311; Magno and Schiff, *Culturally Responsive Leadership*; Carolyn J. Riehl. "The Principal's Role in Creating Inclusive Schools for Diverse Students: A Review of Normative, Empirical, and Critical Literature on the Practice of Educational Administration," *Review of Educational Research* 70, no. 1 (2000): 55–81; James Ryan, *Leading Diverse Schools*, col. 2 (Springer Science and Business Media, 2003).

9. Howard, "As Diversity Grows, So Must We."
10. Riehl, "The Principal's Role in Creating Inclusive Schools."
11. Muhammad Khalifa, "A Re-New-ed Paradigm in Successful Urban School Leadership: Principal as Community Leader," *Educational Administration Quarterly* 48, no. 3 (2012): 424–67.
12. Raj Chetty, John N. Friedman, and Jonah E. Rockoff, "Measuring the Impacts of Teachers II: Teacher Value-Added and Student Outcomes in Adulthood," *American Economic Review* 104, no. 9 (2014): 2633–79; Paul Watkins, "The Principal's Role in Attracting, Retaining, and Developing New Teachers: Three Strategies for Collaboration and Support," *Clearing House: A Journal of Educational Strategies, Issues and Ideas* 79, no. 2 (2005): 83–87.
13. Susan Headden, "Beginners in the Classroom: What the Changing Demographics of Teaching Mean for Schools, Students, and Society," Carnegie Foundation for the Advancement of Teaching, September 2014, https://www.carnegiefoundation.org/wp-content/uploads/2014/09/beginners_in_classroom.pdf.
14. Linda Darling-Hammond, "Excellent Teachers Deserve Excellent Leaders," in *Education Leadership: A Bridge to School Reform* (Wallace Foundation, 2007), www.wallacefoundation.org/knowledge-center/school-leadership/key-research/Pages/Bridge-to-School-Reform.aspx.
15. Meng Tian, Mika Risku, and Kaija Collin, "A Meta-Analysis of Distributed Leadership from 2002 to 2013: Theory Development, Empirical Evidence, and Future Research Focus," *Educational Management Administration and Leadership* 44, no. 1 (2016): 146–64; Philip A. Woods, "Democratic Leadership: Drawing Distinctions with Distributed Leadership," *International Journal of Leadership in Education* 7, no. 1 (2004): 3–26.
16. Magnus O. Bassey, "Teachers as Cultural Brokers in the Midst of Diversity," *Journal of Educational Foundations* 10, no. 2 (1996): 37–52.
17. Geneva Gay, "Building Cultural Bridges: A Bold Proposal for Teacher Education," *Education and Urban Society* 25, no. 3 (1993): 285–99.
18. Luis Moll, Cathy Amanti, Deborah Neff, and Norma Gonzalez, "Funds of Knowledge for Teaching: Using a Qualitative Approach to Connect Homes and Classrooms," in *Funds of Knowledge* (Routledge, 2006).
19. Geneva Gay, *Culturally Responsive Teaching: Theory, Research, and Practice*, 2nd ed. (Teachers College Press, 2010), 106.

Chapter 6

I wish to acknowledge the research assistance of Dr. Dustin Pappas who took a deep dive into the philosophy of democracy.

1. Principal Margaret Court is a composite of more than twenty different school principals who were part of my research in studying newcomers in two international settings.
2. Claudia Ruitenberg, "The Practice of Equality: A Critical Understanding of Democratic Citizenship Education," *Democracy and Education* 23, no. 1 (2015): 1–8.
3. Gert Biesta, *Learning Democracy in School and Society* (Sense, 2011), 1.
4. Lynn Davies, "Education and Violent Extremism: Insights from Complexity Theory," *Education and Conflict Review* 2 (2019): 21.
5. Peter Gronn, "Administrators and Their Talk," *Educational Management and Administration* 21, no. 1 (1993): 30–39, https://doi.org/10.1177/174114329302100105.

Chapter 7

1. Nour Halabi, *Radical Hospitality: American Policy, Media, and Immigration* (Rutgers University Press, 2022).
2. Nancy Deutsch, "A Second Home," in *A Place to Call Home: Afterschool Programs for Urban Youth*, ed. Barton J. Hirsch (American Psychological Association, 2005), 41–56; Cheuk Fan Ng, "Canada as a New Place: The Immigrant's Experience," *Journal of Environmental Psychology* 18, no. 1 (1998): 55–67, https://doi.org/10.1006/jevp.1997.0065.
3. Halabi, *Radical Hospitality*.
4. Bryan Mann and Jaclyn Dudek. "Education Policy Is Spatial Policy: Using Spatial Imaginaries to Enhance Education Policy Research," *Policy Futures in Education* 22, no. 5 (2024): 826–45, https://doi.org/10.1177/14782103231186296.
5. Travis J. Bristol and Marcelle Mentor. "Policing and Teaching: The Positioning of Black Male Teachers as Agents in the Universal Carceral Apparatus," *Urban Review* 50, no. 2 (2018): 218–34, https://doi.org/10.1007/s11256-018-0447-z; Connie Wun, "Schools as Carceral Sites: A Unidirectional War Against Girls of Color," in *Education at War: The Fight for Students of Color in America's Public Schools*, ed. Arschad Imtiaz Ali and Tracy Lachica Buenavista (Fordham University Press, 2018), 206–27.
6. Maria Lewicka, "Place Attachment: How Far Have We Come in the Last 40 Years?," *Journal of Environmental Psychology* 31, no. 3 (2011): 207–30, https://doi.org/10.1016/j.jenvp.2010.10.001; Maria Vittoria Giuliani, "Theory of Attachment and Place Attachment," in *Psychological Theories for Environmental Issues*, ed. Mirilia Bonnes, Terence Lee, and Marino Bonaiuto (Ashgate, 2003), 137–70; Setha M. Low and Irwin Altman, "Place Attachment: A Conceptual Inquiry," in *Place Attachment*, ed. Irwin Altman and Setha M. Low (Plenum Press, 1992), 1–12.
7. Leila Scannell and Robert Gifford, "Defining Place Attachment: A Tripartite Organizing Framework," *Journal of Environmental Psychology* 30, no. 1 (2010): 1–10, https://doi.org/10.1016/j.jenvp.2009.09.006.

Chapter 8

1. Local Authorities in England are municipal bodies that are responsible for economic, social, and environmental governance in their area, including schools. Local Authorities consist of elected councilors.
2. Refugee Council, *Quarterly Asylum Statistics* (UK, 2022).
3. "Operation Warm Welcome Under Way to Support Afghans Arrival in the UK," Government of the United Kingdom, September 1, 2021, https://www.gov.uk/government/news/operation-warm-welcome-underway-to-support-afghan-arrivals-in-the-uk.
4. Ofsted is the Office for Standards in Education, Children's Services and Skills, in England. A nonministerial department that reports to the UK Parliament, it is responsible for inspecting and evaluating a range of educational institutions and social services across a four-point scale of "outstanding," "good," "requires improvement," and "inadequate." Ofsted, Government of the United Kingdom, 2023.
5. Halleli Pinson and Madeline Arnot, "Local Conceptualisation of the Education of Asylum-Seeking and Refugee Students: From Hostile to Holistic Models," *International Journal of Inclusive Education* 14, no. 3 (2010): 247, https://doi.org/10.1080/13603110802504523.

6. Mary Mendenhall and Lesley Bartlett, "Academic and Extracurricular Support for Refugee Students in the US: Lessons Learned," *Theory into Practice* 57, no. 2 (2018): 109, https://doi.org/10.1080/00405841.2018.1469910.
7. Angharad Reakes, "The Education of Asylum Seekers: Some UK Case Studies," *Research in Education* 77, no. 1 (2007): 92, https://doi.org/10.7227/RIE.77.7.
8. Linda Morrice, Linda Tip, Rupert Brown, and Michael Collyer, "Resettled Refugee Youth and Education: Aspiration and Reality," *Journal of Youth Studies* 23, no. 3 (2020): 388; Reakes, "Education of Asylum Seekers," 109.
9. Rachel Hek, "The Role of Education in the Settlement of Young Refugees in the UK: The Experiences of Young Refugees," *Practice: Social Work in Action* 17, no. 3 (2005): 151, https://doi.org/10.1080/09503150500285115.
10. Yeonjai Rah, Shangmin Choi, and Thu Suong Thi Nguyen, "Building Bridges Between Refugee Parents and Schools," *International Journal of Leadership in Education* 12, no. 4 (2010): 347, https://doi.org/10.1080/13603120802609867.
11. Joanna McIntyre and Christine Hall, "Barriers to the Inclusion of Refugee and Asylum-Seeking Children in Schools in England," *Educational Review* 72, no. 5 (2020): 583, https://doi.org/10.1080/00131911.2018.1544115.
12. Khalid Arar, Deniz Orucu, and Gulnur Ak Kucukcayir, "Culturally Relevant School Leadership for Syrian Refugee Students in Challenging Circumstances," *Educational Management Administration & Leadership* 47, no. 6 (2019): 960, https://doi.org/10.1177/1741143218775430.
13. Omer Caliskan, "Ecology of Social Justice Leadership: How Schools Are Responsive to Refugee Students," *Multicultural Education Review* 12, no. 4 (2020): 267, https://doi.org/10.1080/2005615X.2020.1842656.
14. Lauri Johnson, "Culturally Responsive Leadership for Community Empowerment," *Multicultural Education Review* 6, no. 2 (2014): 145–70.
15. Arar et al., "Culturally Relevant School Leadership for Syrian Refugee Students," 960.
16. Angela Rose, "The Role of Teacher Agency in Refugee Education," *Australian Educational Researcher* 46 (2019): 75, https://doi.org/10.1007/s13384-018-0280-0.
17. McIntyre and Hall, "Barriers to the Inclusion of Refugee and Asylum-Seeking Children," 583.
18. Rose, "Role of Teacher Agency in Refugee Education," 75.
19. Arar et al., "Culturally Relevant School Leadership for Syrian Refugee Students," 964.
20. Khalid Arar and Izhar Oplatka, "Community-Based Leadership," in *Advanced Theories of Educational Leadership*, ed. Khalid Arar and Izhar Oplatka (Springer, 2022), 49.
21. Muhammad Khalifa, *Culturally Responsive School Leadership* (Harvard Education Press, 2020), 1–232.
22. Arar and Oplatka, "Culturally Relevant Leadership," 74.

Chapter 9

1. Heidi L. Ballard, Angela Calabrese Barton, and Bharat Upadhyay, "Community-Driven Science and Science Education: Living in and Navigating the Edges of Equity, Justice, and Science Learning," *Journal of Research in Science Teaching* 60, no. 8 (2023): 1613–26, https://doi.org/10.1002/tea.21880.
2. Daniel Morales-Doyle, *Transformative Science Teaching: A Catalyst for Justice and Sustainability* (Harvard Education Press, 2024).
3. Minjung Ryu, Mavreen Rose S. Tuvilla, and Casey Elizabeth Wright, "Resettled Burmese Refugee Youths' Identity Work in an Afterschool STEM Learning Setting," *Journal of*

Research in Childhood Education 33, no. 1 (2019): 84–97, https://doi.org/10.1080/02568543.2018.1531454; Minjung Ryu, Shannon Mary Daniel, Mavreen Rose S. Tuvilla, and Casey Elizabeth Wright, "Refugee Youth, Critical Science Literacy, and Transformative Possibilities," in *Proceedings of the International Conference of the Learning Sciences 2020* (International Society of the Learning Sciences, 2020), 569–72; Edna Tan and Beverly Faircloth, "One World: Refugee Youth Incubating Epistemologies Toward Rightful Presence with/in Community-Driven STEM," *Journal of Research in Science Teaching* 60, no. 8 (2023): 1627–56, https://doi.org/10.1002/tea.21846; Susan G. Harper, "Engaging Karen Refugee Students in Science Learning Through a Cross-Cultural Learning Community," *International Journal of Science Education* 39, no. 3 (2017): 358–76, https://doi.org/10.1080/09500693.2017.1283547; Joseph A. Johnson and Mihwa Park, "Creating School Scientific Communities Among Urban Refugee ELL Populations," *European Journal of Science and Mathematics Education* 10, no. 1 (2022): 87–103, https://doi.org/10.30935/scimath/11380.

4. Megan Bang, Beth Warren, Ann S. Rosebery, and Douglas Medin, "Desettling Expectations in Science Education," *Human Development* 55, nos. 5–6 (2012): 302–18, https://doi.org/10.1159/000345322; Molly Shea and Jose Sandoval, "Using Historical and Political Understanding to Design for Equity in Science Education," *Science Education* 104, no. 1 (2020): 105–29, https://doi.org/10.1002/sce.21555; Natalie R. Davis and Janelle Schaeffer, "Troubling Troubled Waters in Elementary Science Education: Politics, Ethics, and Black Children's Conceptions of Water [Justice] in the Era of Flint," *Cognition and Instruction* 37, no. 3 (2019): 367–89, https://doi.org/10.1080/07370008.2019.1624548; Tia C. Madkins and Maxine McKinney de Royston, "Illuminating Political Clarity in Culturally Relevant Science Instruction," *Science Education* 103, no. 6 (2019): 1319–46, https://doi.org/10.1002/sce.21542.
5. Norma González, Luis C. Moll, and Cathy Amanti, eds., *Funds of Knowledge: Theorizing Practices in Households, Communities, and Classrooms* (Routledge, 2006).
6. William G. Wraga, "What's the Problem with a 'Rigorous Academic Curriculum'?: Setting New Terms for Students' School Experiences," *Clearing House* 84, no. 2 (2011): 59–64, https://doi.org/10.1080/00098655.2010.511307.
7. Ballard, Calabrese Barton, and Upadhyay, "Community-Driven Science and Science Education."
8. Morales-Doyle, *Transformative Science Teaching.*
9. Morales-Doyle, *Transformative Science Teaching.*
10. Thomas M. Philip, foreword to *Teaching Toward Rightful Presence in Middle School STEM*, by Edna Tan and Angela Calabrese Barton (Harvard Education Press, 2023), viii.
11. Roozbeh Shirazi, "Between Hosts and Guests: Conditional Hospitality and Citizenship in an American Suburban School," *Curriculum Inquiry* 48, no. 1 (2018): 95–114, https://doi.org/10.1080/03626784.2017.1409592.
12. Tan and Calabrese Barton, *Teaching Toward Rightful Presence in Middle School STEM*, 4.
13. John Dewey, *Democracy and Education: An Introduction to the Philosophy of Education*, introduction by Patricia H. Hinchey (Simon and Brown, 2018).
14. Django Paris and H. Samy Alim, *Culturally Sustaining Pedagogies: Teaching and Learning for Justice in a Changing World* (Teachers College Press, 2017).
15. Morales-Doyle, *Transformative Science Teaching.*
16. Morales-Doyle, *Transformative Science Teaching.*
17. Heather F. Clark, Symone A. Gyles, Darlene Tieu, Shriya Venkatesh, and William A. Sandoval, "Exploring Science Teachers' Efforts to Frame Phenomena in the Community,"

Journal of Research in Science Teaching 61, no. 9 (2024): 2104–32, https://doi.org/10.1002/tea.21945.

Chapter 10

1. L. A. Shepard and T. B. Reed *A Research Agenda for Year-Round Schools: Executive Summary* (1975); B. Heyns, "Schooling and Cognitive Development: Is There a Season for Learning?," *Child Development* 49, no. 1 (1978): 149–65, https://doi.org/10.2307/1128610; J. Johnston, J. Riley, C. Ryan, and L. Kelly-Vance "Evaluation of a Summer Reading Program to Reduce Summer Setback," *Reading and Writing Quarterly* 31, no. 4 (2015): 334–50, https://doi.org/10.1080/10573569.2013.857978.
2. Johnston et al., "Evaluation of a Summer Reading Program to Reduce Summer Setback"; Shepard and Reed, *Research Agenda for Year-Round Schools.*
3. W. Saunders, C. Goldenberg, and D. Marcelletti, "English Language Development Guidelines for Instruction," *American Educator* 37, no. 2 (2013): 13–25.
4. San Leandro USD English Learner Department, "Structured Language Protocols," June 2012, accessed September 23, 2025, https://studylib.net/doc/18382054/structured-language-protocols---san-leandro-unified-schoo.
5. L. M. Shea, J. H. Sandholtz, and T. B. Shanahan, "We Are All Talking: A Whole-School Approach to Professional Development for Teachers of English Learners," *Professional Development in Education* 44, no. 2 (2018): 190–208, https://doi.org/10.1080/19415257.2016.1274267.
6. S. L. Woulfin and J. G. Rigby, "Coaching for Coherence: How Instructional Coaches Lead Change in the Evaluation Era," *Educational Researcher* 46, no. 6 (2017): 323–28, https://doi.org/10.3102/0013189X17725525.

Chapter 11

1. Dorothy M. Steele and Becki Cohn-Vargas, *Identity Safe Classrooms, Grades K–5: Places to Belong and Learn* (Corwin Press, 2013).
2. Laura E. Hernández and Linda Darling-Hammond, "Creating Identity-Safe Schools and Classrooms" (Learning Policy Institute, 2022), https://learningpolicyinstitute.org/media/3843/download?inline&file=WCE_Identity-Safe_Schools_Classrooms_REPORT.pdf.
3. Hernández and Darling-Hammond, "Creating Identity-Safe Schools and Classrooms."
4. "What Is a Refugee?," UNHCR (United Nations High Commissioner for Refugees) US, accessed December 12, 2024, https://www.unhcr.org/us/what-refugee.
5. Yen Le Espiritu, *Body Counts: The Vietnam War and Militarized Refugees* (University of California Press, 2014); Khatharya Um, "Exiled Memory: History, Identity, and Remembering in Southeast Asia and Southeast Asian Diaspora," *Positions: Asia Critique* 20, no. 3 (2012): 831–50.
6. "Thai in the U.S. Fact Sheet," Pew Research Center, April 29, 2021, https://www.pewresearch.org/socialtrends/fact-sheet/asian-americans-thai-in-the-u-s/.
7. Van T. Lac, "From the Flatlands of Oakland to the Ivory Towers of Higher Education: A Counter-Narrative of a Southeast Asian Refugee," *Journal of Southeast Asian American Education and Advancement* 15, no. 2 (2009): article 7; Amanda Keddie, "Refugee Education and Justice Issues of Representation, Redistribution, and Recognition," *Cambridge Journal of Education* 42, no. 2 (2012): 197–212; Jill Koyama, "Constructing Gender: Refugee Women Working in the United States," *Journal of Refugee Studies* 28, no. 2 (2015): 258–75.

8. Josue Lopez and Erica Fernandez, "'You Never Know When You Will See Him Again': Understanding the Intersectional Dimensions of Immigration, Indigeneity, and Language for Unaccompanied Indigenous Minors," *Journal of Cases in Educational Leadership* 23, no. 1 (2020): 6.
9. Espiritu, *Body Counts*; Linn Biorklund and Jennifer Hyndman, "Refugee Studies Has Always Been Critical," in *Routledge Handbook of Immigrant and Refugee Studies*, 2nd ed., ed. Anna Triandafyllidou (Routledge, 2022).
10. Hernández and Darling-Hammond, "Creating Identity-Safe Schools and Classrooms."

Chapter 12

1. Karen L. Mapp and Paul J. Kuttner, "Partners in Education: A Dual Capacity-Building Framework for Family-School Partnerships" (SEDL [Southwest Educational Development Laboratory], 2013).
2. Jill Koyama and Fortidas Rwehumbiza Bakuza, "A Timely Opportunity for Change: Increasing Refugee Parental Involvement in US Schools," *Journal of Educational Change* 18, no. 3 (2017): 311–35.
3. Teresa S. McKay, *Effective Family Engagement Policies: A Guide for Early Childhood Administrators* (Routledge, 2021).
4. José M. Bolívar and Janet H. Chrispeels, "Enhancing Parent Leadership Through Building Social and Intellectual Capital," *American Educational Research Journal* 48, no. 1 (2011): 4–38.
5. Anne T. Henderson and Karen L. Mapp, *A New Wave of Evidence: The Impact of School, Family, and Community Connections on Student Achievement* (National Center for Family and Community Connections with Schools, 2002).
6. Maia Bloomfield Cucchiara and Erin McNamara Horvat, "Perils and Promises: Middle-Class Parental Involvement in Urban Schools," *American Educational Research Journal* 46, no. 4 (2009): 974–1004.
7. Bolívar and Chrispeels, "Enhancing Parent Leadership Through Building Social and Intellectual Capital," 6.
8. Guadalupe Valdés, "Dual-Language Immersion Programs: A Cautionary Note Concerning the Education of Language-Minority Students," *Harvard Educational Review* 67, no. 3 (1997): 391–430; Angela Valenzuela, "Subtractive Schooling, Caring Relations, and Social Capital in the Schooling of US-Mexican Youth," in *Beyond Silenced Voices: Class, Race, and Gender in United States Schools*, ed. Lois Weis and Michelle Fine (State University of New York Press, 2005), 83–94.
9. Koyama and Rwehumbiza Bakuza, "A Timely Opportunity for Change."
10. Jerome Cranston, Shauna Labman, and Stephanie Crook, "Reframing Parental Involvement as Social Engagement: A Study of Recently Arrived Arabic-Speaking Refugee Parents' Understandings of Involvement in Their Children's Education," *Canadian Journal of Education* 44, no. 2 (2021): 371–404.
11. Cranston et al., "Reframing Parental Involvement as Social Engagement."
12. Rebecca Georgis, Rebecca J. Gokiert, Donna Mae Ford, and Mulki Ali, "Creating Inclusive Parent Engagement Practices: Lessons Learned from a School Community Collaborative Supporting Newcomer Refugee Families," *Multicultural Education* 21, nos. 3–4 (2014): 23; J. Lynn McBrien, "The Importance of Context: Vietnamese, Somali, and Iranian Refugee Mothers Discuss Their Resettled Lives and Involvement in Their Children's Schools," *Compare* 41, no. 1 (2011): 75–90; Rahat Zaidi, Christine Oliver, Tom Strong, and Hanan

Alwarraq, "Behind Successful Refugee Parental Engagement: The Barriers and Challenges," *Canadian Journal of Education* 44, no. 4 (2021): 907–37.

Chapter 13

1. Tea Rozman Clark, Julie Vang, and Tom Kaczynski, *Our Stories Carried Us Here: A Graphic Novel Anthology* (Green Card Voices, 2021).
2. "Figures at a Glance," UNHCR (United Nations High Commissioner for Refugees), updated June 13, 2024, https://www.unhcr.org/us/about-unhcr/who-we-are/figures-glance.
3. Convention Relating to the Status of Refugees (1951), United Nations Human Rights, Office of the High Commissioner, 2, accessed August 29, 2025, https://www.ohchr.org/sites/default/files/refugees.pdf.
4. "Resettlement Handbook," UNHCR, accessed August 29, 2025, https://www.unhcr.org/resettlement-handbook/.
5. "Fact Sheet: U.S. Refugee Resettlement," National Immigration Forum, updated November 5, 2020, https://immigrationforum.org/article/fact-sheet-u-s-refugee-resettlement/; "Iraqi and Afghan Special Immigrant Visa Programs," Congress.gov, https://www.congress.gov/crs-product/R43725.
6. Julia Ann McWilliams and Sally Wesley Bonet, "Continuums of Precarity: Refugee Youth Transitions in American High Schools," *International Journal of Lifelong Education* 35, no. 2 (2016), https://doi.org/10.1080/02601370.2016.1164468; Linda Morrice, Linda K. Tip, Rupert Brown, and Michael Collyer, "Resettled Refugee Youth and Education: Aspiration and Reality," *Journal of Youth Studies* 23, no. 3 (2019), https://doi.org/10.1080/13676261.2019.1612047.
7. Morrice et al., "Resettled Refugee Youth and Education."
8. Marco Antonsich, "Searching for Belonging: An Analytical Framework," *Geography Compass* 4, no. 6 (2010), https://doi.org/10.1111/j.1749-8198.2009.00317.x; Beth R. Crisp, "Belonging, Connectedness, and Social Exclusion," *Journal of Social Inclusion* 1, no. 2 (2010); Ignacio Correa-Velez, Sandra M. Gifford, and Adrian G. Barnett, "Longing to Belong: Social Inclusion and Wellbeing Among Youth with Refugee Backgrounds in the First Three Years in Melbourne, Australia," *Social Science and Medicine* 71, no. 8 (2010), https://doi.org/10.1016/j.socscimed.2010.07.018.
9. Linda P. Juang, Jeffry A. Simpson, Richard M. Lee, Alexander J. Rothman, Peter F. Titzmann, Maja K. Schachner, et al., "Using Attachment and Relational Perspectives to Understand Adaptation and Resilience Among Immigrant and Refugee Youth," *American Psychologist* 73, no. 6 (2018), https://doi.org/10.1037/amp0000286; Emrah Cinkara, "The Role of L+ Turkish and English Learning in Resilience: A Case of Syrian Students at Gaziantep University," *Journal of Language and Linguistics Studies* 13, no. 2 (2017).

Chapter 14

1. University Canada West, "What Is the Difference Between Colleges and Universities in Canada," UCW blog hub, March 15, 2024, https://www.ucanwest.ca/blog/education-careers-tips/what-is-the-difference-between-colleges-and-universities-in-canada/.
2. "Refugee Data Finder," UNHCR: The UN Refugee Agency, last updated June 12, 2025, https://www.unhcr.org/refugee-statistics .
3. Snežana Ratković, D. Kovačević, C. A. Brewer, C. Ellis, N. Ahmed, and J. Baptiste-Brady, *Supporting Refugee Students in Canada: Building on What We Have Learned in the Past 20 Years* (Social Sciences and Humanities Research Council of Canada. St. Catharines:

Brock University, 2017); Louis Volante, Don Klinger, Özge Bilgili, and Melissa Siegel, "Making Sense of the Performance (Dis)Advantage for Immigrant Students Across Canada," *Canadian Journal of Education* 40, no. 3 (2017): 329–61, https://journals.sfu.ca/cje/index.php/cje-rce/article/view/2557; Sandra Taylor and Ravinder Kaur Sidhu, "Supporting Refugee Students in Schools: What Constitutes Inclusive Education?," *International Journal of Inclusive Education* 16, no. 1 (2012): 39–56.

4. Raghad Ebied, "Settlement Workers in Schools' (SWIS) Support for K–12 Refugee Students: A Resilience and Compassion-Based Approach" (PhD diss., Western University, 2023), 127.
5. B. Lavelle, L. Flook, and D. Ghahremani, "A Call for Compassion and Care in Education: Toward a More Comprehensive Prosocial Framework for the Field," in *The Oxford Handbook of Compassion Science*, ed. Emma M. Seppälä, Emiliana Simon-Thomas, Stephanie L. Brown, Monica C. Worline, C. Daryl Cameron, James R. Doty (Oxford University Press, 2017), 1–19; K. Pieloch, M. McCullough, and A. Marks, "Resilience of Children with Refugee Status: A Research Review," *Canadian Psychology/Psychologie canadienne* 57, no. 4 (2016): 330, https://doi.org/10.1037/cap0000073.
6. Ebied, "Settlement Workers in Schools."
7. Lavelle et al., "A Call for Compassion and Care in Education."
8. Lily Kaufmann, "Integration in Canada: A Systematic Review of the Youth Experience," *International Journal of Intercultural Relations* 84 (2021): 52–64, https://doi.org/10.1016/j.ijintrel.2021.06.010.
9. Ratkovic et al., "Supporting Refugee Students in Canada."
10. "Settlement Workers in Schools," Cross Cultural Learners Center, accessed October 8, 2025, https://www.lcclc.org/settlement-workers.
11. Ebied, "Settlement Workers in Schools," 2.
12. Ebied, "Settlement Workers in Schools," 46; P. Hopkins and M. Hill, "The Needs and Strengths of Unaccompanied Asylum-Seeking Children and Young People in Scotland," *Child & Family Social Work* 15, no. 4 (2010): 399–408, https://doi.org/10.1111/j.1365-2206.2010.00687.x
13. Pieloch et al., "Resilience of Children," 331.
14. Research and Evaluation Branch, Immigration, Refugees, and Citizenship Canada (IRCC), "Evaluation of the Settlement Workers in Schools (SWIS) Initiative," Government of Canada, update July 13, 2022, https://www.canada.ca/en/immigration-refugees-citizenship/corporate/reports-statistics/evaluations/settlement-workers-school-initiative.html.
15. Ebied, "Settlement Workers in Schools," 103

Chapter 15

1. Sophia Rodriguez, T. Monreal, and J. Howard, "'It's About Hearing and Understanding Their Stories': Teacher Empathy and Socio-Political Awareness Toward Newcomer Undocumented Students in the New Latino South," *Journal of Latinos and Education* 19, no. 2 (2018): 181–98, https://doi.org/10.1080/15348431.2018.1489812.
2. "Central America Refugee Crisis," USA for UNHCR (United Nations High Commissioner for Refugees), accessed August 27, 2024. https://www.unrefugees.org/emergencies/central-america/.
3. Nicole Ward and Jeanne Batalova, "Central American Immigrants in the United States," *Migration Policy Institute*, May 10, 2023, https://www.migrationpolicy.org/article/central-american-immigrants-united-states-2021.

4. "Central American Minors (CAM) Program," U.S. Citizenship and Immigration Services, accessed March 7, 2024, https://www.uscis.gov/CAM#_blank.
5. *Children on the Run* (UNHCR, 2016), https://www.unhcr.org/us/media/children-run-full-report.
6. Sophia Rodriguez, Lisa Lopez-Escobar, and Katya Murillo-Valencia, "The Bureaucratic Paradox: Newcomer Unaccompanied Children, Educational Access, and Strategies for Increasing Flourishing Through an Ecosystem of Care," in *Teaching and Learning in the New Latino Diaspora* (Teachers College Press, 2024).
7. "Central American Minors (CAM) Program." U.S. Department of State, accessed August 27, 2024, https://www.state.gov/refugee-admissions/central-american-minors-cam-program/.
8. Rodriguez et al., "Bureaucratic Paradox."
9. Sophia Rodriguez and Eric Macias, "'Even Being a Citizen Is Not a Privilege Here': Undocumented Latinx Immigrant Youth and Perceptions of Racialized Citizenship," *Sociology of Race and Ethnicity* 9, no. 1 (2023): 21–36, https://doi.org/10.1177/23326492221114812.
10. Sean D. Cleary, Ryan Snead, Daniela Dietz-Chavez, Ivonne Rivera, and Mark C. Edberg, "Immigrant Trauma and Mental Health Outcomes Among Latino Youth," *Journal of Immigrant and Minority Health* 20 (2018): 1053–59, https://doi.org/10.1007/s10903-017-0673-6.
11. Rodriguez et al., "Bureaucratic Paradox."
12. Leticia Alvarez Gutiérrez, Taeyeon Kim, Sonny Partola, Paul J. Kuttner, Amadou Niang, Alma Yanagui, et al. "Community-Centered School Leadership: Radical Care and Aperturas During COVID-19," *AERA Open* 8 (2022): 23328584221096465, https://doi.org/10.1177/2332858422109; Monisha Bajaj and Sailaja Suresh, "The 'Warm Embrace' of a Newcomer School for Immigrant and Refugee Youth," *Theory into Practice* 57, no. 2 (2018): 91–98, https://doi.org/10.1080/00405841.2018.1425815; Courtney Pollack, Maria Theodorakakis, and Mary E. Walsh, "Leveraging Integrated Student Support to Identify and Address COVID-19-Related Needs for Students, Families, and Teachers," *AERA Open* 7 (2021): 23328584211058473, https://doi.org/10.1177/23328584211058473; Sophia Rodriguez, Lisa Lopez-Escobar, and Staci Pippin-Kottkamp. "Toward Race-Conscious Care-Based Healing to Support Latino Immigrant Youth," *Educational Policy* 39, no. 4 (2024), https://doi.org/10.1177/08959048241265509; Sophia Rodriguez, Benjamin Roth, and Leticia Villarreal Sosa, "'Sometimes, It's About Breaking Rules': School Social Workers' Role as Nepantleras and Equity for Undocumented Students," *Social Service Review* 94, no. 4 (2020): 748–80, https://doi.org/10.1086/712044.
13. Sophia Rodriguez and Emily R. Crawford, "School-Based Personnel Advocacy for Undocumented Students Through Collective Leadership in Urban Schools: A Comparative Case Study," *Journal of Research on Leadership Education* 18, no. 3 (2023): 347–77, https://doi.org/10.1177/19427751221081887.
14. Emily R. Crawford, David Aguayo, and Fernando Valle, "Counselors as Leaders in Advocating for Undocumented Students' Education," *Journal of Research on Leadership Education* 14, no. 2 (2019): 119–50, https://doi.org/10.1177/1942775117739301.
15. Principal, interview with authors, October 8, 2023.
16. Principal, interview, October 8, 2023.
17. Bajaj and Suresh, "'Warm Embrace' of a Newcomer School"; Lisa M. Dorner, Kelly Harris, and Blake Willoughby, "Policy Enactment During a Pandemic: How One School Responded to COVID-19 in Negotiation with a Nonprofit Partner," *AERA Open* 8 (2022):

23328584221078328, https://doi.org/10.1177/23328584221078328; Alexandra E. Pavlakis, J. Kessa Roberts, and Meredith P. Richards, "When the Old Will No Longer Do: School and Community Practices for Student Homelessness amid COVID-19," *AERA Open* 7 (2021): 23328584211064305, https://doi.org/10.1177/23328584211064305.
18. Counselor, interview with authors, February 4, 2022.
19. Counselor, interview with authors, November 7, 2023.
20. Emily R. Crawford and Fernando Valle, "Educational Justice for Undocumented Students: How School Counselors Encourage Student Persistence in Schools," *Education Policy Analysis Archives* 24, no. 98 (2016): 98, https://doi.org/10.14507/epaa.24.2427; Joanna Dreby, "The Burden of Deportation on Children in Mexican Immigrant Families," *Journal of Marriage and Family* 74, no. 4 (2012): 829–45, https://doi.org/10.1111/j.1741-3737.2012.00989.x; Carola Suárez-Orozco, Marie Onaga, and Cécile de Lardemelle, "Promoting Academic Engagement Among Immigrant Adolescents Through School-Family-Community Collaboration," *Professional School Counseling* 14, no. 1 (2010): 2156759X1001400103.
21. Assistant principal, interview with authors, November 7, 2023.
22. Sophia Rodriguez, "'We're Building the Community; It's a Hub for Democracy': Lessons Learned from a Library-Based, School-District Partnership and Program to Increase Belonging for Newcomer Immigrant and Refugee Youth," *Children and Youth Services Review* 102 (2019): 135–44, https://doi.org/10.1016/j.childyouth.2019.04.025.
23. Christine Jean Yeh, Samantha Stanley, Crystal A. Ramirez, and Noah E. Borrero, "Navigating the 'Dual Pandemics': The Cumulative Impact of the COVID-19 Pandemic and Rise in Awareness of Racial Injustices Among High School Students of Color in Urban Schools," *Urban Education* (2022): 4208592210978-, https://doi.org/10.1177/00420859221097884.
24. Randi Capps, Jodi Berger Cardoxo, Kalina Brabeck, Michael Fix, and Ariel G. Ruiz Soto, *Immigration Enforcement and the Mental Health of Latino High School Students* (Migration Policy Institute, 2020).
25. Assistant principal, interview November 7, 2023.
26. Margary Martin and Carola Suárez-Orozco, "What It Takes: Promising Practices for Immigrant Origin Adolescent Newcomers," *Theory into Practice* 57, no. 2 (2018): 82–90, https://doi.org/10.1080/00405841.2018.1425816.
27. Martin and Suárez-Orozco, "What It Takes."
28. Rodriguez, "'We're Building the Community,'" 2019.
29. Rodriguez et al., "Toward Race-Conscious Care."

Chapter 16

1. Gaudet is a pseudonym for the city where the study took place.
2. US Census Bureau, *QuickFacts* (2019).
3. "By All Means Initiatives," Harvard EdRedesign, Harvard Graduate School of Education, accessed August 31, 2025, https://edredesign.org/our-work/by-all-means-initiative.
4. Megan F. King, Vivian F. Renó, and Evlyn M. L. M. Novo, "The Concept, Dimensions, and Methods of Assessment of Human Well-Being Within a Socioecological Context: A Literature Review," *Social Indicators Research* 116 (2014): 681–98, https://doi.org/10.1007/s11205-013-0320-0.
5. Betty S. Lai, Gabrielle Oliveira, Rebecca Lowenhaupt, Mauricio Montes, and Alexa Riobueno-Naylor, "The Important Role of Schools Following Disaster Events," National Academy of Medicine, December 9, 2024, https://doi.org/10.31478/202412a.

6. For examples of this research, see Sarah A. Havlik, Cheryl Sanders, and Elizabeth Wilson, "Preparing Students Experiencing Homelessness for College: Considerations for Counselors and Other Supportive Personnel," *Journal of College Access* 4, no. 1 (2018), https://scholarworks.wmich.edu/jca/vol4/iss1/3; Joseph F. Murphy and Karen J. Tobin, "Homelessness Comes to School," *Phi Delta Kappan* 93, no. 3 (2011): 32–37, https://eric.ed.gov/?id=EJ964320.
7. For data, see Cirenia Chavez Villegas, Arash Bordbar, Tristan McConnell, Becky Telford, Charlie Dunmore, Laura Bowles, et al., comp. and prod., *UNHCR Education Report 2023: Unlocking Potential—The Right to Education and Opportunity,* United Nations High Commissioner for Refugees (UNHCR), 2023, https://www.unhcr.org/media/unhcr-education-report-2023-unlocking-potential-right-education-and-opportunity.
8. Khalid Arar, *School Leadership for Refugees' Education: Social Justice Leadership for Immigrant, Migrants, and Refugees* (Routledge, 2020), https://doi.org/10.4324/9780429021770; Emily R. Crawford, "The Ethic of Community and Incorporating Undocumented Immigrant Concerns into Ethical School Leadership," *Educational Administration Quarterly* 53, no. 2 (2017): 147–79, https://doi.org/10.1177/0013161X16687005.
9. Jongyeon Ee and Patricia Gándara, "The Impact of Immigration Enforcement on the Nation's Schools," *American Educational Research Journal* 57, no. 2 (2020): 840–71, https://doi.org/10.3102/0002831219862; Rebecca Lowenhaupt, Dana B. Dabach, and Angela Mangual Figueroa, "Safety and Belonging in Immigrant-Serving Districts: Domains of Educator Practice in a Charged Political Landscape," *AERA Open* 7 (2021), https://doi.org/10.1177/23328584211040084.
10. Aymen Taysum and Khalid Arar, "Turbulence, Empowerment, and Marginalized Groups: A Comparative Analysis of Five International Governance Systems," in *Turbulence in Six International Education Governance Systems*, ed. Aymen Taysum and Khalid Arar (Emerald, 2018), 237–71.
11. Khalid Arar, Deniz Örücü, and Sedat Gümüş, "Educational Leadership and Policy Studies in Refugee Education: A Systematic Review of Existing Research," *Educational Review* 76, no. 4 (2022), https://doi.org/10.1080/00131911.2022.2066632.
12. Lowenhaupt et al., "Safety and Belonging in Immigrant-Serving Districts"; Sofia Rodriguez, "Community-School Partnerships as Racial Projects: Examining Belonging for Newcomer Migrant Youth in Urban Education," *Urban Education* (2020), https://doi.org/10.1177/0042085920959126.
13. John M. Bryson, Barbara C. Crosby, and Melissa M. Stone, "The Design and Implementation of Cross-Sector Collaborations: Propositions from the Literature," *Public Administration Review* 66, no. S1 (2006): S44–S55, https://doi.org/10.1111/j.1540-6210.2006.00665.x; Sarah Dryden-Peterson, Elizabeth Adelman, Michelle J. Bellino, and Vidur Chopra, "The Purposes of Refugee Education: Policy and Practice of Including Refugees in National Education Systems," *Sociology of Education* 92, no. 4 (2019): 346–66, https://doi.org/10.1177/0038040719863054; Gabriela Oliveira, "Im/migrant Children's Stories in Elementary School: Caring and Making Space in the Classroom," *Diaspora, Indigenous, and Minority Education* 15, no. 4 (2021): 224–32.
14. Richard Rothstein, *Class and Schools: Using Social, Economic, and Educational Reform to Close the Black-White Achievement Gap* (Economic Policy Institute, 2004); Aaron Schutz, "Home Is a Prison in the Global City: The Tragic Failure of School-Based Community Engagement Strategies," *Review of Educational Research* 76, no. 4 (2006): 691–743.
15. Sarah Bruhn and Roberto G. Gonzales, "Geographies of Belonging: Migrant Youth and Relational, Community, and National Opportunities for Inclusion," *Social Sciences* 12, no. 3

(2023): 167; Cameron Duff, "Networks, Resources, and Agencies: On the Character and Production of Enabling Places," *Health and Place* 17, no. 1 (2011): 149–56.

16. Jennifer Ridgley, "Cities of Refuge: Immigration Enforcement, Police, and the Insurgent Genealogies of Citizenship in U.S. Sanctuary Cities," *Urban Geography* 29, no. 1 (2008): 53–77.
17. Bruhn and Gonzales, "Geographies of Belonging," 167; Duff, "Networks, Resources, and Agencies," 149.
18. Anne-Marie Boyer, Katherine R. Cooper, Shaun M. Dougherty, Rong Wang, and Michelle Shumate, "Predicting Community Adoption of Collective Impact in the United States: A National Scan," *Nonprofit and Voluntary Sector Quarterly* 51, no. 4 (2020), https://doi.org/10.1177/0899764020964583; William Impellizeri and Victor J. Lee, "A Comparison of IHEs and Non-IHEs as Anchor Institutions and Lead Agents of Promise Neighborhoods Projects," *Education and Urban Society* 54, no. 7 (2021): 823–47, https://doi.org/10.1177/00131245211049736; Holly M. Kingston and Fátima Da Cunha, "Embedding Social Relations into Primary Care: A Population-Based Approach," *Lifestyle Medicine* 3, no. 4 (2022), https://doi.org/10.1002/lim2.71; Peter M. Miller, Mark K. Scanlan, and Karen Phillippo, "Rural Cross-Sector Collaboration: A Social Frontier Analysis," *American Educational Research Journal* 54, no. 1 (2017): 193–215, https://doi.org/10.3102/0002831216665188.
19. Rebecca Lowenhaupt, Whitney Hegseth, Gabrielle Oliveira, and Betty Lai, "Co-Designing a Children's Cabinet: A School District–University Partnership for Youth Well-Being Post-Pandemic," *Journal of Educational Administration* 62, no. 6 (2024), https://doi.org/10.1108/jea-11-2023-0290; "Every Child and Family Is Known (ECFIK) One-Pager," Harvard EdRedesign, Harvard Graduate School of Education, September 1, 2024, https://edredesign.org/sites/default/files/documents/2025-02/ECFIK%20Fact%20Sheet.pdf.
20. Lara Gautier, Erica Di Ruggiero, Carly Jackson, Naïma Bentayeb, Marie-Jeanne Blain, Fariha Chowdhury, et al., "Learning from Intersectoral Initiatives to Respond to the Needs of Refugees, Asylum Seekers, and Migrants Without Status in the Context of COVID-19 in Quebec and Ontario: A Qualitative Multiple Case Study Protocol," *Health Research Policy and Systems* 21, no. 1 (2023), https://doi.org/10.1186/s12961-023-00991-x; M. Rein and L. Stott, "Working Together: Critical Perspectives on Six Cross-Sector Partnerships in Southern Africa," *Journal of Business Ethics* 90, no. S1: 79–89, https://doi.org/10.1007/s10551-008-9915-9; L. Stadtler and Ö Karakulak, "Broker Organizations to Facilitate Cross-Sector Collaboration: At the Crossroad of Strengthening and Weakening Effects," *Public Administration Review* 80, no. 3 (2020): 367.
21. Mohamed H. Awad, "Place and the Structuring of Cross-Sector Partnerships: The Moral and Material Conflicts over Healthcare and Homelessness," *Journal of Business Ethics* 184 (2023), https://doi.org/10.1007/s10551-023-05360-w; Bryson et al., "Design and Implementation of Cross-Sector Collaborations," 48; Anna Dubois and Lars-Erik Gadde, "'Systematic Combining'—A Decade Later," Journal of Business Research 67, no. 6 (2014): 1281, https://www.sciencedirect.com/science/article/pii/S014829631300132X.
22. Miller et al., "Rural Cross-Sector Collaboration," 196.
23. James S. Coleman, "Social Capital in the Creation of Human Capital," *American Journal of Sociology* 94, no. S1 (1988): S95–S120; Nan Lin, *Social Capital: A Theory of Social Structure and Action* (Cambridge University Press, 2001); Carrie R. Leana and Frits K. Pil, "Social Capital and Organizational Performance: Evidence from Urban Public Schools," *Organization Science* 17, no. 3: 359; https://pubsonline.informs.org/doi/abs/10.1287

/orsc.1060.0191; Mario L. Small, *Unanticipated Gains: Origins of Network Inequality in Everyday Life* (Oxford University Press, 2009).

24. Chris Brown, Alan Daly, and Yi-Hwa Liou, "Improving Trust, Improving Schools: Findings from a Social Network Analysis of 43 Primary Schools in England," *Journal of Professional Capital and Community* 1, no. 1 (2016): 69–91.
25. Lowenhaupt et al., "Safety and Belonging in Immigrant-Serving Districts."
26. Elana D. Buch, *Inequalities of Aging: Paradoxes of Independence in American Home Care* (New York University Press, 2015); Joan C. Tronto, "Care as the Work of Citizens: A Modest Proposal," in *Women and Citizenship*, ed. Marilyn Friedman (Oxford University Press, 2005), 1–23; Rosemarie Rivera-McCutchen, *Radical Care: Leading for Justice in Urban Schools* (Teachers College Press, 2021).
27. Eden Tesfa and Rebecca Lowenhaupt, "Caring Through Crisis: Newcomer Students and Their Educators During the COVID-19 Pandemic," *Voices in Urban Education* 51, no. 1 (2022).
28. Alejandro Portes and Rubén G. Rumbaut, *Immigrant America: A Portrait*, 3rd ed. (University of California Press, 2006), https://www.jstor.org/stable/10.1525/j.ctt1pq07x.

Chapter 17

1. "UNHCR Global Trends," UNHCR (United Nations High Commissioner for Refugees), 2024, https://www.unhcr.org/us/global-trends.
2. "Unaccompanied Children Released to Sponsors by State and County, FY 2014–Present," Migration Policy Institute, 2024, https://www.migrationpolicy.org/programs/data-hub/charts/unaccompanied-children-released-sponsors-state-and-county.
3. Julie Sugarman, "The Impacts on English Learners of Key State High Schools Policies and Graduation Requirements," Migration Policy Institute, 2021, https://www.migrationpolicy.org/sites/default/files/publications/high-school-policies-els-2021_final.pdf.
4. Julie Sugarman, "The Unintended Consequences for English Learners of Using the Four-Year Graduation Rate for School Accountability," Migration Policy Institute, 2019, https://www.migrationpolicy.org/sites/default/files/publications/ELGradRates-FINALWEB.pdf.
5. Lisa Dorner, "Contested Communities in a Debate over Dual Language Education: The Import of 'Public' Values on Public Policies," *Educational Policy* 4, no. 25 (2011).
6. Aída Walqui, Haiwen Chu, and Mary Schmida, "How Can Schools Support Secondary Newcomers Academically, Socially, and Emotionally?" WestEd and Fort Worth Independent School District, 2016, Institute of Education Science, US Department of Education, https://files.eric.ed.gov/fulltext/ED605666.pdf.
7. John A. Powell, "Whites Will Be Whites: The Failure to Interrogate Racial Privilege," *University of San Francisco Law Review* 34, no. 3 (2000).
8. Walqui et al., "How Can Schools Support Secondary Newcomers Academically, Socially, and Emotionally?"
9. Christopher M. Weible and Paul A. Sabatier, *Theories of the Policy Process* (Routledge, 2018).
10. Paul A. Sabatier, "An Advocacy Coalition Framework of Policy Change and the Role of Policy-Oriented Learning Therein," *Policy Sciences* 21 (1988).
11. Lisa Dorner, Kim Song, Sujin Kim, and Lina Trigos-Carrillo, "Multilingual Family Engagement: Shifting the Focus from What Families Need to How They Can Lead," *Literacy Today* (November–December 2019), https://www.lisamdorner.com/wp-content/uploads/Dorner-EtAl-Literacy-Today-2019.pdf; Ann M. Ishimaru, Kathryn E. Torres,

Jessica E. Salvador, Joe Lott II, Dawn M. Cameron Williams, and Christine Tran, "Reinforcing Deficit, Journeying Toward Equity: Cultural Brokering in Family Engagement Initiatives," *American Educational Research Journal* 53, no. 4 (2016): 850–82; Rebecca Lowenhaupt and Nicholl Montgomery, "Family Engagement Practices as Sites of Possibility: Supporting Immigrant Families Through a District-University Partnership," *Theory into Practice* 57, no. 2 (2018).

12. For more on such use of social media, see "ELL Strategies for Success: How to Use Technology to Engage Multilingual Families," ¡Colorín Colorado!, accessed September 1, 2025, https://www.colorincolorado.org/article/how-use-technology-engage-multilingual-families.
13. "Actor Mapping—Standard Tool Overview," Protect Humanitarian Space, Norwegian Refugee Council, accessed August 30, 2024, https://www.protecthumanitarianspace.com/sites/default/files/2023-11/Actor%20mapping %20tools%20and%20methods%20.pdf.
14. Sarah Diem and Anjalé D. Welton, *Anti-Racist Educational Leadership and Policy: Addressing Racism in Public Education* (Routledge, 2020).
15. As an example of state policy, see Missouri Graduation Handbook, https://dese.mo.gov/media/pdf/graduation-requirements.

Acknowledgments

The editors extend our heartfelt gratitude to the chapter authors for their thoughtful collaborations, deep engagement, and dedication to this project. We also wish to express our profound appreciation to the countless preK–12 educators, leaders, newcomer students, families, community organizations, and school staff whose voices, experiences, and resilience are at the heart of this book. Their stories and perspectives breathe life into these pages, and it is our sincere hope that this book honors their contributions.

We are especially grateful to Shannon Davis at Harvard Education Press for her steadfast support and thoughtful guidance throughout this process. Her keen editorial eye, patience, and encouragement have been invaluable at every stage. Finally, we extend our sincere thanks to our reviewers, all preK–12 practitioners who lead by example every day in showing what it looks like to create inclusive schools for newcomers. These reviewers so generously dedicated their time and expertise to strengthening this work: Bryan Vanosdale, Shelly Fair, Lynn Tarvin, Monika Hasanbasic, Kristie Beck, Edward Franco, Ty Collins, and Tiffanie Beasley. Their careful reading, insightful feedback, and commitment to excellence have made this book stronger, and we truly appreciate their efforts.

We also dedicate this volume to all the school leaders, teachers, staff, and faculty who support newcomer students, sometimes at great personal and professional risk. Your work is a beacon of hope in challenging times. Finally, to the newcomer students and families: You are seen, you are valued, and you are not alone. We stand with you, and we dedicate this work to your strength, your dreams, and the future you deserve.

Emily, Bryan, Meredith, and Ryan

About the Editors

Emily R. Crawford, PhD, is an associate professor in the Department of Educational Leadership and Policy Analysis at the University of Missouri, Columbia. Her research explores issues related to leadership and immigration in Pk-12 public schools across geographic contexts. Her work has been published in a number of top journals, including *Educational Administration Quarterly*, *Educational Policy*, and *Equity and Excellence in Education*. She has coedited two books: *Educational Leadership of Immigrants: Case Studies in Times of Change* and *Critical Consciousness in Dual-Language Bilingual Education: Case Studies on Policy and Practice*.

Bryan Mann, PhD, is an associate professor and founding director of the Geography of Education Policy Analysis Lab at the University of Kansas. His research explores the intersection of geography and education policy. This work revolves around a few simple questions with complex answers and profound implications: Where do children enroll in school, and what drives these trends? What policy mechanisms shape enrollment patterns to enhance educational and social equity? These motivating questions guide research on several education policy areas, including enrollment patterns as they relate to segregation and diversity, school choice, and alternative models of education.

Meredith Bittel, MS, is a PhD candidate in the Department of Educational Leadership and Policy Studies at the University of Kansas. She received her MS in architectural engineering and worked as a professional engineer in Seattle and Kansas City before joining the Peace Corps as an education volunteer in Guinea, West Africa. Currently, she is a research assistant for Accessible Teaching, Learning, and Assessment Systems, working to develop dynamic learning maps for science. Meredith's research centers on equity and science education in a global context (i.e. how science is culturally accessible to some more than others), with the larger goal of supporting democratic goals in science education.

Ryan Rumpf, EdD, is an educational leader with twenty years' experience as an English-language development teacher, coordinator, and newcomer center administrator. He is passionate about designing and facilitating effective educational systems for multilingual students, especially those just beginning their journeys in English.

About the Contributors

Nishat Tasnim Akhi is a PhD student in curriculum and instruction with a specialization in educational leadership and policy at Boston College. She completed her master's in economic policy and global markets at Central European University, Vienna. Currently, she works as a research assistant on the interdisciplinary study of cross-sector collaboration for immigrant well-being and is pursuing her own research focused on higher education access, immigration, and internationalization.

Ryan Alvarez, EdD, is an adjunct professor at Touro University California in its Doctorate in Education Leadership program and a teacher at Washington Unified School District in Sacramento. His current research emphasizes English learners spanning from elementary school to community college. His experience in teaching consists of elementary English language development, physical education, and higher-education leadership and policy studies.

Liliana Belkin, PhD, is a senior lecturer in the School of Education at the University of Roehampton, London, UK. She is a faculty member on the master's degree programs in Education Leadership and Management and Special and Inclusive Education. Her research experience and interests focus on social justice issues related to marginalized groups of youth accessing education.

Alex Bittel, MA, is a PhD candidate in the Department of Educational Leadership and Policy Studies at the University of Kansas. He holds degrees in ecology and evolutionary biology and has worked in agriculture and taught chemistry in Guinea as a Peace Corps volunteer. His research interrogates the fundamental goals and function of science education in society, particularly the role that it plays (or fails to play) in shaping the public's conceptualization, relationship, and engagement with science and science issues. Given that every country in the world connects science and science education to important economic, social, and individual development goals, he is interested in taking a global, institutional perspective on this issue.

Ira Bogotch, PhD, is a professor of educational leadership at Florida Atlantic University and has studied the welcoming of Syrian newcomers to schools in Ontario, Canada, and North Rhine, Westphalia, Germany, from 2017 to 2019. In this chapter, he applies those empirical research experiences to theories and practices of school leadership specifically in terms of expanding the meanings of democracy in education.

Kristina F. Brezicha, PhD, is an associate professor of educational leadership at Georgia State University. Her research interests focus on how education supports individuals' abilities to equitably participate in the democratic processes at both the local and national level domestically and internationally. She has presented in numerous conferences such as American Educational Research Association, Comparative and International Education Society, and University Council for Educational Administration, and has published her work in journals such as *Educational Administration Quarterly*, *Equity and Excellence in Education*, and *Journal of School Leadership*.

L. Lynn Stansberry Brusnahan, PhD, is a professor in the Department of Special Education at the University of St. Thomas. Her research focuses on autism and socioculturally sustaining educational practices. She is the parent of an adult son with autism. Stansberry Brusnahan is an author or editor of several books, including *Diversity, Autism and Developmental Disabilities: Guidance for the Culturally Responsive Educator* (2021) and *Disability, Intersectionality, and Belonging in Special Education* (2024).

Amie B. Cieminski, EdD, is an associate professor of Educational Leadership and Policy Studies at the University of Northern Colorado, Greeley. She began her educational career as a secondary school Spanish teacher and served in many leadership roles, including school principal, principal supervisor, and professional learning director. Her research interests are leadership development, school improvement, and inclusive leadership.

Anne O. Davidson, PhD, is an assistant professor of Culturally and Linguistically Diverse Education and Literacy in the School of Teacher Education at the University of Northern Colorado, Greeley. She is focused on advancing equitable access for all students in inclusive educational spaces, drawing on her experience as a special education teacher and instructional coach supporting diverse learners in kindergarten through age twenty-one.

Lisa M. Dorner, PhD, is a professor in the Department of Educational Leadership and Policy Analysis and the Director of the Cambio Center at the University of Missouri, Columbia. Always striving to work alongside communities to disrupt inequities, her research focuses on the politics and discourses of bilingual education, educational policy enactment, and immigrant childhoods, especially children's and families' integration in "new" spaces. Read more on her website, lisamdorner.com.

Raghad Ebied, PhD, is a faculty member with the Center for Leading Research in Education and Faculty of Education at Wilfrid Laurier University, where she has taught courses on antidiscriminatory education and global educational philosophies, research, and practices examined through an equity, inclusion, and compassion-based lens. She completed her PhD in critical policy, equity, and leadership studies at the Faculty of Education at Western University with a focus on compassionate and resilience-based approaches to support refugee students in schools. She has completed compassion cultivation training with Stanford University and Resilience Expert Training with Dalhousie University and is a contributing author to *Leading for Equity and Social Justice: Systemic Transformation in Canadian Education* (2022).

Katrine S. Gosselin, PhD, is an assistant professor at the University of Northern Colorado, Greeley, with expertise in significant-support needs and autism in the School of Special Education. Her foci include intervention for students with complex learning and communication needs, access for all students, Universal Design for Learning (UDL), co-teaching, and collaborative practices that support district and school teams in facilitating meaningful inclusion for all students.

Hongjie Guan, MSE, is a PhD student in the Department of Educational Policy Studies at Georgia State University in Atlanta. Her research interests include intercultural communication, bilingual education, and culturally responsive leadership. She earned a master's degree in education at Johns Hopkins University.

Damaris Gutierrez, MEd, currently serves as a middle school administrator in Northside Independent School District in Texas. She is a National Board certified teacher in English as a New Language and has worked with students and families that have refugee and asylee status for ten years at the elementary and middle school levels. In addition, Gutierrez has worked at the district level to support Bilingual and English as a Second Language programs.

Afsana Hamidy, MA, is an MA student in International Child Rights and Development at King's College London, UK. She has an MA in special educational needs and disabilities (SEND) and Inclusive Education from the University of Roehampton, London. She works with unaccompanied asylum-seeking children in the UK. Her research interests focus on social justice issues related to refugees accessing education.

Daniah Hammouda, MS, is a doctoral student at the University of Kansas in Educational Policy Studies and also teaches high school English in Kansas. She is passionate about researching school segregation, promoting educational equity, examining race in education, applying critical frameworks, and advocating for decolonization of educational practices.

Hassan Hassan, EdD, is the principal of Banaadir Academy Charter School. He was born in Somalia and moved to Minnesota more than twenty years ago as a teenager. He has held many different roles in K–12 education, from teaching, supervising, and coaching to leading. During his career as an educator and as a researcher, he has focused on diversity, inclusion, curriculum development, and public engagement by working with diverse students and staff.

Melissa Hauber-Özer, PhD, is an assistant professor of Qualitative Inquiry in the College of Education and Human Development, University of Missouri,

Columbia, where she teaches graduate-level qualitative research methods courses. Her research employs critical participatory, ethnographic, and narrative methodologies to examine issues of educational access and equity for linguistically and culturally diverse learners.

Deeqaifrah Hussein, EdD, is the Executive Director of Special Education for Minneapolis Public Schools, where she coaches and collaborates with teachers and administrators on program standards using evidence-based practices for students with disabilities. Dr. Hussein has nineteen years of experience in the field of education and holds three administrative licenses (special education director, principal, and superintendent). She is on the boards of the Autism Society of Minnesota, Somali Parents Autism Network, and Senate Autism Council.

Nasir Kaihan is a doctoral student in education policy and evaluation at Arizona State University, where he also serves as the Assistant Director of Monitoring and Evaluation for the Education for Humanity Initiative. He is originally from Afghanistan and is a former Fulbright fellow. Nasir has over twelve years of experience working in international development with different international and multilateral organizations, such as the Americas Research Network, UNESCO, the American University of Afghanistan, and USAID. His career and research interests lie in refugee education, with a narrowed focus on parent/family involvement. Nasir has led, attended, and presented at more than ten conferences and workshops in the US and internationally. Nasir is the founder/principal director of the Alekain Foundation, which exists to create pathways to high school and undergraduate education, empowerment, and hope for women and girls in Afghanistan, who are denied their fundamental right to learn, and ensure they unlock their potential, and uplift generations to come. He is a collaborator and co-organizer of Learning and Educating Across Refugee/(Im)migrant Networks (LEARN)—a project of the Learning Future Collaboratives ASU's MLFTC—and was an associate editor for *Current Issues in Education* between 2022 and 2023.

Jill Koyama, PhD, a cultural anthropologist, is vice dean and professor in the Division of Educational Leadership and Innovation in Arizona State University's Mary Lou Fulton Teachers College. Her research is situated across several integrated strands of inquiry: the productive social assemblage of policy; the controversies of globalizing educational policy; the politics of immigrant and refugee education; and community organizing and activism. For the past fifteen years, Koyama's research has centered on how, even under dire circumstances and inhospitable politics, displaced people access and create resource-rich networks, make learning-centered spaces for themselves and their families, and take civic action in the United States.

Sophia Piral Lee, MPA, is a Fulbright alumna from Guatemala currently pursuing a PhD in educational leadership and policy analysis at the University of Missouri, Columbia. Working with immigrant children from Latin America studying in the United States, she is developing research on their families, their teachers, and their access to education free of stigma, discrimination, and violence. She is a bilingual teacher, International Project Management Association (IPMA)-certified project manager, certified nonprofit manager, social impact and sustainability mentor, strategic communicator, and advocate who enjoys community-based work aiming for better conditions for poblaciones vulneradas in the United States.

Grace Jia Liang, PhD, is an associate professor of educational leadership at Kansas State University. Her research interests focus on school leadership, equity for women and minoritized populations, leadership capacity building and career positioning, and leaders' dispositions and practices in community engagement. She holds a PhD in educational administration and policy from the University of Georgia.

Daniel D. Liou, PhD, is an associate professor of educational leadership and innovation at the Mary Lou Fulton Teachers College at Arizona State University. His research examines the sociology of expectations in fostering conditions of equity and justice across the prekindergarten to university educational pipeline.

Rebecca Lowenhaupt, PhD, is an associate professor of educational leadership and higher education at Boston College and works with aspiring educational leaders and policy makers on organizational, instructional, and sociocultural aspects of their practice. Her research has focused on leadership in the context of immigration, and she has explored topics ranging from organizational change and principalship to family engagement and instructional leadership. She has received funding for her research from the National Science Foundation, the W. T. Grant Foundation, and the Spencer Foundation.

Nathern Okilwa, PhD, is an associate professor in the Department of Educational Leadership and Policy Studies at the University of Texas at San Antonio. Both professional and personal experiences have shaped Okilwa's scholarly interests and commitment to educational outcomes for marginalized students. Some of Okilwa's areas of scholarly interest include educational access and equity for underserved students, educational policy, sociocultural influences, school leadership, and international organization of schooling.

Staci Pippin-Kottkamp is a PhD student at the University of Maryland, College Park, studying urban education. Her background in multilingual education and refugee resettlement informs her current research interest in the transition of newcomer youth from public schools to postsecondary education.

Gisell Ramírez is a PhD student at the University of Maryland, College Park, in the urban education program. She has worked with immigrant youth and families in urban schools. Her research interests focus on newcomer Latino youth, immigrant families, and systems of support in schools.

Sophia Rodriguez, PhD, is an associate professor of urban education at the University of Maryland College Park and soon to be associate professor of educational leadership and policy studies at New York University. Her integrated research agenda addresses issues related to racial equity, urban education, leadership, and policy and centers minoritized youth voices. Her current longitudinal projects, funded by the Spencer and W. T. Grant Foundations (2019–27), use mixed methods and ethnographic designs to investigate how community-school partnerships, teachers, leaders, and critical school-based personnel promote equity and advocate for immigrant youth. Her work has appeared in *AERA Open*, *Educational Policy*, *Educational Researcher*, *Teachers College Record*, and *Urban Education* and in the *Washington Post*.

Stacey Tran, MA, Director of English Learners and Support Programs in Washington Unified School District in Sacramento, California, has dedicated her twenty-five-year career to advocacy for multilingual learners. Her passion for professional learning and expanding opportunities for the most marginalized students has led to the creation of the Newcomer Center and the Summer Institute discussed in chapter 10. With a background in instructional coaching and a focus on effective language instruction, Tran strives to support educators and shape inclusive learning environments for all students.

Index